AN ICL
ANTHOLOGY

CU00823259

AN ICL
ANTHOLOGY

ANECDOTES AND RECOLLECTIONS
FROM THE PEOPLE OF ICL

EDITED BY
Hamish Carmichael

Laidlaw Hicks Publishers
SURBITON
1996

First published in Great Britain
in 1996 by Laidlaw Hicks Publishers
63 Collingwood Avenue, Surbiton, Surrey, KT5 9PU

ISBN 0-9527389-0-2

British Library Cataloguing-in-Publication Data.
A catalogue record for this book is
available in the British Library.

Printed in Great Britain

Page design and typesetting by
TRAX, ICL Enterprises, Windsor.

Contents

Foreword

Hamish Carmichael has had a very happy thought in taking the initiative to collect anecdotes and recollections from the people of ICL, and so to edit and produce this Anthology.

Those of us who were and who still are privileged to work in the most exciting and significant industry so far created by the human race will recall that our colleagues came together from BTM, Powers Samas, and the computer activities of GEC, EMI, Ferranti, English Electric, LEO, Elliotts, Singer and other companies. The strategy of consolidating all the parts making up ICT was the work of Cecil Mead. The creation of ICL was – I suppose fairly – the desire of Harold Wilson's government; their chosen method was a combination of stick and carrot, termed by Tony Benn 'a golden rod'. As I recall, the rod caused some pain and the gold contribution was minuscule. Nevertheless, the combined efforts of all the people overcame the problems with the enthusiasm of pioneers.

ICL is unique in many ways, but there is one outstanding characteristic: its recognising and rewarding – as it always has – long service. More than 15,000 people have served for 21 years or more, and over 360 for more than 42 years. No wonder there are many anecdotes!

The computer business itself is also unique in that only two countries, Britain and the United States, can fairly claim not only to have invented the computer but to have spurred virtually every advance and innovation which the last fifty years have witnessed. The talents of people from all parts of ICL have contributed more to the state of the art than any other single company.

ICL people, past and present, can be proud of their achievements, and as they flip through this Anthology their memories will be triggered with more and more recollections, and Hamish is likely to be inundated with more and more material justifying or even demanding further editions of this work. I wish it well.

Arthur Humphreys, November 1995

Introduction

This book is really based on gratitude: first and foremost to my former colleagues in many parts of ICL. If the company's products provided a career full of continuing interest and excitement, it was my fellows in ICL who always provided the ideal atmosphere in which to exploit them. Their attitude was always stimulating, very occasionally exasperating, and nearly always amusing and enjoyable. Although there are a few historical articles as scene-setting, this is not an attempt at a serious work of history. It will have succeeded if it reminds people of the flavour of their times in ICL and its constituent companies.

Although, when I joined in 1958, the great days of the pioneers were already in the past, it was a fine time to see a great industry shake itself into order and start to grow, in what Lord Peter Wimsey called 'the "ampelopsis" manner: first year, tender little shoots; second year, fine show; third year, all over the place'. How lucky we are to have been part of it.

As for the compilation, the book effectively wrote itself. A few requests for material brought in a wonderful flood of contributions, which may have slowed to a comparative trickle, but which has certainly not yet stopped. I think this supports my contention that ICL, although it has always thought it was producing computers, has actually had some of its greatest successes in producing raconteurs. Except on a very few topics, such as the Galactic Storage Device and Mike Forrest, there has been remarkably little duplication.

My thanks to everybody whose various inputs I have joyfully accepted. Particular thanks to Chris Cheetham, who not only supplied many gems from his own varied experience, but who kindly read the whole compilation with great care, and saved me from many errors of taste, accuracy, and orthography. Further hearty thanks to the great family of Anon, several of whom are represented by several masterpieces.

On the arrangement of the material, there have been two types of advice. One said I should aim for a thematic structure, with chapters on Quirks of Machines, Foibles of Customers, The Things Salesmen Say, and the like. Another suggested that I should aim at a balanced anthological structure (shades of well-balanced trees), with meatier items embedded in snippets à la Reader's Digest. Instead of either of these I have gone for a simple-minded and approximately chronological sequence, which I hope produces an acceptable mixture of material. But do please note that 'approximately'; I am only too well aware that better-informed people will have many occasions to say: 'Oh no, *that* didn't happen *then*'. Maybe it didn't, but I hope it doesn't matter too much.

I hope that the chosen arrangement helps to illustrate the different strands of the ICL character: the fifty-year rivalry between British Tabulating Machines and Powers Samas (long dormant but even now perhaps not finally extinguished); the engineering flair of Ferranti; the far-sighted boldness of LEO; the somewhat reticent steadiness of English Electric; and the striking originality of Singer.

An apology is perhaps due on the score of accuracy. What I have put together is largely what people have told me, without any formal checking on their veracity. Many of these stories have been filtered through the years, and perhaps been improved in the re-telling and, anyway, human memory is an active process without the boring restrictions of parity checks and such. So there are, I already know, instances where A and B were jointly involved in some memorable activity, and A has sent me a version of what happened, on seeing which B has said: 'Oh no, it wasn't like *that* at all'. Well, to all the Bs among you I can only respond that you had the chance to get your version in first.

One other apology, and then I've done. There are many mentions – or hints – of particular people whose permission to mention them I have not sought. But all are included for reasons of respect or affection or both; there has been no room for malice. 'No no, I do but jest, poison in jest; no offence i' the world'.

Formal acknowledgments for permission to quote copyright material are due to the British Computer Society, the National Physical Laboratory, the Institution of Professionals, Managers and Specialists, and to *Punch* Publications Limited. Rod Smith of the Science Museum kindly provided photographs of old equipment. I thank ICL for its permission to plunder historic copies of *Tabacus*, the *ICT House Magazine*, and associated publications, and Bernard Bassett for having the good sense to preserve an archive of them and the kindness to let me borrow them. For practical help in producing this book I owe thanks to Denis Blandford of Peritas, and to Alan Thomas of ICL Enterprises.

Many people have allowed me to see a wide variety of cherished documents, which has been a great help and very interesting. In that connection may I issue a general plea: don't unthinkingly throw anything away! Precious little survives of the documentation of the last forty years, because of the speed with which programs and ideas are superseded. 'Oh, that's old hat', we say, and toss it in the bin. Yet historians of technology are going to look back on our times and wonder what it was like, and how we performed our marvels, and are going to have to rely far too much on guesswork. What we so casually discard is probably equivalent to one great library of Alexandria every five years, vandals that we are.

I hope you will find in this collection both some old favourites and some new delights. No doubt you will also notice many omissions. But then, if you suppose that each ICL person and each ex-ICL person knows one unique good story (which must be on the conservative side), and if you reckon how many tens of thousands of such people there are, a book of this size can only be like dipping a teaspoon in a vast tankful of possibilities. Who knows, with your help another dip might easily be possible.

Finally, I can never completely express my thanks to my wife Yvonne, who with commendable patience has tolerated her menfolk's obsession with computers for many years, and who while I have been producing this book has been, as always, an unfailing help and support.

Hamish Carmichael, Tolworth, November 1995.

Prologue

The interview that wasn't

H.C.

It was a Thursday morning in May 1958, and three of us had been sent along by the University Appointments Board to the lounge of the Randolph Hotel in Oxford, to be interviewed for a coveted technical trainee's job with Powers Samas. We were all there, as specified, by 11 a.m., and settled in three distant corners of that vast room, each of us glowering at our rivals.

Eleven o'clock came, but nothing happened. Half past eleven, and still nobody came and nothing happened. Then it got to twelve noon, and by this time we had all surreptitiously checked the letter, confirming that we were there at the right time, in the right place, and on the right day, but still nobody came and nothing happened. By half past twelve we were getting pretty desperate, but each of us was resolved not to be the first one to weaken.

Finally, at 12.40, in breezed A. Allen Knight, then Manager of Training Branch for Powers Samas.

He called us together from the far corners of the room, and announced airily: 'Sorry, I seem to be a little late! Look, there are jobs for all three of you if you want them! Let's go and have some lunch!'

I never saw the other two again.

The joining letter that didn't

H.C.

It told me to turn up at 9.00 a.m. on 8 September 1958 at the Powers Samas Training School in Fulwood Place, a small side street on the north side of High Holborn.

So I did. My first job! Great excitement! But no 'Welcome' on the mat. No warm greetings. No 'Come in, my boy, glad to see you.'

Instead, puzzlement, blank looks, and a hint of hostility. 'Why have you come here today? Don't you know your course doesn't start for another fortnight?' I showed the letter. It was plain and unambiguous. It confirmed I was being paid from that very day. So they were going to have to find something for me to do.

Brainwave! I was shoved into the Punch Training Room among the girls for a week, to learn how to punch forty column cards on a Universal Automatic Key Punch, and how to use the Powers Samas Verifier and Interpreter. It was actually very valuable training, and stood me in good stead for many years.

The second week I was promoted! I got to help train the new intake of girls in how to punch forty column cards on a UAKP, and how to verify and interpret them.

Subsequent promotions were never so fast nor such fun.

One British Tabulating Machine Co

A brief history   **ICT House Magazine**

Abridged from the ICT House Magazine *Number 1, February 1959*

The British Tabulating Machine Company Limited, usually known as 'BTM' or 'Hollerith', came into being in December 1907, to continue the work of a syndicate known as The Tabulator Limited which had been formed in 1904 by Mr R.P. Porter (a friend of Dr Herman Hollerith), Mr (later Sir) Ralegh B. Philpotts and others. In fact, things really started even earlier, in 1902, when Porter and Philpotts agreed to send C.A. Everard Greene to America to learn about the Hollerith punched card machines first used in the US National Census of 1890. And that happened because Hollerith had offered his friend Porter the rights to exploit his inventions in Britain and throughout the British Empire (apart from Canada).

In the early days Thomas Kesnor & Company, of Fulham, manufactured certain machines for the company and others were imported from America and assembled in England, being altered for sterling and imperial weights as necessary. They comprised a simple hand Key Punch, a lever-operated Gang Punch, and a hand-operated pin-type Tabulator. The cards measured some $7^3/_8$ by $3^1/_4$ inches (as they did throughout the punched card era), a size derived by Hollerith from the American dollar bill. They had only 37 columns (as opposed to the eventual 80) and used round holes. The first Automatic Sorting Machine followed in 1908. The Automatic Tabulator also became available in 1908 and operated at 150 cards per minute.

The first regular installation of Hollerith machines was in 1906 at Messrs Vickers, Sons & Maxim at Sheffield. This was followed over the next few years by the Lancashire and Yorkshire Railway at Horwich, the Great Western Railway at Swindon, The Calico Printers Association, and the British Westinghouse Electric and Manufacturing Company in Manchester.

In 1911 the Registrar-General used punched card equipment for the first time for the compilation of the Population Census of England and Wales. The Scottish authorities decided likewise. The company manufactured the 50 million cards needed from English-made paper and, in conjunction with

Kesnor's, built the special Key Punches and Census Counting Machines, both of which were of English design. The compilation work was completed in three years, which was no mean feat for such a small concern. When the contract was signed, the company had a small but very enthusiastic team of five people!

Another important event in 1911 was the first overseas contract, in South Africa, shortly followed by another in Buenos Aires. Both were in railways, confirming that railways were still in the forefront of technology at that time. In 1917 the third overseas country (Egypt) installed machines for its population Census.

In 1913 the company moved into its own workshops in Verulam Street, off Gray's Inn Road.

During the 1914–18 war a number of employees joined HM Forces but, despite this and other difficulties, a big expansion of business took place, many munitions factories installing the punched card system for accounting and statistical work. During this time the capacity of the card was increased from 37 to 45 columns, and the company moved again to larger premises in Belvedere Road, Lambeth.

The business was now growing steadily and, realising the need for better manufacturing facilities, the company selected land in Letchworth Garden City and built a modern factory, with space for future expansion, in 1921.

In 1922 the first Training School for Service Engineers was set up under the aegis of the company's Engineer.

A major improvement in the product took place in 1923, when the Tabulating Machine was first fitted with automatic total control and printing mechanism, two developments which increased its usefulness and demand for accounting work. The tabulating speed remained at 150 cards a minute when printing totals only, or 75 cards a minute when listing every card.

In 1923 the nominal capital of the company was £100,000, the number of installations had passed 100, and the total number of employees was 132, of whom 8 were overseas.

Dr Hollerith's original design of the Vertical Sorting Machine, which operated at 250 cards per minute, was superseded by a new horizontal design in 1926, operating at 400 cards per minute. During the following year the first Subtracting Tabulator was designed and built, which greatly widened the scope in the field of commercial accounting.

In 1929 the 80-column card, with slotted holes, was introduced. In this year too, the company's Head Office was moved from Aldwych to Victoria House, Southampton Row.

By 1933 the total number of employees in the company had grown to 643, including 40 overseas, and the number of installations was 149.

In 1934 the Rolling Total Tabulator introduced as standard the concept of detachable and interchangeable plugboards.

At the outbreak of World War II the number of employees was just over 1,200, of whom 425 were production workers in the factory and 139 overseas, the latter number being a fair measure of the much increased activity overseas.

Between 1939 and 1945 the company's products were in constant demand to meet the needs of Government and industry in a great variety of ways, and many installations were supplied to the Armed Services, both at home and overseas. In addition, the company undertook in its various works in Letchworth, then five in number, the manufacture of such widely varying products as bomber aircraft frames and watchmakers' lathes, as well as special early electronic equipment, many details of which apparently still remain classified.

Number 17 Park Lane became the company's Head Office in 1948, the Victoria House premises being retained to house the London and South of England sales force. To cope with ever increasing demand, a factory site was acquired at Castlereagh, near Belfast, and manufacturing operations started there in 1949.

In 1951, 217 members of staff with 21 years' service or more attended a dinner of the Majority Club given in Letchworth by the Directors, who expressed their pride in the fact that 61% of the company's relatively small staff in 1930 was still in service in 1951.

At the Business Efficiency Exhibition held at Birmingham in 1952 the company exhibited one of its first Electronic Multiplying Machines. At this date the company's capital had grown to £2,500,000 and the number of employees approached 5,000.

Summing up at the time of the merger with Powers Samas to form ICT: 'BTM's staff has grown to nearly 9,000. Undoubtedly the most important development during recent years has been the intensive research on electronic computers and production activity on a large scale. With over 40 computer installations now in action, it is obvious that electronics will play an ever increasing part in our future business.'

Census, 1917 *Sarah Hamilton*

1917 was the year of the first ever census in Egypt, all done with Hollerith punched cards. Mind you, they had to be shipped to Italy for processing, because there were no sorters or tabulators in Egypt.

Circling the credits, 1920s   Bernard Bassett

The convention of identifying credit items on internal accounts by drawing circles round them goes back to Arthur Howarth, for many years chief Accountant for BTM, who was colour blind and so couldn't tell black from red.

The 13-period calendar, 1920s   Bernard Bassett

This convention, surely the most rational way ever invented of measuring time for internal accounting and management purposes, should probably be credited to Arthur Howarth.

It was a great pity that Geoff Cross could never be made to understand that 'Period 5' didn't mean 'May'. Switching the year end to 31 December, and trying to adopt the irregular months of the public calendar for accounting purposes, was probably the daftest bit of vandalism in the whole of the American era.

Conversely, the internal calendar's survival for payroll purposes until 1994 was probably one of the best achievements of trade unionism within ICL.

IBM: The great crate supplier, 1930s   Bernard Bassett

In the days when BTM was acting as a UK and Empire sales arm for machines manufactured by IBM, tabulators used to arrive from across the Atlantic in massive packing crates. Then the labels on the machines had to be changed from 'IBM' to 'Hollerith', and the alpha printing mechanism had to be converted to UK standards. But, much more important, it got to the stage when there was hardly a BTM house in Letchworth that didn't have a garage, or a coal bunker, or a chicken hut constructed out of IBM tabulator crates. Some thought they were the best products ever to come out of IBM.

Bassett Enterprises: The inspiration, 1937   Bernard Bassett

The working week in British Tabulating Machines at Letchworth was five and a half days, with every fourth Saturday morning off. Then one week there was a call for volunteers to work an extra Saturday morning during their time 'off'.

Being young and keen, I put my name down and turned up on the day. The vital extra work turned out to be no more than selling potatoes to the factory workforce on behalf of Mr Ralegh Philpotts, the Chairman (of whom it was suggested that he was really a farmer and ran BTM as a sideline).

Bassett Enterprises: Early days, 1937-38   *Bernard Bassett*

I started my own sideline in artificial manure, for friends locally who were keen gardeners and allotment holders, and based my pricing on £7. 10s. 0d. per ton. Typical quantities were 2 lb. or 5 lb. in bags. Then, blow me, Mr Ralegh Philpotts went and ordered a whole ton, to be delivered to his farm in Devon. This raised several problems, not least transport, because all I had was a pushbike. I had to hire a lorry from a friend for a special weekend trip at a cost of £2. 10s. 0d., which completely wiped out all my profit.

When I griped about this in the office next Monday, my boss gave me an unsympathetic lecture on always setting price levels with a margin for contingencies, and then dismissed the affair. But I found an unexpected bonus of £2. 10s. 0d. in my next pay packet.

A twenty-six year job, 1938-1964   *Bernard Bassett*

As a youngster, I was given the job of transferring the ledger address information from Addressograph plates to punched cards. We had at last acquired tabulators which could print alpha! Then I was called up.

In 1947, typically demob-happy, I had plans to go up to Cambridge to improve my qualifications but the company said: 'No, sorry, you haven't finished that address conversion job'. So I took up where I'd left off nine years previously.

Years passed, and the idea of having address information in punched cards became passé in its turn. So we started converting the addresses to 1301. But then someone suggested that 1301 was being superseded by 1500 for internal purposes, so we stopped one conversion and started another. Which was going along very nicely until someone invented the 1900, so we stopped one conversion and started another. And we finished that one, thank God.

Code-breaking, law-breaking, 1939   *George Thomson*

BTM abounded in characters, Freddy Freeborn being one of many. At the outbreak of the 1939-45 war, Freddy was seconded to Bletchley Park as a manager on the Enigma code-breaking project. Eric Goode was one of the Hollerith Technical Servicemen seconded to work with him. Shortly after his arrival at Bletchley Park, Eric received his call-up papers from the RAF. He went to tell Freddy who asked to see them, threw them in the wastepaper basket, and told Eric to forget about it. Some weeks later, two RAF Service Policemen came to the gates of Bletchley Park to take Eric into custody. Freddy's instructions to Eric, when he was appraised of the situation, were: 'They can't come in; you must not go out'. Two RAF SPs were encamped outside the gates for several weeks until the matter was resolved in Freddy's favour.

Be prepared! c. 1941 — *Gordon Collinson*

During the war, Jock Neill was responsible for the gun which, from the roof of number 1/1 Factory, Letchworth, was going to defy the full might of the Luftwaffe and protect the factory from dastardly enemy action. Of which, as it turned out, there wasn't a lot (though there was a heck of a lot of trouble later from the dust kicked up when the air raid shelter fell down).

Until, of course, the day when a solitary marauding Dornier 17 (the 'pencil' Dornier) came over and strafed Baldock railway station (it does suggest a certain weakness in target identification procedures, doesn't it?).

At the sound of the first shots, Jock sprinted into action. Sadly the gun itself was not actually mounted in the firing position, but down inside the factory for cleaning. Seizing it as fast as he could, he beat the Olympic record to the roof, mounted the weapon and frantically scanned the horizon, only to see the twin tail of the distant bandit already disappearing over Hitchin and, worse still, to realise that the breech-block of the gun had become detached during the scramble upstairs. Oh well, better luck next time!

Something nice about IBM! c. 1942 — *Bernard Bassett*

Ralegh Philpotts received a cable from Thomas J. Watson, President of IBM, asking for the names and addresses of all BTM staff. Though puzzled, he complied, compiled the information and sent it off, whereupon for Christmas all BTM staff received very welcome food parcels.

Did you know? 1944 — The Tabulator

From The Tabulator, *Golden Jubilee Issue, 1958*

A mobile Hollerith installation was landed on the Normandy beaches on D-Day plus six.

Second class gratitude, 1945 — *George Thomson*

When the war ended Freddy Freeborn was awarded an OBE for his work at Bletchley Park, but was most upset that the medal was simply sent to him through the post. As he complained afterwards, it wasn't even registered!

Something in the wind? 1946 — Gordon Collinson

Doug Gray was in charge of Specifications Department in Letchworth which ran the production end of the 'Serial' programme.

Life seemed pretty tame to some of us ex-RAF types and, for some reason, it struck us as a good idea, one time when Doug was away, to unstitch part of the upholstery of his office chair, insert a kipper, and replace the stitching.

Thereafter, whenever he sat down, the heat of his body would so work upon the kipper that it 'blossomed' (see Kipling, *Stalky & Co*). Doug took to opening the windows, and then the door, and wearing a puzzled expression. We kept our heads down, our faces straight, and got on with our work. Until, after a couple of weeks, we ourselves could stand it no longer, and took advantage of another absence to remove the by now very elderly fish. But to the day he retired he never traced the phenomenon to its source.

A bumpy start, 12 October 1947 — Ray Kilroy

After a formal interview I was delighted to be told that I would be engaged as a trainee Technical Serviceman with the British Tabulating Machine Company.

Sure enough, a letter arrived at home a few days later setting down my terms of employment and instructing me to report to Victoria House on 12 October prior to going to Hollerith House, Letchworth, for a three month initial training course.

On the due date I duly presented myself to the Personnel Manager, Mr Bill Kemp, all keen and raring to go. Imagine my dismay when he told me he was sorry, but the Training School was closed down, as all the staff were manning the stand at the Business Efficiency Exhibition. He could see my disappointment and said immediately: 'Don't worry; you are on the payroll from today. Go home and wait for us to send for you.' Three weeks later I received the call.

Has anyone else in the history of ICL joined the staff with a compulsory three week paid holiday?

Democracy, 1950 — George Thomson

I joined the old British Tabulating Machine Company in June 1950, well remembering my first day when we all assembled in the then Head Office at 17 Park Lane for an introductory address by a rather pompous prat (who shall remain nameless). In the course of his talk he made the fatuous remark that: 'We are a democratic company; the Chairman calls the office boy by his christian name'. My suggestion that 'it would be even more democratic if the office boy were to call the Chairman by his christian name' was not well received.

Letchworth may have been dry, but Arlesey wasn't, 1950
George Thomson

We entrained at King's Cross for the Training School Hostel (male) at Arlesey Bury and its redoubtable housekeeper, Miss Seawright (a former Dame at Eton), who always referred to Cedric Dickens as 'young Master Dickens'. The following day we started our Technical Service course at the school in Gernon Road, Letchworth, under the late irascible John Armstrong.

All I can remember of the course was drinking a lot of beer in the Rose and Crown at Arlesey. One Saturday morning, at the behest of Miss Seawright, we had to entertain Sir Ralegh Philpotts, the then company Chairman, who was dressed in deerstalker hat, Norfolk jacket, jodhpurs, and riding boots, gear which he frequently wore to the office. In the August I met my future wife who was on another TS course. One of my drinking companions was Eric Waldmeyer who, with Gus Thibaut, was to be murdered in the riots in Cairo in 1952 when King Farouk was deposed and General Neguib took over.

The saga of the High Speed Reproducer, 1950
Jack Howlett and Tommy Cox

It was at the LOTUS Shoe Company in Stafford that a BTM High Speed Reproducer broke its Geneva Gear, late one Friday afternoon in the autumn of 1950. This was Jack's contract. The company was owned by the Bostock Brothers, one of whom, Gilbert, was in charge of the Accounts and Hollerith department and also a personal friend of Vic Stammers, a Director of BTM.

As Mr Bostock was going to spend the Saturday morning, more or less single-handed for reasons of confidentiality, producing the senior staff payroll, we knew for sure that the machine must be fixed by then.

Because the necessary part was not available from spares, we decided to take it out of a similar machine at 16 MU, RAF Stafford. This was Tommy's contract. So that evening we made a visit to the Officers' Mess to obtain permission from the Wing Commander which, after a few drinks that lasted till closing time, he gave, subject to his own High Speed Reproducer being back in full working order by 8 a.m. on Monday.

It was probably Friday midnight before work on the broken H.S.R. started and nearly 7 a.m. on Saturday before it was completed.

When he turned up about 8 a.m. and realised that we had been there all night, Mr Bostock kindly laid on coffee and rolls.

During the morning the Birmingham office rang to say that they had located a spare Geneva gear at Meadow Dairies near Nottingham but, in order to get it, we would first have to go to the home of Stan Birchell in Derby and identify ourselves, as this was his contract.

So after a wash and brush up we set off on the trip to Derby, a matter of some 30 miles. Trouble struck 20 miles later in the form of running out of petrol. Two hours later, after we had walked miles in the rain to get some fuel and then cleaned out the carburettor, which had picked up nasty sludge from the bottom of the tank, we continued to Stan's home, only to be told that he hadn't come home yet from a call to the Nottingham Council offices. So that was the next general destination, for which we started at about 7 p.m. but we didn't know in which particular office Stan would be working.

We did know that Stan drove a black Standard car and had learned that if you stamped on its back bumper the driver's door would spring open. There were many black Standards in the Town Hall car park, and we had tried several before the policeman arrived. Well, if you were a conscientious officer would you have accepted our attempted explanation? Providentially, when we put the bumper to the test on the car where he had caught us, the driver's door sprung open. Scratching his chin, the law accepted our story and left.

We now had to wait for Stan to return or to leave a message saying why we were there. Eventually he appeared, with his inspector Les Hopkins (who later became an instructor at the Letchworth Field Engineering Training School) and found us sitting in his car.

As none of us had eaten we adjourned to the nearest hostelry for refreshment, so it was not until after closing time that we got to Meadow Dairies, where the security man told us that he had been waiting for us all day.

It was already the early hours of Sunday morning when we arrived home in Stafford, and went blissfully to sleep, knowing that we still had to fix the H.S.R. at 16 MU, RAF. This we completed without more ado on Sunday afternoon.

And that would have been the last of it, except that Meadow Dairies refused to pay the overtime which their security guard had claimed for waiting for us all day until 11 p.m. It was a very irate Stan Wells, BTM chief inspector for the Midland Region, who eventually had to shell out, saying: 'One couldn't really expect those two ******s to arrive until after the pubs shut!'

Paper management, early 1950s   *George Thomson*

Tony Lang was the Technical Serviceman responsible for the RAF's Hollerith installations which were scattered around the country. Tony would appear in the Victoria House office each Monday morning to hand in his expense claim for the previous week, collect his expenses for the week before that, and deal with any correspondence that had accrued in his absence. The rest of the week was spent touring round the country visiting his various installations.

Tony's method of dealing with paperwork was simplicity itself. With anything that was not absolutely essential, the carpet was rolled back, the papers piled in a heap in the middle of the floor, sprinkled with lighter fuel, and set alight. When the flames were out, the carpet was replaced.

Tony was succeeded by Teddy Grieve, who carried a lot of weight. Shortly after his arrival, the occupant of the office below was surprised to be showered in plaster and. looking up, he saw the underside of a carpet appear through a hole in the ceiling. Tony had burned so many papers that the floorboards had been charred to the extent that they had given way under Teddy's weight.

Lubrication, c. 1951   Albert Brook

Simmonds Brewery in Reading ordered a major BTM 80 column installation, but when we came to install it we found that the salesman had got it wrong: he specified unit counters instead of sterling. Changing this was a major job, involving Albert, Pat and Stan in a lot of weekend working. Which was complicated by the further facts that only Stan had a car and there were no eating facilities on site. So a convention evolved that someone would cook some chips at home, allow the fat to cool, and then bring in the pan plus the fat plus the chips plus a primus. The caretaker was sympathetic and pointed out that one of his weekend jobs was to change over the barrel in the managers' mess and, since the lads were obviously working so hard, they might like to have a glass or two out of the old barrel before he changed it. When he later came to change it the one or two glasses had grown to several more and the barrel was empty; which meant that he lost part of his perks for that weekend. The invitation was never repeated.

Bog-smacked, 1950s   Graham Morris

The paper feed mechanism on a Senior Rolling Total Tabulator went berserk, and oversped at an astonishing rate, flinging a stream of paper high and far behind it. The watching Irish Engineer's comment was : 'Bejabers! Ectoplasm!'

Hysteresis hysterics, 1953 *Stephen Hare*

'HEC' was the short name for the Hollerith Electronic Computer, later marketed as the '1201'. The recording heads used on its magnetic drum were stamped from thin mu-metal strip, a process which adversely affected their magnetic properties. According to conventional wisdom, the way to restore them was by heat treatment, heating them up to a specified temperature and then cooling them very slowly over a long period of time. One of the team of engineers was Bill Davies, who devised an electric oven with a motor-driven variac transformer which gradually reduced the voltage over three or four days, all very elaborate and technical! It was a great disappointment to find out that, when all this had been done, the heads would not work.

At this time BTM retained Dr Booth from Birkbeck College as a consultant and he would visit us every two or three weeks. The HEC logic system using a magnetic drum as permanent storage was based on his design concepts and his students had built an embryo system at his laboratory. Hence it was natural to refer the problem to him. His solution was simple. In a workshop near the lab there was a gas cylinder and burners used by the fitters for brazing. He merely took one of these magnetic heads in a pair of pliers, waved it about in the flame for a few seconds and then invited us to try it. Amid much scepticism and disbelief, we carefully wound the required turns of wire and set it up on the drum and of course it worked perfectly.

I believe by the time the machine went into production a more professional method was found.

Putting one's foot on it, 1953 *Stephen Hare*

The laboratory prototype HEC was put together using flat chassis construction mounted on Post Office racks and cross-wired; that part was commonly referred to as the 'rats' nest'. When the company wished to exhibit their first stored program electronic computer at Olympia in 1953 we were required to build a HEC as an integrated unit with covers. This was where Dick Chandler, the foreman of the tin bashers' model shop, became involved. He built a long framework (about eight feet long), with columns at 19 inch intervals. We fitted the power supplies at the bottom to give stability. When all was assembled and being tested it was found that the power supplies had too much ripple voltage at full load. At that late stage it wasn't practical to do a redesign so the solution was to fit more electrolytic capacitors. As there was no room within the framework, Dick fitted outrigger wheels at the ends of the machine with sub-frameworks to mount these large capacitors. These were then covered with formed sheet metal shrouds, which we called the 'spats'. This was

13

fine until some visitor unwittingly placed a foot on one of these convenient footrests, when there was a tremendous explosion as the bending cover shorted out the bank of capacitors! Solution? Stick a sheet of fibre on the inside of the cover. This machine then toured the Exhibitions with eye-catching demonstrations such as playing noughts and crosses and bidding bridge hands, having been programmed by R.L. Michaelson, Brian Dagnall and Harold Ashforth. Eventually it ended up at Head Office in Old Park Lane.

Not Pygmalion likely, 1953 *Stephen Hare*

In the laboratory we were trying to find out how to life-test electronic valves (which the Americans called 'vacuum toobs'), in order to weed out those which were liable to early failure. A technician by the name of Derek Cook had assembled a rack full of several hundred of these valves ready to switch on for the experiment. Just at that moment the Director of Research, Dr Womersly (ex-NPL), came in with some prestigious visitors. What an embarrassment when the whole lot went up in a brilliant flash! The heater transformer had been connected up back to front. Ever afterwards, in describing this incident, Dr Womersly would exclaim in his Mancunian accent: 'Ee! It lit up just like a blooming Christmas tree!'

Drum minors, 1950s *Ted Evison*

Setting up the drum on a HEC 4 (or 1201) was tricky. One stage in the process crucially depended on the use of Rizla cigarette papers; but it *had* to be the *blue* Rizla paper, the red just wasn't right for the job.

Glasgow decorations, 1954 *George Thomson*

In 1954, I was transferred to the Glasgow office. Two of the 'characters' on the staff were Leslie Alan Wight (known as China Wight because he had spent some months in Hong Kong) and Frank deLuca Kennedy.

Leslie Wight was then in his fifties, having joined the Glasgow office of BTM about 1934 when the staff consisted of himself, Reggie Wigram and a secretary. They moved into a new office which Reggie thought was rather drab, so Leslie was sent out with the petty cash to purchase a suitable picture with which to decorate it. He returned some two hours later with a limited-edition signed artist's reproduction water-colour of a group of nudes by Sir William Russell Flint. Reggie deemed it unsuitable for the office and instructed Leslie to get rid of it. He took it home where it had pride of place in his living room. Leslie loved to tell visitors how Hollerith came to pay thirty pounds for his Russell Flint.

Tales from Holborn Bar, c. 1955   *Vernon Hardman*

A very senior and respected sales manager (Seymour Dearden) in London in the BTM company was the epitome of the upper class English gentleman; tall, distinguished, elegant, languid. The story was told that he had survived the rigours of a Japanese prisoner of war camp by exploiting this appearance and demeanour. After the terrible beatings and privation appeared to have absolutely no effect, his captors largely ignored him.

On one occasion he visited a customer at the behest of, and in the company of, a young trainee. In those days in the capital managers travelled by taxi whereas trainees normally went by more humble public transport. However, on this occasion they shared a taxi. Similarly, trainees rarely met senior managers and, when they did, would rarely speak unless spoken to. As a result there was a long silence in the taxi, finally broken by the manager with the (to him) obvious conversational opener: 'Do you beagle?'

Tales from a bar in Holborn, c. 1955   *Vernon Hardman and Richard Dean*

The same manager (Seymour Dearden) was seen, by appointment, by another young man. The latter carefully and politely expounded his case for a salary increase. The manager suggested that better money management might help. For example, a Number 1 account for essentials, a Number 2 account for savings, and a Number 3 account for spending money. However, the young man protested that the money was simply inadequate to exist on in London.

This elicited the kindly, not to say avuncular, but singularly unhelpful response: 'Can't your Mummy and Daddy help you... ?'

But the young man was equal to this and responded: 'But, Sir, I'm an orphan'. Pause for thought.

'Ah well, only thing to do. Last resort. Rich widow... Did it myself.'

How the Computer came to Letchworth, 1956–58   Tabacus 85

Condensed from Tabacus 85, October 1958

Two facts: The first is that nearly 100 Computers have been installed in Great Britain now - and the nameplate 'Hollerith' appears more frequently than any other. The second is that we have got one ourselves! The advantages of the tool that we as a company have fashioned, and which we have christened 'HEC

4', are potentially so great that we cannot afford not to put it to use in our own business. But like all other tools, its effectiveness depends upon the skill with which it is used and its suitability to the job in hand.

In the early days of 1955, our Sales Division set up a Department whose function it was - and is - to advise on the uses of Hollerith equipment for Production Control work as distinct from those many activities classified under the general heading of Accounts. This was not really a new idea: quite a number of our customers had been using our machines for such things as Stores Balancing and Programme Breakdown. In fact both at Number 1 and Number 8 factories, the exercise of turning a machine production programme into terms of piece parts and materials had been carried out with the aid of Hollerith for some years. The new Department was created to enable a proper specialisation of the study of production control requirements to be made. It was not long before the rather complicated arithmetic associated with production control work suggested the use of the very latest and most complex of Hollerith machines - the Computer.

In fact, it was soon accepted that some of the more desirable procedures involved in controlling production could be managed only with the aid of a Computer if they were to be prepared swiftly enough to be of real value. The great enemy of all production control men is TIME. The circumstances of production change rapidly. If a plan is required, to establish the loading of work into a factory or to tell a supplier in what quantities and at what times you want your pieces delivered, then that plan has got to be made swiftly and made known to everyone concerned. If it takes a long time to work out then, by the time it is issued, it is out of date and of little practical value.

It was in this field of production control that it was felt there was a worthwhile outlet for the abilities of the Computer we were making and, if this was to be true for our customers, so it must be for us, for our own factories.

At the beginning of 1956, a preliminary survey was made in Number 1 factory of our own production control problems. This confirmed the view that a great deal of worthwhile use could be made of a Computer and so, towards the end of that year, a 1201/588 HEC 4 was ordered by Production Division.

Early in 1957 we started to get together a team of people to do the work involved in introducing a Computer system of Production Control. Of the six members of the team, four came from Production Division, one from Accounts, and one from Sales. To most of the six the Computer was initially a bit of a mystery. This was quickly put right with a few Computer Training Courses at Moor Hall, Cookham. Thus equipped and with high enthusiasm the team set to work to produce a workable scheme.

The most important realisation at this stage was that this was not the sort of job that a group of long-haired back-room boys could do by themselves.

Right from the beginning of the exercise, with informal talks between team members and others in the factory organisation, and with rather more formal talks to the Foremen; to the Shop Stewards; to the Superintendents; and to the Division Executives, the team explained what its objectives were, what benefits they should bring and how they should be achieved. And, in return, the real experts proffered advice, criticism and guidance, so that the scheme, when completed, would be a compound of all the knowledge and experience gained over the years by all those who have a direct interest in a decent scheme of production control.

Another very important point settled at the beginning was that the complete scheme should be introduced to No 1B factory first and subsequently extended to No 1 itself. In March this year the team had sufficiently completed their plans for the Management to decide on a starting date for the scheme to be introduced into 1B factory. And by late April THE ROOM had appeared.

Since the only site that could be used was more or less a sun-trap, all the walls and ceilings are packed with fibreglass insulation. This was fitted between the studding of the walls and for a week or so, before the outer walls were put up, scarcely a soul walked by without prodding an inquisitive finger into the fibreglass wadding, with the result that there were a great many sore fingers in Letchworth during this period.

On Saturday 3 May the Computer arrived. Early that morning a giant forklift truck from Messrs Shelvoke and Drewry, our neighbours in Icknield Way, picked up the 1201 unit from its resting place in Shipping and Transport and gently carried it round on its steel forks to a spot just beneath the fire escape platform at the east end of No 1 factory. There, while the many interested spectators watched with bated breath, the truck steadily lifted the Computer the 18 or 20 feet up to the platform. As it went up it rocked gently and, every few feet, the angle of the forks was altered slightly to control this. There was, however, a great sigh of relief when the 1201 came finally to rest on the platform, from where it was rolled along to the Computer Room.

There followed a period of nine weeks during which the machine and its operating programmes were tested. During this period everybody concerned learned a great deal about air conditioning, humidity, heat output, and various other technicalities. Air conditioning is one of those subjects on which a very large number of people are experts - which is probably the reason for our being unsuccessful with the three air conditioning units originally installed.

We have hardly had a heat wave sort of summer, but there have been a good many days during the past three months which were warm enough to give our Computer apoplexy. That is, our air conditioners didn't get the heat away from the Computer fast enough, and its thermostats cut out. After several weeks of this and several waves of experts we resorted to the good old extractor fan which sucks 900 cubic feet of air per minute through the 1201 and keeps it cool and contented.

One of the sights at Letchworth during this period was to see the old jam tins standing outside the Computer Room catching the drips from the air conditioners, which produce a surprising amount of water from the air they condition. This gave rise to a good deal of ribald comment about 'Computer Output' and the like.

The date set for the start of Computer Production Control in 1B arrived - Monday 11th August. Although various members of the Computer team might have been seen on the previous day feverishly biting their nails and hoping they had not forgotten something, there was nothing spectacular about the start. The complete system of production control had been changed, as it were, overnight, but it was quietly absorbed by the factory and, apart from one or two minor shudders during the first week, work went on without pause. The following weeks have been spent in getting the detail 'bugs' out of the system and, so far as the team are concerned, learning just how a Computer system of control should be introduced - by doing it the hard way.

As a result of this exercise, our company is the very first in England and among the first three or four in the world to use a Computer for the complete production control system of one of its factories.

A successful piece of remarkable daring for its time, and well ahead of most other companies (apart from J. Lyons & Co). There's a delightful period feel to the language: 'Computer' always has a capital 'C'; 'programme' hasn't yet lost its final 'me'; 'bugs' live in inverted commas; the word 'application' hasn't yet been invented; and so on. H.C.

Gamesmanship: 1, 1955-56   *George Thomson*

Every year the BTM golf tournament for the Everard Greene Trophy was played, comprising a preliminary round in each region and a final round at a Hertfordshire course. In 1955 or 56 the Scottish regional round was played at Lanark. Leslie Wight was persuaded to take part despite his protestations that he had not played since before the war. On the morning of the match he turned up wearing a Fair Isle pullover, plus-fours, hand-knitted stockings and black and white brogues, carrying a small round canvas golf bag holding half a dozen assorted hickory-shafted clubs whose iron heads were rather rusty. He stepped onto the first tee, placed a brand new Dunlop 65 on a plastic tee (we had half expected him to play a gutta percha off a heap of sand), selected a club, let go his bag which promptly fell in a heap, spreadeagling his other clubs, stepped up to his ball, waggled his club a bit, then belted the ball right down the middle of the fairway. He was round in close to regulation figures, winning by a mile but refusing to represent Scottish Region in the final. Back in the clubhouse for lunch he informed us that he hadn't played since 1934 when his handicap was down to two, but as he wasn't getting any better he had given it up. However, he had to confess that he had cheated a bit, since he had gone down to Troon the previous Sunday for a little bit of practice.

Gamesmanship: 2, 1955 *George Thomson*

Frank deLuca Kennedy, born of a Scottish father and an Italian mother, had been the IBM manager in Italy just before the war. In 1955 I was with him on a course at Moor Hall. We were sitting in the lounge one evening when a rather supercilious tech. service trainee, dressed in whites and swinging a tennis racket, entered enquiring: 'Anyone for a game of tennis?' As there were no other takers, deLuca offered his services, which were initially declined with the words: 'Aren't you a bit too old for me?' but, as there were still no takers he condescendingly accepted the offer. deLuca disappeared to his room to appear a few minutes later having removed his jacket, collar and tie (we still wore detachable collars in those days), using his tie to hold up his trousers as he had removed his braces, grey flannel trousers tucked into his socks, on his feet a pair of disreputable sand shoes and carrying a racket that had seen better days. As this ill-assorted pair left the room, I told the assembled company: 'This we must see!' I don't think I have ever seen such a one-sided contest. The TS trainee was beaten out of sight. I don't think deLuca lost a point; he certainly never broke sweat. What I knew (and nobody else there knew) was that F. deLuca Kennedy had represented Italy and had reached the second week of the men's singles at Wimbledon before the war and was then still playing county class tennis regularly.

Tales from Holborn Bar, c. 1957 *Vernon Hardman*

A young technical adviser (Dick Evans) was on duty on the stand at a BEE (Business Efficiency Exhibition) at Olympia. He was engaged in a highly technical discussion with two visitors, and they were standing next to a punched card reader which was connected to the processor by a highly visible length of cable. A third gentleman, in the proverbial raincoat, and clearly unconnected with the other two, interrupted from time to time with, to put it politely, very mundane and not always very appropriate questions. These were dealt with expeditiously but courteously by the young representative before he resumed the main discussion with the other two.

There was at one point a particularly long silence on the part of the third gentleman, during which he appeared to be listening intently to the conversation while staring fixedly at the floor. Suddenly he raised his head and interrupted: 'Yes, yes, I understand all that, Mr... er... er...' (peering at the name on the representative's lapel badge), 'but what I don't understand' (pointing at the cable on the floor) 'is how those big cards get through that little pipe.'

What rotten luck, 1957   *George Thomson*

Bradenham Manor, near West Wycombe, was built in the reign of Elizabeth I. Around 1830 Isaac Disraeli (father of Benjamin) added a Georgian wing and had the original Elizabethan front faced in the Georgian style. This unfortunately interfered with the ventilation and as a result, shortly after the company took possession, dry rot was found in the beams beneath one of the rooms. The floor boards were lifted, exposing the affected beams which were merely roughly shaped whole oak tree trunks. They became quite an attraction. I was showing some visitors round and made the remark: 'We will now go to the one place in the company where you can actually see the dry rot'. Unfortunately this was repeated and reached the topmost echelons of the company. It was not really appreciated.

Romance in the air, 1957 and much later   *George Thomson*

There must have been something about Moor Hall, as I could name quite a few couples who first met there and subsequently married, including one particularly noteworthy pair. Many moons later I happened to meet them both at a party and, late on in the evening, was alone in a corner with the wife when she started the following conversation:

'You never knew the half of what went on at Moor Hall'.

'What makes you say that?'

'You never did anything about it'.

'The fact that I did nothing about it didn't mean that I didn't know what was going on'.

'You didn't know that I was sleeping with X (her husband)'.

'Of course I knew. And I also knew that you slept with Y and Z (naming two other TS trainees)'.

She turned on her heel and walked away without another word. Some time later the husband met me and asked:

'Why does my wife seem to be avoiding you?'

'I don't know. It might have been something I said'.

The ready answer, 1959   ICT House Magazine

'What's this?' asked the customer, pointing to the neon on the 550 control panel that was marked 'Marg Test'.

'That, Sir? It's so that it can tell Stork from butter.'

Cookham, c. 1959   H.C.

In the late fifties, when George Thomson was running Moor Hall, his introductory speeches of greeting to each new intake of trainee technical advisers were memorable, not least for a passage which ran something like this:

'This academic establishment exists for the purpose of awarding Degrees, which exist at three levels: there's the BSC, the MSC, and the PHD. Which, being interpreted, stand for Bull Shit Champion, Mair o' the Same Category, and Piled Higher and Deeper.'

In the thirty-five following years, I have never encountered a Doctor without mentally saying to myself: 'You're just a Piled Higher and Deeper'. It has been very comforting.

Cookham, c. 1959   Bert Molsom

On another occasion, the Principal at Moor Hall was explaining at a Lecturers' Meeting the latest reorganisation of the company, and in particular the new structure of the Sales Division, which would apparently imply much greater emphasis on training for OXO (which we all knew well as an ingredient of beef gravy). Repetition of this strange term led to increasing confusion and mystification, until eventually a bold lecturer interrupted and asked for an explanation of the connection between OXO and the reorganisation of the Sales Division. The Principal, somewhat red-faced, had to explain that he was *not* referring to OXO, but to the new United Kingdom Sales Organisation — UKSO!

Croquet, c. 1959   Bert Molsom

The Grange and Bradenham Manor were both superior residential training establishments, with well-kept croquet lawns, which were fully used during the summer months by both staff and customers. To non-players, croquet has an image of gentle serenity and English good manners. In fact, its rules embody a legal amount of vicious maltreatment of one's opponents which doesn't seem to happen in any other game; there are suspicions that this is why it is so popular at theological colleges.

At the Grange on one occasion I was in the house after lunch, when one of the students dashed in from the croquet lawn calling: 'Quick! Quick! Come quickly! Mr X has gone mad and is going to murder Mr Y!' Happily it never quite got to that stage, but relations were decidedly strained for some time.

Two Powers Samas

A brief history   **ICT House Magazine**

Abridged from the ICT House Magazine *Number 1, February 1959*

In 1907 James Powers, a little-known engineer, was selected by the Director of the US Census to prepare suitable machinery for the 1910 Census, and was called to Washington to start the work which resulted in a new and successful type of statistical equipment.

Throughout his association with the US Government Powers was given the right to apply for patents on his many inventions and, when in 1911 his specialised services were completed, the Powers Accounting Machine Company was formed. Working in New York, Powers devoted his time to the development of machines for commercial purposes, and between 1911 and 1913 he invented the first machine to feed and punch cards automatically, as well as the first Horizontal Sorting Machine and the first Printing Tabulator. The latter was to prove of particular interest to insurance and commercial companies.

Meanwhile a selling company, the Accounting and Tabulating Machine Corporation, had been formed to handle the distribution throughout the world of the products of the Powers Accounting Machine Company, and towards the end of 1913 a set of Powers machines was taken to Europe and demonstrated there. So favourably were they received that sales agencies were immediately organised in various countries. Among them was the American-owned company registered in UK as the Accounting and Tabulating Corporation of Great Britain Limited.

Manufacture of Powers machines on a commercial basis began in 1914. First came a motor-driven punch arranged with a keyboard of 45 slides, one for each column of the card, and known as the Slide Punch. Two years later came an Automatic Key Punch with only twelve keys, providing the punching equivalent of touch typing.

Between 1913 and 1918 the Prudential, the earliest commercial users of Powers machines in Britain, carried out many experiments in the application of different punched card machines to their business, and eventually decided to standardise on Powers because that company had at the time the only machine which printed its tabulated results. Moreover, as they did not wish their organisation to become dependent on the resources of a factory situated so far away, they negotiated the purchase of the whole of the patent, manufacturing, and marketing rights of Powers machines in the British Empire. On 1 January 1919 the Accounting and Tabulating Corporation of Great Britain Limited became a wholly British company.

The Prudential then established the Croydon factory and research organisation in Aurelia Road, where one of the first achievements was the design and manufacture of the alphabetic printing unit for the tabulator, a world first and many years ahead of competitors.

From 1921 onwards the company concentrated on expanding the application of punched card machines, particularly in accountancy, a field which had previously been considered beyond their scope. This led to the introduction of the first combined alphabetic and numeric printing units as well as fully automatic direct subtraction, both essential for invoicing and ledger posting work.

In 1932 a revolutionary departure was the introduction of a new range of machines which functioned with a card $4^5/8 \times 2$ inches in size, the forerunner of 36-column and 40-column ranges whose comparatively low cost opened up completely new markets. In 1936 came 'Powers One', an even smaller range using 21-column cards. This type of machine became widely used, particularly by Co-operative Societies (in fact, the standard Co-op application only required ten and a half columns, so one week's cards could be turned end for end and re-used for a second week).

An associated company had built up a large business in the sale of Powers machines in France under the trade name SAMAS or, in full, the Société Anonyme des Machines à Statistiques. In 1929 a consolidated British selling company was created for both home and overseas sales, known as Powers Samas Accounting Machines Ltd. In 1936 the manufacturing company changed its name from the Accounting and Tabulating Corporation of Great Britain Limited to the neater title of Powers Accounting Machines Ltd.

[*Though in early 1995, while preparing this book, I was talking to Robert Moscrop in the bar of a hotel in Purley, and we mentioned the Aurelia Road factory. 'Ah', said a young chap standing close by, 'You mean the old Acc and Tab', a name which had officially ceased to exist fifty-nine years earlier. H.C.*]

During the war, the company manufactured parts and assemblies for bomb-sights, fuses, aircraft instruments, tools, gauges, etc., not only for the Air Ministry but also for the Army and the Royal Navy. But war-time requirements did much to widen the appreciation of punched card equipment. During the latter part of the war the Government introduced PAYE, and special arrangements were made to meet this challenging task.

In the early days, the world-famous engineering firm of Vickers Ltd. had become Powers users, and not a few of the developments of the machines had been initiated to meet the needs of this customer. Indeed the first steps in the development of punched cards from a statistical system into an accounting system were achieved in co-operation with Vickers.

In September 1945 the Prudential Assurance Company, while remaining the largest user of Powers equipment, and while still retaining a substantial financial interest as debenture holders until 1947, decided to dispose of its shareholding, and control of the Powers organisation passed to Morgan Grenfell and Vickers. This arrangement continued until 1955, when Powers Samas Accounting Machines became a wholly-owned subsidiary of Vickers.

The post-war period was one of great expansion for the company. On the one hand, a successful drive was organised to capture overseas markets which were considerably widened by the termination of a territorial agreement, dating originally from 1919, with Remington Rand, who had bought the American Powers Company between the wars. On the other hand, the electronic field presented an exciting new challenge. The company entered this field in 1946, the results being the EMP (Electronic Multiplying Punch), the P.C.C. (Programme-Controlled Computer), and the Samastronic high speed Tabulator-Printer.

Too close for comfort, 1940s   Des Tracey

Early on in the war I was on deferred service, working flat-out building tabulators for factories and the forces. One Friday evening I had an early finish (about 5 p.m.) and cycled home to Woodside Green, Croydon. As I approached the traffic lights in Lower Addiscombe Road a German bomber dropped a string of bombs, one landing a few hundred yards in front of me in the middle of the road. It fractured a gas main and sent flames shooting high. Shortly after I reached home I heard that another bomb of the string had landed right in the entrance of the Powers Samas factory in Aurelia Road, the very entrance I had walked through only about ten minutes earlier. This one caused casualties, including the unfortunate gatekeeper.

The Afrika Korps in action, 1940s   Des Tracey

After being called up I eventually found myself as a Corporal in Cairo, working with a couple of civilian engineers, Alf Stokes and A. Withers. The large 65-column installation worked twenty-four hours a day, seven days a week, dealing with Army stores, records, pay and everything else. Then the Army decided to move the installation out of Cairo and split it into three; I was allocated to the unit at GHQ Middle East, somewhere out in the desert near the Great Bitter Lake. The Egyptian civilian staff we had been using either wouldn't move or would not be wanted at the new locations, but as staff were an urgent problem the authorities decided to use German prisoners of war. Trusted ones were selected and brought into Cairo for training, which normally took place during the night shift. When I was on night duty I had to sign for the prisoners and for the containers of soup and bread rolls, the only food allowed them for the night's work. It did not take the Germans long to find out that next door to the machine room was the ATS canteen. Sure enough, one night while doing a check I found two of them missing; they had broken into the canteen and were helping themselves. They also found out that if they put their fingers into a machine and held a lever the machine would go wrong. Not deliberate enemy action, you understand, just a way of ensuring they could curl up on the floor and have a sleep.

Sand punching, 1940s   Des Tracey

From Cairo we took the machines allocated to GHQ in three army trucks, each with an armed guard, installed them, and drafted in RAOC clerks for training as operators. Data preparation was to be by hand punches, and the ATS girls to work these were due to land at Port Said from the UK in the next few days. When they arrived, we found that not one of them was a punch operator; they had all been trained as cooks. With Monty's staff breathing down our necks, the re-training was rapid.

The unkindest cut of all, 1940s   Des Tracey

I was lucky in spending most of my time in the army servicing Powers machines. There was one 65 column installation where a civilian operator put her head between a Tabulator and its Summary Card Punch to clear a wreck. Then, silly girl, instead of switching off she pressed the operating lever to cause the SCP to do one cycle, and her hair went round in the gears. It was quite some time before she would accept that the only way out was to cut her hair.

Powers in peacetime, c. 1950
Ron Driver

I joined straight from the Royal Navy (I had been a pilot in the Fleet Air Arm, a much less dangerous occupation). My appointment was as a Trainee Technical Adviser and Accountant, subject to obtaining a BCom or professional Accounting qualification by external studies.

My first boss was Hector Prytz, the Area Sales Manager for Kent, Sussex, South London and part of the Central London postal districts; a very shrewd businessman with good negotiating skills. One of the first things he taught me was that in spite of the (then) licensing laws you could always get a drink 'where they make the laws and where they keep them'. To prove it we walked down from the Holborn Office to the Law Courts in the Strand and, sure enough, he knew where the bar was and it was indeed open.

Great Expectations, c.1950
Ron Driver

One of the first sales investigations I was engaged on was at a very dirty metal works in Greenwich, next door to a very smelly dog biscuit factory. At this time I was working with Michael 'Stoke' Newington. One Friday afternoon Prytz turned up on site to 'see how we were getting on' (and probably for a quick Friday getaway). About four o'clock the Managing Director put his head round the door and said: 'We usually have a little celebration at the end of the week, would you like to join us?' 'YES PLEASE', said Prytz, and then to me: 'No need for you to come'. Off went a smiling Area Manager and Senior Technical Adviser. Later a totally unsmiling Newington arrived back in the office. 'They meant a prayer meeting!', he said.

What happened to 'both'?
H.C.

The User Manuals and Technical Guides for all Powers Samas products were produced under the guidance of Herbert Gerstl. They were in most respects admirable models of conciseness and clarity. But there was one problem.

From somewhere unidentified and unspecifiable, Gerstl had acquired the unshakeable conviction that in English the word 'both' must always be immediately preceded by one comma and immediately followed by another.

This had the curious effect that as you were studying a passage of some complexity you would be suddenly affected by, both, a complete interruption of the flow and a complete distraction from the sense.

The mapping job, 1954   ICT House Magazine, *August 1962*

A magnificent book was presented by the Botanical Society of Great Britain to Roy Smith, Systems Adviser of Essex North-West Area. It contained an article with the following description of his work, whose success had earned the Society's gratitude:

'At a late stage in the planning of the Maps Scheme, when it had already been agreed that the use of punched card machinery was essential for the preparation of the data for mapping, the idea arose that it might be possible to use the punched cards themselves to produce the maps mechanically. The problem was presented to L.R. Smith of Powers Samas and within days he had solved it and was able to demonstrate the technique when the project was launched in April 1954. So thorough was Mr Smith's analysis of the problem that the technique has been altered little since it was first developed.

'The forty column cards are prepared for mapping by sorting all those for one species on the first figure of the grid reference. The cards are divided into four groups, each for a vertical strip of the British Isles. The four groups, proceeding from west to east across the map, have the first figure of the grid reference as follows:

 8 and 9
 0 and 1
 2 and 3
 4, 5 and 6

'Each of these groups is twenty ten-kilometre squares wide except the last which is twenty-five - the maximum number of print positions available on the tabulator used.

'Within each strip the cards are arranged in vertical order. 100 master cards are interspersed between them, one for each of the 100 possible vertical positions. (By insetting the Channel Islands, Orkneys and Shetland, the British Isles can be shown on a map as less than 1000 kilometres from north to south).

'The cards are transferred to a standard tabulator modified only so that the vertical and horizontal throws are equal. An outline map is set at a fixed position in the tabulator, and the 100 master cards operate the paper-advance mechanism, so that the map turns through 100 positions, one for each 10-kilometre square of northing, during the course of a run. When a species card punched with a grid reference is fed into the tabulator the map remains stationary, the card is sensed, and the appropriate sector of the print unit is operated to bring up a symbol in the correct position.

'The map is re-positioned for each of the four vertical strips in turn.

'By this means a map of 3,500 dots can be produced in less than an hour, and an average map of about 1,000 dots in twenty minutes. During the scheme the tabulator has been used to place the solid dots on the maps; circles and other symbols have been added by hand.'

When I first heard of this job I was told that in certain maps showing the distribution of wild flowers during the middle decades of the 19th century you could see that a certain species, initially common around the little village of Euston, had ten years later reached Bletchley, and from there spread to Crewe, much as in our times salt-tolerant plants are spreading inland from the coasts along the verges of motorways. H.C.

Tales from Holborn Bar, c. 1956   *Vernon Hardman*

It was *de rigueur* for London-based sales and support staff (as they might be called today) to wear suits and for managers, in particular, to wear hats. Those who worked in the City, and some of those in the West End, would wear pin-striped suits and bowler hats as a matter of course.

A young salesman from the City was temporarily transferred to the Edinburgh office. Sharp at nine o'clock on the appointed Monday morning he presented himself at the Powers Samas reception desk, which was on the fifth floor of a large building. He was attired in his normal suit, wearing his normal bowler hat, and carrying his normal briefcase. History does not record whether he also carried a tightly rolled umbrella, but is seems highly likely that he did.

Before he had a chance to announce himself, the receptionist looked up, gave him a welcoming smile and said, in what he was later to learn was a Morningside accent (à la Miss Jean Brodie for the uninitiated): 'Good morning, Sir! I'm sorry, but you have come to the wrong office. The insurance company's reception is two floors down'.

Initiative, 1956   *Sarah Hamilton*

Egypt was at war with Israel, the UK, and France. At that time, all staff salaries were actually flown in from England, as were all spare parts. But one immediate consequence of the war was that our Egypt offices were closed down by the Government (because it was a British company) and no supplies of any kind could be obtained from England.

Fortunately, the enterprising Egyptian Country Manager of the time managed to keep things going for a full eight months until the situation returned to normal. He arranged for spares to be delivered from India, he ran all the operations from his own home and the homes of his staff, and he persuaded every customer with leased equipment to pay an extra year's hire in advance, to cover the cost of spares and staff salaries.

That sinking feeling, 1950s   Des Tracey

I was Senior Engineer at the Portsmouth Royal Dockyard installation, located in the grounds of Warblington House, Havant, when a new job came up which required many thousands of cards, all of which had to be interpreted. There was ample machine capacity, except for the interpreting part of the job, and to make sure that we got the order we had to provide another Interpreter at short notice. One which was just about to be delivered to another customer was whipped off the test floor, crated, and sent hotfoot by BRS. I was asked to stay late and see it in. A high open lorry appeared at 7.30 p.m. and backed up to the machine room, going onto the grass as it did so. We manoeuvred the Interpreter down some planks (no hydraulic tailgates in those days), wrestled it into place, and I signed for it. It was only then that the driver noticed that the weight of the rest of his load, several tons of drain covers, had sunk him to the axles in the ground. Oh, it took hours for a towing vehicle to arrive, and I had to stay with the driver until it did. We parted with the mutual hope that we would never meet again.

High old times, 1950s   Des Tracey

Just before the merger with Hollerith, our Southampton sales office obtained an order for a 40-column installation from Jersey Airlines. The machines were to be sited at the Airport in Jersey. As it was the first installation in the Channel Islands, and not large enough to warrant a resident engineer, Sales negotiated a deal under which seats for engineers on call would be provided at the airline's expense. We soon found out that they could get you there ASAP, but coming back you had to wait for a vacant seat.

The machines involved were a Tabulator with Summary Card Punch, Sorter, three UAKPs and a Verifier. With only a few days warning I learned that they would go out on the last flight one Saturday evening, and I was asked would I go to Gatwick to advise. The machines had been delivered, *uncrated*, to the freight department of Jersey Airlines, who were wondering how to treat these strange objects. In the early evening the Dakota arrived from Jersey, unloaded its passengers, and taxied over to the freight shed. Work began at once, as the same plane was due out on another scheduled flight with passengers including a honeymoon couple. All the seats were whisked out, and planks were laid to protect the carpet. A forklift brought the machines up to the door, from where they were manhandled into place and anchored to the floor fittings which a few minutes earlier had secured the seats. A lot of other freight was also loaded, then a screen was hung across the cabin to conceal it all, and the exact number of seats required were reinstalled near the tail. As this all took quite a bit longer than expected, a hostess appeared at intervals from the terminal to check on progress. 'Oh, put another thirty minutes on the departure time' was the chief loader's standard reply. Each time we would hear the Tannoy announce: 'Due to technical problems there will be a further delay', and two anxious faces would appear at the terminal windows. Eventually the crew arrived, looked at the loading sheets, and the Pilot commented ominously: 'Oh, maximum load!'. The crew then had to sidle sideways between the freight in order to get to the cockpit. We taxied to the last inch of the runway, then full throttle, and away to the island.

As the installation got busier a further Tabulator was ordered, and was delivered to Bournemouth Airport. But this was a freight only flight, so there was less pressure on timing. The machine was loaded, and the necessary chains were fixed to the floor anchorages. Next came a lorry load of meat carcasses, which were stacked all round the machine. I went along as the only passenger. All Powers Engineers know that our tabulators were top heavy; every time we banked on the flight to Jersey I could hear the chains taking the strain and protesting.

Later on there was a major job to do in Jersey and, while another engineer and I were waiting at Bournemouth Airport for our flight, over the public address system came the announcement: 'Would the two engineers flying to Jersey Airport please report to reception.' Derek and I reported as requested. 'Look, we see that you're engineers and that you're flying free of charge to Jersey, so would you be good enough to look at the fault on the aircraft?' Having declined for obvious reasons we had to wait for another plane to arrive from Jersey.

Hot-starting started in Crayford, 1956   *Ben Gunn*

There were two prototype P.C.C.s in the Crayford labs, which were switched on at nine every morning for work to start. In order to increase the life of the valves, the filament power was turned up progressively by an automatic control. One night in November, someone stayed late and wired a jumping cracker to the filament supply, winding some fuse wire round the touch paper. Next morning Jock Burney, the maintenance man, switched on as usual, and within seconds the machine was belching smoke and emitting loud bangs. The look of panic on his face as he dashed around looking for the fault will never be forgotten.

Now it really can be told, 1956 — Ben Gunn

The prototype P.C.C. was demonstrated at one of the early Business Efficiency Exhibitions, and because it was a prototype it was thought it might be subject to the occasional error. Any error would be embarrassing; therefore precautions were taken. In each card of the demonstration pack were pre-punched the operands of a computation. The machine would read the factors from a card, perform its miracles of electronic calculation, and punch the answer into the same card as it reached the output stage of the machine. Unbeknown to most people the correct answer was in fact fed into the machine from the previous card. So all the machine had to do was read the answer and wait for the problem to arrive.

Beat that! 1957 — Jeff Banks

The Board of Directors of Powers Samas visited the Dartford Works on 26 July 1957. The documentation prepared for their visit included a history of the site, starting with the Wheat Mill and Malt Mill mentioned in Domesday Book.

There are no earlier references in this Anthology. H.C.

Excelsior! 1950s — Des Tracey

Poultry farmers are used to packing things tight in small spaces. The 21-column installation for a firm in Salisbury was to be based in a country house, and up a narrow stair. When the machines were delivered and we looked at the problem, it seemed impossible; indeed, the driver was all for taking the machines straight back with him. But the salesman got into a timely flap, and out came his wallet. Under this influence, the tabulator was laid on the driver's back, one engineer went in front to pull and guide it, I took the weight below and behind, and the driver *crawled* up the stairs. It's probably still up there.

Lubrication, 1950s — Des Tracey

The Data Processing Manager at the Brewery in Weymouth was an ex-Powers employee, and he well knew how important it was to keep on the good side of the engineers. Consequently a crate of beer was always kept in the cupboard and a bottle was made available on every visit. Needless to say whenever we were in the area a call would be made to ensure that his machines were in tiptop condition. They always were.

The Whyteleafe Firework Society: 1, 1950s   Ben Gunn

A Firework Society was formed at Whyteleafe. I still have the Society's seal, used to authenticate any special messages: it bears the emblem of two crossed rockets and a bomb with the legend *Per Sal Petrum Ad Aeternitam*. The Society was anti-establishment (of course) and usually took the credit or blame for most non-company activities. The first major event was on 5 November with the purchase, by popular subscription, of a very large Catherine wheel; its diameter was 4 to 5 feet! This was mounted on a frame to hang from the roof immediately outside the window of Major Guttridge's office. At the appointed time (it was dark) the device was lowered to window level and ignited. It was *most* spectacular, but the Major did not appreciate it as much as the rest of the audience. Hearing the Guy Fawkes running along the roof, he gave chase but failed to catch him.

The public birth of the P.C.C., 1955   H.C.

The launch of this machine to the astoundable world of Powers Samas customers took place in one of London's great theatres. For the occasion the stage had been cleared, and all that could be seen at the back of it was a conventional 'sky-cloth', painted just the right shade of cerulean blue. Now whether he had planned the script that way, or whether the circumstances gave him the perfect cue, we shall never know.

Anyway, onto this dramatically bare platform, in front of this vividly coloured backcloth, and facing this eagerly awaiting throng, emerged 'Paddy' Winter, who was in charge of Public Relations for Powers Samas. A lovely man, sweet of smile and mellifluous of voice. He was going to introduce this revolution in technology.

How did he do it? Well, you have to use your imaginations now, to ensure that you can synchronise in your mind's eye the dominating and theatrical combination of gesture and voice. He raised both hands majestically until they were together, at arm's length and on tip toe, as far above his head as they would go, and then slowly he swept his fully-stretched arms down to the horizontal on each side. As he did this, he uttered the immortal words: 'Ladies and Gentlemen! Under the w h o l e c a n o p y o f H e a v e n, there has never been a machine like the P.C.C.!'

The Colman verses, 1958   Cecil Kellehar

These arose as a result of Donald Smith, Colman's Finance Director, saying at a business lunch that in the 1800s their sales representatives travelled on horseback. One would go to, say, Thetford, stable his horse at the Bell Hotel and put up a notice outside saying: 'Messrs Colman's representative is within and will be pleased to take your orders.'

'What a marvellous way of doing business!' I said.

'Kellehar,' he replied, 'If ever you come to us on a horse, we'll give you an order'.

In 1958 I was trying to sell them an early computer to replace their Powers Samas punched card equipment. Negotiations were dragging on and so, in desperation, I hired a horse from Captain Palmer and rode up to the offices in Carrow with the contracts in my briefcase. They were signed!

From Colman's, *September 26th 1958:*

At that time I was breeding pigs and keeping chickens as a hobby. Who penned the following lines remains a mystery; Donald Smith stoutly denied authorship.

A certain Mister Kellehar,
Quite an enterprising fellehar,
Has introduced a novel selling force:
While others ride in Zephyrs
He deserts his pigs and heifers
To sell us a computer – from a HORSE!

Mounted on a broiler
He'll sell a patent oiler;
A Hereford would justify a Tab.
A Sorter would be easy
From a Jersey or a 'Friesie';
An Auto-Punch a guinea-pig could nab.

Why not an alligator
For a new Interpolator?
A rhino for a Samastronic do?
If we ever want an ERNIE
He'll have a lovely journey –
Why, blimey, he'll bring half the ruddy ZOO!

To Donald Smith, September 27th 1958:

May I thank you for your letter,
It could hardly have been better;
Your resourcefulness in rhyme is much admired.

But there's very little doubt
That if I try to carry out
Your suggestions, then I'll very soon be FIRED.

It isn't that we're mean
Or unwilling to be seen
In the company of cow or other creature;
It's merely that we feel
You'll demand a Conger Eel
For an Independent Designating Feature.

Your final business terms
May claim larger pachyderms
To be ridden from the attic to the basement;
I respectfully suggest
That we let the matter rest
Till replacement is succeeded by replacement.

Rank offence, 1959 *Arthur Humphreys*

I went to the Powers Samas research establishment at Whyteleafe with 'Red' Marples (a great character from the drawing office; his nickname derived from his staunch, and sometimes somewhat bolshie, trade unionism). 'Mr Humphreys and Mr Marples have come to see Mr Guttridge', he said to the receptionist. 'Mr Guttridge, indeed!' she replied; 'You mean *Major* Guttridge'. 'In that case', said Marples, 'You tell Major Guttridge that his visitors are Mr Humphreys and *Staff Sergeant* Marples'.

The Whyteleafe Firework Society: 2, 1959 *Ben Gunn*

At Christmas, following the merger between Powers and BTM, there was no tree in the entrance hall at Whyteleafe, and indeed no other sign of the festive season. The Firework Society took a dim view of this and decided to go ahead with some DIY. Bob Gibson owned a Rolls Royce, so we set off and purchased a tree the length of the car and lashed it outside on the side opposite to the security booth at the gate. We got through the gate OK, unloaded the tree at the rear entrance, and raced it up the back stairs to the lift room. Here it was placed in a tub, decorated with tinsel, and the lights were fitted. The next problem was to get it into position in the reception area without our being caught by the Chief Security man, Mr Card. One of us was given the task of getting him out of the reception area long enough for the tree to be carried down the main stairs and plugged in. Imagine his surprise, after leaving the area for no more than 90 seconds, to find a fully decorated Christmas tree in position, bearing a prominent message which read : 'Happy Christmas to all at ICT, and a VERY VERY PROSPEROUS New Year to all the staff.' Definitely one up to the Society.

Alas, regardless of his doom...   *Ben Gunn*

Peter Brett of the development team announced that he was getting married and that drinks would be on him at lunch-time in the pub at Whyteleafe. This was an occasion he would never forget. We acquired a chain and padlock, plus a 75lb. ball from a fly press in the workshop. With the aid of a young lady, who diverted his attention by sitting on his knee and sweet-talking him, we managed to padlock the ball and chain to his ankle. At the pub he wasn't much concerned. But then everybody left, and he found that he had to carry the weight back to work. That was not so much fun, at least for him; the other passengers on the bus thought it was hilarious.

Tact at Croydon, 1959   *H.C.*

The testing floor at the Aurelia Road factory was run by a splendid but formidable lady called May. Was her surname Phelan? I believe it was, or something like it. She had a glass-fronted cabin of an office set diagonally in one corner of the space, and raised several feet above the surrounding floor. From the top of the steps leading to it, i.e. from what South Africans would call its 'stoep', she could issue orders to any part of the testing floor without any fear of being misunderstood. She had what the Royal Navy used to refer to as a North Atlantic voice, meaning that mere gales could never get in the way of effective communication.

Not long after the merger, I was among the erks driving Samastronic printers under test on that spacious floor, and we were doing meticulously what we were told. May was in full song. While this was all proceeding according to Cocker, a charge-hand in a white coat sidled up to the foot of the steps and surreptitiously suggested: ' 'ere, May, quieten dahn a bit! Sir Cecil's coming rahnd'.

Back on the instant came the stentorian riposte: *'Sir Cecil 'oo?'*

Whereupon, precisely on cue, a dapper little silver-haired gentleman emerged from around the nearest corner, complete with his entourage, smiled beatifically up at her, bowed, and said: 'Weir, Madam!'

Oh! Calamity! 1959   H.C.

There was a modest little company making a modest little profit trading in a modest little way by dealing in aircraft parts. It was based in a proto-industrial estate on the fringes of the scruffy bit of reclaimed swamp that called itself Portsmouth Airport.

For no reason that I could ever discover the directors had been persuaded that the business had grown to the stage where its reputation would in future depend on the modernity of their company being confirmed by their adoption of punched card technology for all logistic and financial processing. So they had invested in a set of re-conditioned 36-column machines, comprising a single UAKP, one sorter, and the massive threatening form of a tabulator.

The whole of the administrative processes of this firm had hitherto been run by a couple of ladies; they had now been volunteered by their management to run this new-fangled automatic equipment. I was taken down there by the young salesman, and introduced by him as the Technical Adviser who would get them going, see them started, give them immediate support for some weeks, and see them launched into independence.

I've no doubt they were really extremely competent, and I suppose they were probably in no more than their early fifties, but at the time they seemed to me immensely old, and they were all of a twitter!

Some clot had mentioned 'card wrecks' to them, and it was as though they were facing the end of the world.

'Oh, you don't need to fret about that!', said wonder-boy young salesman. 'Look, I'll cause a wreck, and show you how easy it is to deal with!'

So he took a card at random, and mangled its leading edge in such a way that it would feed out of the hopper but still be guaranteed to wreck somewhere in the middle of the machine.

The start button was pressed, the card was correctly fed, there was that brief horrid squeal which indicated trouble, and the tabulator stopped.

'Right Ho!', said the wonder-boy young salesman; 'This is the procedure, and it's really straightforward: We switch the power off, OK? And we take out all the un-fed cards, noting exactly where we've got to, and we put them safely aside. Then, using the hand-wheel, we turn the machine over until all sensing pins are entirely clear of the card track, so that we know the card is free from all of the pins. (And, look!, we can tell when we've reached that condition by watching the picker knife when it's as far forward as it can go, we know the card-track is clear). Then, using this hefty screwdriver, we prise the feed-rolls apart to give us some room to work in. Then we insert this object - called a 'wreck-knife', - and wiggle it about until we can catch hold of the wrecked card or any of its fragments, with the hooked end. And then we carefully pull them out. Finally, before restarting the machine we reassemble the card fragments on a convenient desk, to make sure that we haven't left any bits that are going to cause trouble later. And we re-punch the damaged card, and etc. etc.'

The exposition was masterly. The two old dears followed each step of the way with trusting faith and increasing confidence. Until, mehercule, the actual extraction of the deliberately-induced wrecked card. At this point, wholly hostile to the script, and at the very first wiggle of the inserted wreck-knife's handle, there was a musical little 'twang' sort of sound, the wonder-boy young salesman was seen aghast holding the unattached stubby little wooden handle, and the vital blade of the wreck knife was left irretrievably buried in the guts of the machine.

Two hours, I think it took, to do the round trip to another installation to borrow their wreck-knife in order to retrieve the remnants of our wreck-knife.

Looking at where the responsibilities lie, now as much as then, Oh, I am glad that I've never been a salesman.

The Whyteleafe Firework Society: 3, 1960   Ben Gunn

That year, as 5 November came closer, a notice was posted banning *all* fireworks. At the time the cold war was in full swing, with ballistic missiles pointing in all directions and plentiful satellite launchings. As the fifth arrived, strict security reigned, and management were convinced that they had succeeded. But at 5.30 p.m. spotlights came on in several upper windows, illuminating a monster rocket sitting on the lawn in front of the Directors' window. It was proudly labelled 'I.C.T.B.M'. Then from loudspeakers at other windows came the countdown: '10, 9, 8, 7, 6, 5, we have ignition' and then 'ABORT, ABORT, ABORT'. On 'we have ignition' enormous clouds of smoke billowed out from below the rocket, with plenty of red flames and flashes. As the flames reached their peak an *enormous* explosion rocked the whole site. The floodlights went out, and there was silence apart from the ominous tinkle of broken glass. We had used Drain Testing Smoke Generators driven by Vent-Axia fans for the smoke, and some thunder flashes for the warhead. Unfortunately, the warhead calculations went a bit wrong, with the result that the complete head of the wooden structure was blown to pieces and several windows bore the brunt. Next morning management were presented with sufficient funds to cover the cost of repairs. Another victory for the Fireworks Society.

Sweet harmony
Ben Gunn

E.C.H. Organ had been appointed Director in charge of all research, and it was announced that he was coming to speak to all senior staff in the Whyteleafe restaurant at 5.30 p.m. Alongside the terse official notice there blossomed a much larger and more decorative poster. It read, (more or less, and taking some liberties with Beethoven's sequence):

GRAND E.C.H. ORGAN RECITAL
BEETHOVEN'S SIXTH SYMPHONY – THE PASTORAL

1. Awakening of pleasant feelings on arrival in the country
2. Scene at the brook
3. The storm
4. Shepherds' hymn after the storm
5. Peasants making merry

After ECHO had finished his storm, and the drink was flowing, (i.e. the fifth movement), Peter Simpson took him to see the poster. He liked it.

Well, goodness gracious me! 1960s
Robert Moscrop

The 4/5 Powers Samas Tabulator was being installed at the headquarters of the Rajasthan Transport Authority. Such a great event could not be allowed to happen without due ceremony. So in the presence of all the burra sahibs the holy man made puja, at its climax raised high the dish of sanctified rice and, with a rapt expression, poured it over the platen and print hammers straight into the heart of the machine. The first print run was deferred for four weeks while the engineers retrieved it, grain by painstaking grain.

Transfer time optimisation
Ben Gunn

When John Drew became development supremo of both Letchworth and Whyteleafe, travel and co-operation between the sites increased considerably. This was helped by John's offer of a crate of beer to the person who took the least time to make the journey during working hours. At both ends this was taken very seriously, and a clock card was used to book out of one site and into the other. Train timetables were pored over for optimum times and connections. Routes through the centre of London were tested for traffic conditions at different times, as it was thought that the car might be the quickest way (less traffic, of course, in those days but equally, no M25).

The winning team, led by Cyril Williams, went to the trouble of hiring a helicopter from Biggin Hill and landing at an airfield near Letchworth, with the airport transfers at each end made as a pillion passenger on a motorbike. Peter Simpson stumped up a consolation prize for the car group. At least it got North and South talking to each other.

Goodbye Whyteleafe   Arthur Humphreys

The time came when 'ECHO' Organ decided that Advanced Research needed to be rationalised in Stevenage, and hence that Whyteleafe would have to close. He made a presentation to the Board on his reasoning, and when the vote was taken it was accepted. 'A pity, really', said Sir Edward Playfair, 'Mollie and I will miss seeing the place on our way to Glyndebourne'.

The End, 1962   ICT House Magazine, Number 38

On Wednesday 31 January 1962 a page of company history was turned when the last mechanical tabulator to be produced at Croydon Works left the assembly floor. The machine was one of three Restyled Tabulators for the Madras Office of the Life Insurance Corporation of India. The 21- and 40-column mechanical tabulator story continues at Dartford, but at Croydon the book is closed.

Three I C T

The beginnings of ICT, 1958   H.C.

At the great Computer Exhibition held at Olympia in October 1958 (the one when the prototype Rank Xeronic printer delighted us all by the chance that it might catch fire), the Powers Samas stand was manned by a small but select group of handsome, well-dressed, elegant and charming young gentlemen.

Just round the corner, in an adjoining aisle, the British Tabulating Machine Company stand was staffed by a more numerous but equally select group of very good-looking, marvellously well-dressed, superbly elegant and extremely charming young ladies.

After a week in such fortunate proximity, several very promising relationships had already been established.

So much so, that when the Boards of the two Companies announced the merger that was to form ICT, many of us thought that they were just rubber-stamping what had already been decided at a much more practical level.

Defusing the situation, c. 1959   *Bernard Bassett*

It was one of those very rare cases where there was a dispute between ICT and its customer over the accuracy of ICT's maintenance invoices. Clem Shread went up to Nottingham in person to sort it out. But things, having started tense, got bitter and then acrimonious. As he left in highest dudgeon, Clem suddenly diverted into the machine room, whipped the fuses out of the back of every machine, stuffed them into his pocket, and stormed out. Later he handed over his pocketful to a bemused field engineer. And until the BFE had worked out which fuse went where, analysis of bicycle sales was severely disrupted.

The print that vanished, 1959   H.C.

It must have been in late 1959, during the Business Efficiency Exhibition at Olympia. David 'Duff' Lewthwaite and I were driving a Samastronic on the ICT stand. I was feeding the demo pack of cards repeatedly into the hopper at one end, and Duff was monitoring the printed output at the other. From time to time, just for variety, we swapped ends and roles.

Now before the Exhibition started we had been given a briefing by our manager (Jessie Webster) which included one strongly emphasised and very explicit warning: if a particular salesman (could it have been Roy Hill?) ever came onto the stand, we were to watch him like a hawk and keep him well away from any machine for which we were responsible. Why? Because he was a fiddler; he couldn't keep his fingers off things; he would switch switches and twiddle levers without being conscious that he was doing it, particularly when he was talking to a prospect.

So there we were, separated by the ten feet length of the Samastronic, minding our own business, and waiting for the next refreshment break. Suddenly, I saw Duff's eyebrows shoot up and a look of utter alarm come over his face. Abandoning the card feeding job, I went to the printer end and immediately saw, with at least equal alarm, what had so astonished him. The lines of print, previously so even and regular, were progressively diminishing in width. Some plague was eating them up from one end. What could it be?

Nothing was obviously wrong in front, or at either end. What about round the back? And there, previously hidden from our view, was the predicted villainous salesman, deep in the most animated conversation with some prospect or other. And, as he urged his case with highly professional eagerness, he was moving continually forwards; to which his listener was responding by edging continually backwards. And, as this *pas de deux* progressed, with the right hand punctuating the conversation and stressing arguments with a variety of possibly relevant gestures, unnoticed and unconsciously the left hand was flickering over the back of the printer, and switching off one columnar decoder after another.

Jessie had been right. She usually was.

More and more potatoes, 1959   *Bernard Bassett*

Following the BTM/Powers Samas merger, the sales ledgers of the two companies were consolidated at Letchworth and, in the interests of fairness, the bought ledgers were to be consolidated at Powers Samas House in Holborn. This didn't work out all that well, and some suppliers became increasingly shirty. Cecil Mead set out to investigate in person.

Illustrating the chaos he found, here is just one example: a supplier had supplied a load of potatoes to the canteen in Powers Samas House, and had been paid with a cheque for £40. 0s. 0d. But somehow or other his invoice was paid twice, and he received another cheque for £40. 0s. 0d., which, being an honest fellow, he sent back with an explanatory letter. But the system didn't include any procedure for cancelling a cheque, so it was returned to him. And the only way he could see out of the impasse was to deliver another load of potatoes to the canteen, which they didn't want and didn't have room to store. So the cheque and the potatoes might have been reverberating to this day if the bought ledger hadn't been transferred to join its more orderly counterpart in Letchworth.

Powers power, 1959   *Martin Wright*

A story from the days of *the* merger, when the blood on the walls was in either slotted-shaped or round-shaped splashes.

Upon formation of the new combined Defence Area, the senior salesman from the Hollerith Defence team was sharing an office with his opposite number from Powers Samas. During a lull one day, the Hollerith man enquired of the Powers Samas man how on earth had he managed to win a particular order for a mobile data-processing unit for use in the Middle East.

Said the ex-Hollerith salesman: 'I thought I had the order sewn up. I had proposed a very neat solution, fitting all the punched card equipment into one five-ton truck, with another five-tonner to carry the generator. As well as providing a good solution, I thought I had all the right contacts: I had been at school with the Colonel in the War Office who wrote the requirement; I played golf with the Principal who was evaluating the tenders; and my father-in-law was the Under Secretary at the Treasury responsible for the War Office data processing vote. And yet you got the order!'

'Ah', said the Powers Samas salesman (and remember this was long before the days of political correctness): 'You may have had a beautiful system and all the contacts, but my equipment all fitted into one *three*-ton truck and for electricity the only other thing needed was a wog on a bicycle.'

Card-iac arrest, 1959   *H.C.*

There was a dress firm near the Goat and Compasses, round the back of where LON24 was later built, with a small 21-column installation, the only one where I've found cockroaches actually living in the bottom of the tabulator.

Every dress dispatched to a retail shop went with a little plastic bag attached to its hanger, containing three cards, prepunched with the model number and the price. They were of different colours, and one was a receipt for the customer, one was retained by the branch for its local sales records, and the third was returned to head office for all forms of central accounting and analysis. They were always put into the little plastic bags in the same order, so that every pink central sales card had its face in contact with the plastic and its reverse in contact with one of the other cards.

I can only assume that some slippery factor was picked up on the face of each card from its little plastic bag, and was progressively transferred onto the upper feed rolls of the card track in the tabulator, so that while the lower rolls exercised standard traction on the underside of the card, the upper rolls began to skid. Or maybe it was the other way round; maybe the upper rolls got stickier.

Anyway, having set the tabulator going, I was concentrating on the next sorting job at the other side of the room, and it took a long time before I became conscious of something odd in the sound of the tabulator behind me. It was still running all right, but there wasn't any printing going on. Funny! Emergency stop and investigate. The findings were horrendous. Every card was passing through the control sensing station correctly but then, instead of continuing horizontally into the main sensing station, it was turning upwards through 90 degrees, into a space where it had no right to be, and there stopping. By the time I found them, over three hundred cards had piled up in this mechanical limbo. Their extrication and repunching were less than enjoyable. Over the language that ensued let us draw a decent veil.

On the right lines, 1959   H.C.

The office building was brick-built, only two stories high, and curved gently to stay close to the branch line alongside which it had been built some time in the late nineteenth century. The architect had been Matthew Webb, whose principal job was as locomotive designer for, I suppose, the London and North Western Railway. It is said that when the building was formally opened, the Chairman of the Railway commented: 'Stick to engines, Webb, stick to engines.'

Anyway, it was this building which was to receive two P.C.C.s, programmed to assist in stock control. Part of the first floor had been refurbished as a computer room, and was bright, clean, and shining. The other side of the same floor was still equipped with high sloping green leather-topped clerical desks with matching stools, probably unchanged for eighty years. What a contrast!

We craned the first P.C.C. in using our own contractor, with the utmost delicacy, and it took a fortnight to commission. When the second one arrived, BR said that they now knew how to do it, gaily hefted it over the roof with one of their breakdown cranes, swung it in through the windows, and dropped it the last inch. It worked a treat from first switch-on.

Good intentions, 1959 · H.C.

The Winkle's Eye was a short-lived ancillary machine, designed to be safer and more reliable than chad-stuffing. If a card had a mis-punched hole, the Winkle's Eye (which looked rather like the machines with which you can emboss your address on fancy note paper) would cover it with a neatly cut small circle of coloured Sellotape.

We were trying to test a newly installed P.C.C., when it transpired that the test pack had a mistaken character gang-punched in column 1. Well, there were lots of other things to do, so we carried on with them, not realising that in the background the Installation Manageress was devotedly going through the whole pack with the Winkle's Eye. By the time she'd finished there was so many little Sellotape circles that the column 1 end of the pack was nearly two inches thicker than the column 80 end, and the pack wouldn't feed because the card weight didn't sit right. But didn't she do well?

Nobody has ever liked our invoices, c. 1960 Chris Penfold

I handed to the customer a special invoice for the delivery charges (during the weekend we had put a tabulator into his office in the City of London). He took one look at it and complained very loudly. Why?

The delivery had to be on a Sunday because a crane was needed to lift the machine up to the window of his offices, and the Police wouldn't allow a crane in that narrow street on any other day. Organising a Sunday delivery clearly involves a number of actions, a number of people, and some nifty co-ordination. Unhappily, nobody remembered to organise the crane.

Bang on time the lorry arrived with machine on board; so did the customer; and so did our Engineers, one of whom was sent off to hunt hotfoot throughout the City for a mobile crane. He was lucky: he found one the other side of Tower Bridge, twisted the driver's arm, and got him to bring his crane across the river, to the customer's premises, lift in the machine, and depart.

So why the aggro about the invoice? Well, it did include a charge for the tip which our Engineer had given to the crane driver, and we didn't know that the customer had tipped him too!

Punched card horrors: 1 (the thin ones), c. 1960 Chris Penfold

When you think how many cards must have been manufactured, punched, verified, read on machines, filed and thrown away, it's not surprising that sometimes a few didn't turn out the way they were supposed to.

When I was in Support, one of my customers was an insurance company, using cards filed by Premium Renewal Date. Each year, as each month's renewals became due, the appropriate file was tabulated to produce the Renewal Notices. Shock, horror! Some (albeit a very few) of the printouts were totally meaningless.

What had happened was that a box of thin cards had been used for updates during the year and, whenever *two* thin cards were next to each other in the file for the month, the tabulator read them together as one card, and consequently only printed where the holes happened to coincide.

So, OK, when you know what has happened, how do you put it right? Our solution was to get the Inspector from the Card Works down to the customer's premises, and set him to work with a micrometer checking the thickness of all the thousands of cards in the files, for all twelve months' worth! In fact he didn't really need the gauge: his fingers plus his experience were just as good, as he proved when the customer's DP Manager and I spent all day feeling cards with him. In the end we did find the dozen or so pairs of cards which would have caused trouble in the following months if they had been left on file.

Economisery, c. 1961　　　　　　　　　　　　　　　　　　George Thomson

It was one of those cost-cutting periods, so there was a policy of sending all equipment to the Far East by any means rather than by air. This included a 902 tabulator which eventually reached Hong Kong by way of Alice Springs. On arrival at the customer's premises, it was hoisted up the outside of the building and had reached sixth floor level when it fell out of the slings. The engineers rebuilt it on site; it was quicker than getting another one.

Terreo Danaos et dona ferens, c. 1961　　　　　　　　　　　　　H.C.

Dave H. was a young American programmer in Putney, beavering away at a PERT program for the ICT 1500 (the RCA 301). Being a conscientious chap he would often take work home with him, and so could often be seen leaving Bridge House North in the evening with a tightly rolled PERT chart under his arm.

Being also an enthusiastic Anglophile, and in particular a lover of English pubs, and within that category a devotee of pub games and, focusing even more closely, a darts player of perhaps more keenness than skill, he habitually carried around in a side pocket his personal favourite set of darts.

Thus equipped he was strolling perfectly peacefully through the West End one evening when he came upon some sort of disturbance in the street, with a lot of shouting and flag-waving. Intrigued, he approached more closely to see what was afoot. It turned out that Queen Frederika of the Hellenes was staying at Claridges, and for who knows what reason she was unpopular with a lot of the young Greeks in London.

Now Dave had never heard of Queen Frederika, and couldn't have told a Hellene from a Hellion in a month of Sundays, but it looked like quite a good party, so he joined in, energetically and loudly.

And in due course, of course, Sergeant Dixon and the lads moved in to calm things down. Dave, being now overexcited, took a lot of calming down, and wasn't really pacified until he heard words like 'in possession of an offensive weapon, to wit darts and a blowpipe' being bandied about in menacing tones. Then he went quietly.

It was shortly afterwards that it was discovered that he had been selling 1500 machine time on his own account. Then he went quickly.

The AKP's pudding c. 1960   *David Bell*

The restaurant capacity at this organisation was woefully inadequate, and the punch girls had got into the habit of returning to the punch room with the dessert courses of their lunches to avoid the overcrowding in the canteen. To start with, there were no problems: apples, oranges, even bananas can be consumed in the proximity of sensitive equipment without difficulty. However, as time went on things became more adventurous: bowls of apple crumble or spotted dick, topped with lashings of custard, were regularly to be seen making their way back to data prep and, on the fateful day, there was a large helping of creamed rice pudding topped with an outsize blob of jam.

So the bowl of rice pudding was balanced in the usual place, on the card weight of its owner's AKP. She was unaware that she had left the machine switched on when she went to lunch, and I'm sure she didn't mean to catch the sleeve of her blouse on the multi-punch key as she bent to pick up a spoon.

In what seemed like slow motion, the AKP started to feed cards. The bowl of rice pudding inexorably slipped towards the moving cards, and deposited its entire load onto the card at the wait station. Before anyone could react, this card disappeared into the punch unit, which responded by emitting something akin to a satisfied belch before regurgitating the card, minus rice pudding, into the stacker.

The effect of a bowl of rice pudding on the previously harmonious operation of 5,000+ pieces of assorted mechanalia was devastating. I spent most of the next three days dismantling the punch unit into its individual components and then washing them all in carbon tetrachloride. That I am not to this day a carbon-tet junkie is nothing short of a miracle but, while I survived, the AKP was never the same again. Whether it was vestigial traces of rice pudding, or some undetermined effect on the machine's persona, was never established, but it never regained its previous performance and had to be relegated to the position of spare machine.

The bottom line, c. 1960   *David Bell*

The insurance company used multi-form hoppers on top of its Senior tabulators and so, to avoid having to employ giantesses, they erected 15 inch high staging in front of them and gave the operators bar-stools to sit on. And this was the time of the miniskirt, so the effect was very eye-catching, and could be embarrassing for a young and impressionable engineer.

When I arrived on site to fix a tabulator fault it was clear that I was about to be made a fool of by the assembled gaggle of young ladies, but establishing the nature of the fault turned out to be quite difficult. The young lady whose machine had gone wrong was in fits of giggles, and could only say that every time she tried to run the tab it made a strange tearing sound. Her colleagues were equally unhelpful and seemed convulsed by the same joke.

Initial investigations confirmed that the machine was indeed suffering from some fairly serious problem in the print unit; the type bars were sullenly refusing to move and seemed to be obstructed by some foreign body. When I asked if anything unusual had been put in the printer the entire machine room rocked with mirth, but no more information was forthcoming.

It took quite a while to remove the machine's covers and enough of the print unit to be able to get at the root of the problem, and the joke which everybody seemed to be having at my expense reached its zenith as I retrieved a pair of silk knickers on which had been printed a life insurance policy renewal notice.

It was her birthday, of course, and they'd all had a good lunch in the pub, and were in a very merry mood as she opened the parcel of silk underwear which they had clubbed together to buy her. 'Let's have a look!', they chorused and, wildly excited, she held up each item in turn. Murphy's Law worked perfectly: as she dropped the panties they slipped neatly into the sheet feed and the tabulator, seizing its opportunity, sprang into printing life. The result was remarkably readable.

There was a suggestion that the man whose renewal notice had literally become the 'bottom line' might quite like to receive such a novel notification of what he owed the company. Fortunately, sanity prevailed when one of the company's actuaries observed that the shock of receiving such an object at the breakfast table might cause the 'ultimate policy event'.

For my part, I put everything back together, checked that it all worked, and beat a hasty retreat. And I made sure that I didn't go anywhere near that site for a long time afterwards.

Blame Sir Isaac, c. 1960 — John Holden

In the early 1960s, ICT was selling a latest, state-of-the-art tabulator, and David Brown Tractors purchased one of the first to become available. Their offices were housed in a traditional former textile factory, and the punched card department occupied space on the third floor.

Access for delivery of heavy equipment was not easy but, as DBT had their own plant maintenance department, it was agreed that they would be responsible for getting the heavy tabulator up to the third floor.

Accordingly, the building's service lift was disabled, and a start was made on the task of raising the tabulator up the lift shaft by block and tackle. Unfortunately this was only partially successful: when the machine reached second floor level either the lifting chain broke or the slings which had been inadequately secured came adrift. In any case the tabulator instantly obeyed the law of gravity and crashed to the bottom of the shaft. The gleaming brand-new state-of-the-art technology was transformed into thousands of separate bent and broken pieces.

One of the team of men who had been carrying out this operation had been standing in the bottom of the lift shaft, watching the proceedings far above him, when the machine broke loose. Even though he miraculously escaped serious physical injury, the shock left such a mark that he was never the same again.

In spite of the quoted delivery time of up to one year, ICT produced a replacement tabulator within a week. I believe that company policy was changed from that date to ensure that the company took responsibility for delivery of equipment to its designated site. Nobody wanted another DBT experience.

Bamboozled at Bradenham, c. 1961 — Bert Molsom

The Data Processing industry has been a great creator of abbreviations for various terms. We all know of BITs for binary digits, RAM for Random Access Memory, and ROM for Read-Only Memory. In fact, these are collectively known as TLAs – Three Letter Abbreviations. The habit goes back a long way, and has been responsible for some memorable misunderstandings.

Following the merger of British Tabulating Machine Co and Powers Samas, lectures were arranged to introduce personnel from each of the merging companies to what had previously been their competitor's equipment.

[*I know this well! I was one of the junior Powers Samas lecturers delegated to explain the round hole kit to a series of courses of crusty old slotted hole engineers at Bradenham, a searing experience only relieved by the convention that anyone saying 'you' or 'us' forfeited half a crown into the course swear box, which was drunk on the last night, and a lot of half crowns went a long way in those days. H.C.*]

At one of these lectures I remember a Powers lecturer rattling on about the 80A fitted to their tabulator, and BTM people getting increasingly confused and mystified, until one member interrupted the lecturer to enquire: 'What is this mysterious '80A'?', only to be told that it was an Automatic Totalling Attachment, and that he was referring to an ATA, not an 80A.

How programming began for me, 1961   H.C.

There was no room for the 1301 programming course in any ICT premises, so we started it in the back room of a solicitor's offices just next to Putney Station. It was too cramped. And the trains were noisy.

So we shifted half a mile west to the Church Hall of St Mary's, Putney, and to one of the small rooms off the hall normally used for vestry meetings or storage of the Mothers' Union tea-making equipment. In these more salubrious surroundings Sesh Say set out to turn us into 1301 programmers. And he did a good job of it, judging by the number of people who went on to make successful careers as programmers and by the affection with which they always remember him.

There were, however, distractions. The main hall was used by various showbiz people for rehearsals. It was jolly difficult to pick up the more subtle nuances of transfers to and from the 1301's magnetic drum when the ears were reverberating to the beat of Screaming Lord Sutch and his Band on drums of different sorts (this was at a time when SLS still habitually wore a pair of buffalo horns, and hadn't adopted the top hat of respectability in which he invariably loses his deposit at Parliamentary by-elections).

Then we were also deliberately interrupted by Michael Bentine, Goon, actor, polymath and, latterly, psychic. He broke off the rehearsals for one of his charming and zany 'Small World' programmes in order to explain to us the problems of setting up and managing a family airline in the South American country from which he originated, and also to reminisce about the research into the fundamental physical characteristics of small electronic devices for which he had received his degree at Cambridge. A mind fizzing with originality.

It was a good course. We enjoyed it, and we learned a lot.

The Tandoori printer, c. 1961   Sarah Hamilton

One of our service engineers was called out to deal with a problem at the Hollerith installation of Egyptian Railways. They were having a problem with the printer which, being driven by a bank of resistors, used to get extremely hot in normal service; but this one was getting almost incandescent. He opened the cover to take a look, and discovered an array of gently toasting sandwiches: one of the Railway employees had decided that this was the perfect place to grill his lunch.

Tales from a bar in Holborn, 1961   Vernon Hardman

A junior technical advisor (me), had occasion to visit Powers Samas House to see Pat Williams, the lady who was responsible, among other things, for some elements of invoicing and the associated salesmen's bonus scheme. I had spoken to her on the phone several times, but had not previously met her face to face. During the meeting I noticed on the wall a number of photos of Kenneth Williams, then the great star of revue and radio, later to become even more famous through the series of Carry On films. Towards the end of the conversation, the penny dropped. 'Oh!', said I brightly, 'You must be Kenneth Williams' sister!' There was a long moment of silence and then, fixing her young visitor with a withering look honed by years spent in the WAAF and the Australian outback, and in a voice which could shiver a sergeant-major at fifty paces, Pat replied, slowly but firmly: 'No! Kenneth is *my brother*!' I didn't actually turn to stone but it was a close-run thing.

Programming the P.C.C., c. 1961   Philip Sugden

The P.C.C. had an extremely unconventional way of entering the program into the machine, which could almost be described as a form of hard wiring. The instructions had to be riveted into four large boards, each about 15 × 12 inches, which were thrust into slots in the front of the machine and then clamped in place. The boards were difficult to rivet up and needed a special tool set for the job. They were even more difficult to unrivet. This was a great incentive to desk check and dry run the programs before the first rivet was put in place.

I only ever wrote one program for the P.C.C. and inevitably I made an error: I had failed to notice that part way through the job there was a slight change in the way the summary totals were accumulated. It was only a small error, but one that looked as if it was going to require a major re-rivet. I was saved from this fate by an enterprising engineer who noticed that, if the job was suspended at the point where the totalling method changed, the program could be modified to carry out the correct calculation by the judicious placement of a strip of Sellotape over part of one of the rows of rivets. To the best of my knowledge the program continued to be run in this manner for the remaining life of the installation.

Brieflets: 1, c. 1961   *Gwen Steel*

The engineer at Bristol City Council shook a P.C.C. program board and pronounced that the rivets had been put in by a b***** programmer. He was right, of course.

Brieflets: 2, c. 1961   *Gwen Steel*

It seemed like ages that we were waiting to test programs on a P.C.C., and no boards arrived. The factory had run out of binding tape for their boxes.

Environmental concern, c. 1960   *Adrian Turner*

There was a P.C.C. on the stand at the Business Efficiency Exhibition. In those days the stands were topped off with a gauze 'ceiling'. The P.C.C. was equipped with a cooling fan whose exhaust blew directly up out of the top of the machine. By the end of the week there was a distinct oily circle in the overhead gauze. 'Hmmm', said a quizzical passer-by, 'I thought nowadays you would be running these things on smokeless fuel'.

The start of the 1004, c. 1962   *Bert Molsom*

A party flew over to Frankfurt in the 1960s when ICT was negotiating the purchase of the 1004 from Remington Rand. There were two Sales Managers, and two Lecturers from Training, one from London and the other from Cookham. On arrival, we took the airport bus into the city, where one of the Sales Managers hailed a taxi, and we packed our bags into the boot of the car. On being told the name of the hotel where we had booked accommodation, the taxi-driver gave us a look which said, clearer than any words: 'Mad Englishmen!' Then he pointed across the road to the hotel we required.

One of the Sales Managers on that trip went over in his City bowler hat, a most unusual form of head-dress in Germany at that time. Walking a few paces behind him I was amused to see the delayed reaction of other pedestrians when the unusual form of hat registered with them. Just a few seconds, and then they *had* to look back to confirm what their eyes had seen.

Deflation, c. 1962 — David Hawgood

At the ICT Development Labs in Stevenage, E.C.H. ('ECHO') Organ was Director. He was very proud of his car (registration number HP 8898) and of his own personal reserved car park space.

One day he returned to the Labs, found another car in his precious space, and ordered his chauffeur to let its tyres down.

Later the chauffeur could be seen scurrying like mad from lab to lab trying to borrow a foot pump. The offending car belonged to the Borough Treasurer of West Ham who was about to confirm the order for a 1301 computer.

Punched card horrors: 2 (the twisted ones), c. 1962 — Chris Penfold

Another customer of Insurance Area had a 1500 Computer with a 'hay-stack' card reader (the type which was notorious for needing cards to be in perfect condition if it wasn't to jam). One October the worst happened: there didn't seem to be a single card which could get read by the card reader. Careful examination showed that all the cards were twisted.

What was the cause? The intake for the computer room's air conditioning plant passed through the store room where new boxes of cards were stored. A sudden cold snap that month had rapidly lowered the temperature of the store room. The resulting moisture had caused the cards to swell within the unopened boxes to such an extent that the boxes had actually burst open, leaving the cards all twisted.

Once the problem had been diagnosed it only remained to sort out who was going to have to pay to replace several boxes of cards. You're quite right: we did.

Tales from a bar in Holborn, c. 1962 — Vernon Hardman

On the touchy subject of hats, a very successful salesman in London (Trevor Brown) was being interviewed for his first managerial appointment.

'Mr Brown', said the chairman of the panel, 'We notice that you don't wear a hat. If you were to pass this panel, would you wear one?'

He allegedly replied: 'If you give me the job, I'll wear a bloody crown if you want me to.'

Punching on the 1301, 1963   *Philip Sugden*

Using Assembler, punching a card required a process called 'row binarisation', a process that I never understood properly at the time and cannot begin to remember now. With the Mnemonic Programming Language (MPL) there was the advantage of being able to punch a card with a single instruction. The only drawback was that there were actually two different punch instructions, one of which was only to be used if it was the first (or was it the last?) card in the pack. Dire warnings were given about the consequences of using the wrong one at the wrong time.

Needless to say, it didn't take me long to hit the wrong combination. The 1301 card punch was a development of the pre-existing reproducer/summary card punch (the only significant development was probably the shape of the cabinet). It therefore punched cards a row at a time. There were standing instructions *never* to punch more than 65 columns in any row because of the danger of smashing the punch die. Normally this would be a very unlikely event, but in the case of my programming error all 80 columns in all 12 rows were punched in the same card. This had two immediate consequences: the first was a hell of a noise, clearly audible through the viewing glass in Bridge House South, and liable to give heart failure to any engineer within earshot; the second was that the card was so weakened that its remains immediately wrecked in the punch mechanism.

Either way, confession to an engineer was required rather quickly. Absolution *might* be granted the first time, but scarcely thereafter. I only did it twice, and I must have been lucky because the punch die survived both times. The threatened consequences didn't make it seem worthwhile to go for a hat trick.

Before desktop publishing, c. 1963   *H.C.*

Tony G., an elegant and extremely well-spoken young man, acquired an interest in automated typesetting. There was not a lot of this going on in Advanced Systems Group at Putney, so he left and went to RCA at Cherry Hill in New Jersey. We thought we had lost touch with him permanently until a letter arrived and, as a progress report, brought us a piece of cast metal representing about three column inches of a newspaper story. When this was read in a mirror it proved to be the introduction to a serious scientific article stressing the vital importance of the strictest adherence to the prescribed procedures in order to achieve the safe powering-down of nuclear wastepaper baskets.

What you need, mush, is the proper tool, c. 1963   Mike Forrest

Visiting RCA at Camden we were shown the 601, on which the back-wiring was some 18 inches thick. The business ends of their soldering irons, of which they were very proud, were fitted with lights and were linked to the handle ends by viewing tubes. They did not seem practical.

For I also am one having authority, 1963   ICT House Magazine

Work has been undertaken by the Reverend A.Q. Morton to determine the authorship of the fourteen epistles attributed to St Paul. It is interesting to note that Mr Morton made use of a Ferranti Mercury Computer to establish to his satisfaction that St Paul wrote only five of the fourteen epistles.

It's in the bag, 1963   Terry Osborne

On one occasion I was sent to a subsidiary of the engineering firm Babcock and Wilcox. I was then employed as a support engineer, working on Hollerith calculators, and was required to fix a particularly tricky fault to do with 10d and 11d. While waiting for the operators to test the effectiveness of the repair I looked out of the window into Great Dover Street and, in a telephone box opposite, noticed a large brown sack. I called the site engineer over to the window to have a look and asked him if he had any idea what it might be. 'Beat's me!', he said, and we turned our attention back to the 542 calculator.

About half an hour later we looked out of the window again and were amazed to see the street crawling with police. It transpired that the sack that we had seen earlier had contained about half a million pounds in used banknotes, and was part of the haul from the Great Train Robbery.

I've often wondered what I would have done if I'd gone down and investigated the sack when I first saw it. I rather think I wouldn't still be with ICL now. But would it have been better to spend thirty-two happy years with the company, or the same time lazing about on some tropical island? Knowing my luck, I'd probably still be languishing in the Scrubs.

A problem of sorts, c. 1963   *Michael Brew*

Two civil servants from the Department of the Environment in Hastings (though in those days it was probably still called The Ministry of Public Buildings and Works) each claimed a high level of ICT 1300 programming skill. One day they challenged each other as to who could write the most efficient mag tape sort program. The first to be completed was given a test in front of an audience of the two contenders and sundry impartial judges. It looked very impressive as the four tapes ticked and whirred backwards and forwards. However, after 14 passes of the tapes the author surprised everyone by admitting defeat. 'Well', he said, 'I was only trying to sort ten records!'

Alphabetics, 1963   *Mike Forrest*

When the Ferranti computer division was merged into ICT, the administrator at West Gorton rang Putney and said: 'I've got an 'I' and a 'T'; can you send me a 'C'?'

Prediction, 1963   *Gordon Scarrott*

When Peter Hall joined ICT following the Ferranti acquisition, he got sight of recent ICT Board minutes, one of which contained the joyous comment that: 'Magnetic tape is judged to be only a passing phase, which is unlikely to have a long term impact on the sale of cards'.

The world on broad shoulders, 1963   **ICT House Magazine**

What has been hailed as an important feather in the cap of the British computer industry is provided by the announcement that the United Kingdom Atomic Energy Authority has awarded a letter of intent to our company for the purchase of an Atlas 2 computer.

This machine, which will cost £1,500,000, has been developed in conjunction with the staff of the Mathematical Laboratory of the University of Cambridge, where the first model is now being assembled, and will be installed at the Atomic Weapons Research Establishment at Aldermaston.

The first computer of the Atlas series, the Atlas 1, was developed by the Ferranti Computer Department (now part of ICT) in co-operation with the University of Manchester, and was installed in the University at the end of last year. In August 1961 an order for an Atlas 1 was placed by the Rutherford High Energy Laboratory, at Chilton, of the National Institute for Research in Nuclear

Science. This is due for delivery in 1964. Another Atlas 1 was subsequently ordered by the University of London.

Immobilisation, c. 1963   H.C.

There was a field engineer in the Putney area in the 1960s who had either had his car stolen more times than he found amusing, or was frightened that it would be. Or perhaps he kept losing his car keys. His solution to the problem was simple and effective.

Into the radio slot on the dashboard he inserted a suitably cut down piece of Hollerith plugboard. The wiring loom was replaced by tailored leads to contacts on the back of this, through which all the vital functions of the car were controlled. So if a thief did break into it he'd find no ignition switch, no lighting switch, nothing familiar at all. Whereas the owner, who always went around with a pocket full of spare plugs, knew just where to plug to bring on the ignition, or the sidelights, or the headlights, or whatever, in the appropriate combination.

It was neat, and it certainly worked. But I was never sure why any self-respecting thief would have made that old car a target.

The dirty tapes, c. 1963   Sandy Walker

In the early 1960s we delivered a computer to Budapest, and on a visit there I was asked to take some computer tapes for our programmers. At Budapest airport these caused some mystification for the customs officers. They seemed sceptical of my explanations, and disappeared with them into a back room. After waiting for ten minutes or so I knocked on the door and opened it cautiously. The customs men had unrolled the tapes and were holding them up to the light, foot by foot, to try to see the (presumably pornographic) pictures.

Testing and detesting, c. 1963   Richard Dean

I had taken over responsibility for an account which was developing a suite of programs for the ICT 1500 and went to see how they were getting on. The Project Manager showed me a whole lot of programmers beavering away.

'Very impressive', I said, 'How are you planning to do the system testing?'

'System testing? What's that?'

'Well, you put some data into the first program, let it ripple through the whole suite, and verify the final results when they eventually appear.'

'Oh, we won't need to bother with that; each programmer's testing of his own program will be good enough.'

A strange attitude, I thought, and when I got back to the office told my boss, Maurice Handyside, that it looked as though they were heading for a disaster. At my instigation, he requested a meeting with the Project Manager's boss, so that we could express our misgivings.

The meeting duly took place, Handyside and myself on one side, the Project Manager and his boss on the other. I spoke first, telling the boss that they really ought to have a system test plan.

'What do you say to that?', said he to the Project Manager.

'It's quite simple; we don't need one.'

'Well, there you are, gentlemen', said the boss to us. 'Mr ... , who is wholly responsible for the project, says that he doesn't intend to do any system testing. Thank you for your time and for your concern. I don't need to detain you any longer.'

On the way back to the office I said to Handyside: 'That was a funny sort of meeting, wasn't it?' 'Oh yes indeed', he replied; 'But you have to understand that people have different objectives. He hates the Project Manager's guts and is revelling in the expectation that he will fail'. And fail he did, spectacularly. The system was an utter disaster. The customer had to employ an army of temps for a year, at phenomenal cost, to do by hand what the system should have automated. But the boss got what he was after, and we had proved that it wasn't our fault.

Well, bug me! 1964   *John Deas*

The very large contract for the Atlas 2 for UKAEA was running late; heavy penalties were being paid and things were tense. The ex-Ferranti computer division of ICT was developing the hardware and the operating system; the customer was developing his own Fortran compiler. At the regular progress meeting, the customer nagged away at the question of how many bugs were left in the operating system. Finally the ICT senior manager in charge of the software, Peter Hunt, turned on the customer's Fortran man, Alick Glennie, and asked: 'How many bugs are left in your compiler?' Alick stuck his chin out and said 'Two!', to which there was no answer without calling him a liar. The argument moved on, and in due course the meeting wound ill-temperedly to its end.

Next week things were going well and tempers were better. 'How many bugs in your Fortran compiler now?' asked Peter Hunt. 'Still two', replied Alick with a smile, 'but I will admit that they're a different two'.

Ooops! c. 1964   *David Firnberg*

In the days of Current Planning Department we presented a paper to the Board recommending certain actions. It was only after they had agreed the actions that I noticed we had misplaced a decimal point, and the amount of money involved was ten times greater than stated in the paper.

Nonne? c. 1964   *David Firnberg*

On another occasion I made my presentation to the Board after lunch one day. During it the Managing Director, John Bull, fell asleep. At the end of the presentation I looked at him and said: 'You agree, don't you, Sir?' He said 'Yes'. So I went ahead and did whatever it was that I was seeking his permission to do.

Brieflets: 3, c. 1964   *Gwen Steel*

Being an Electricity Board, they had gone to great trouble to install partitions, air conditioning and everything else in a thoroughly professional manner. But somehow they forgot that the engineers would need to plug in to an electricity supply.

Brieflets: 4, c. 1964   *Gwen Steel*

The management of the Gas Board were all assembled and awaiting enlightenment. The systems engineer told them that all 1900 programs were known by a four-letter word.

Now hear this! c. 1965   *George Thomson*

I attended a conference when the principal speaker was Lord Bowden, founder of UMIST, and John Grant was in the chair. In his introductory remarks (which were lengthy as was his wont) John kept referring to him as Lord Halsbury. When John eventually sat down, those of us who had been able to hear his remarks (never easy) waited with bated breath to see what Lord Bowden would say. We were not disappointed: 'I have been called many things in my time, but never before have I been called Lord Halsbury'. I can't think that was the reason for John emigrating to Australia.

Comica Telephonica, c. 1965 *David Brown*

ICT decided to set up a central Travel Office at Putney and, as the opening day approached, some bright spark suggested: 'Let's give the Travel Office a distinctive telephone extension number'. You can imagine the discussions that ensued before someone concluded: 'You can't get much more distinctive or simple than extension 1.'

All the directories were consulted, and many people were questioned, but no-one could find out to whom that extension was allocated. Eventually they got round to ringing it, to see who would answer. It rang all right, but no-one answered, not even though a call was made every hour throughout the working day.

About a week later, a computer engineer consulted the Company Doctor about tinnitus. He kept hearing a sound like a telephone bell in the computer room though, of course, there wasn't any phone in there. The Doctor established that he was sound in ear and brain, and recommended that other people should work in the same area to confirm or disprove the phenomenon. Which is how the investigation started which revealed that the phone with extension number 1 had been left in the void when the new false floor was built.

These things can be strangely misrepresented at a distance, can't they?

George Thomson

Bob X (and for the life of me I can't remember his surname) had been Chief Statistician with the Government of Singapore in colonial days. Following independence and 'localisation', in 1961 Bob set up a market research company in Singapore with the grandiose title of 'Far East Research Organisation' (FERO). He 'rented' a hand punch, verifier and counter/sorter from ICT but, by 1965, had never paid a single solitary Straits Dollar for either machine rental or cards purchased. I got rather fed up being hounded by my Indian masters to get the monies owed by Bob, so I wrote off everything that he owed ICT and sold him the punch, verifier and sorter for the princely sum of S$1, which I paid out of my own pocket (despite his protestations that what I was doing was illegal, unethical, immoral, etc.). For maintenance he had to make private arrangements with an engineer to do it in his own time. And he had to pay cash for any cards needed. He took rather a dim view of this, and so did ICT India.

In 1964, shortly after the announcement of the 1900 series, Bob was sent to London by one of his clients (Shell) and, whilst there, turned up at Putney as the Managing Director of the Far East Research Organisation and therefore a potential 1900 customer. He complained bitterly about the scurrilous treatment that had been meted out by yours truly. Of course, he was feted at

Putney, and taken in style to Stevenage where again he was given the red carpet treatment. Needless to say I received a rocket from Overseas Sales instructing me to make it up to Bob on his return.

A few days after Bob reappeared in the East, George Redhouse was stopping over in Singapore on his way to the UK from Australia, so I arranged a lunch for the three of us. It can best be categorised as hilarious, as Bob described the red carpet treatment he had received from ICT in London (but complained that he had been sent to Stevenage in a Princess rather than a Rolls). Bob and I treated the whole affair as hilarious. George didn't know whether to laugh or cry.

Bob had also tried it out on IBM, but they had checked him out with their Singapore office, and sent him packing.

Carpet carping, c. 1965 *Bill Foote*

A certain senior manager, who had been accustomed to a plush office in Newman Street, on arriving at his new office in the Putney area complained loudly and frequently about the fact that he only had a small piece of carpet around his desk, whereas previously he had had wall-to-wall carpeting. One Monday morning he arrived to find that he had been moved, carpet, desk and all, to another office (which just happened to have a floor area to match his piece of carpet!).

The one that got away, 1965 *Bryan Clarke*

My sales target problems certainly looked a whole lot brighter when I was asked to quote for a system to compete with the entire National Health Service! How on earth did this come about?

As on other occasions, the doctors were in dispute with the NHS over pay and conditions, and the BMA threatened to leave the NHS en bloc and set up their own rival service. My customers (Pye of Cambridge) had a close relationship with the BMA through the Stanley family who were major shareholders. Through this connection I was asked to act both as a DP consultant to the BMA and a salesman for the NHS rival – but only after being sworn to deepest secrecy.

The secrecy bit proved difficult internally, and formulating costs against a forecast number of subscribers to the new service, configuring multiple 19xx systems, working out the number of staff needed to operate the system and all the 'odds and sods' was quite horrendous.

Needless to say, it never happened. Peace broke out between the Government and the BMA, and all my hard work was quickly forgotten apart from a letter of thanks from the would-be customer. I went back to getting my 1965 target in bite-sized chunks.

How many windings has the Yellow River? c. 1965   David Smith

A 1903 and a 1905 were sold to China. But because of COCOM restrictions (which limited the export of advanced technology items to Communist countries), the Westrex teletype consoles, of American manufacture, had to be replaced by others which we obtained from a subsidiary of Imperial typewriters. Attachment and testing went OK, so everything was shipped. So far as I know these were the only consoles of this type ever attached to any 1900s. Nothing more was heard for a year. Then came a query about the reliability of console typewriters. The reply could only be a diplomatic version of: 'You know more about the reliability of these consoles than we do'.

The art of error messages, c. 1965   H.C.

There was a tape sort program called, I think, #XSMC. This was long before any of the GEORGEs, so one had to allocate tapes to it explicitly using the simple Operator's Executive. One evening I made a typing error, and allocated as the input data file a scratch tape which was intended for use in the intermediate stringing phases. The command 'GO #XSMC' was duly given, and the tapes all briefly stuttered on their decks, but instead of the expected orderly spinning, there was an outburst of frenzied chatter from the teletype console. Springing to its desk I read with astonishment:

'When input records number none
There's not much sorting to be done;
And so to while away the time
We're typing out this little rhyme.'

Algab, 1965   H.C.

We had a splendid colleague from an astonishingly polyglot background: each of his parents spoke four or five languages (with barely one in common), his nurse had spoken a different selection, and he had lived as a child in countries where yet other tongues were current. His sister became miraculously fluent in every one of them. He, by contrast, spoke brokenly in every one he attempted. English idiom was always just out of reach. So on one occasion, asserting the necessity for progress, he firmly pronounced: 'We cannot sit where we stand.' On another, faced with a suggestion which he thought unsound, he dismissed it as 'half a baked idea.'

G'day mate, 1960s   Arthur Humphreys

Sir Edward Playfair was on a visit to Australia, and called in at the office in Newcastle, north of Sydney, for a talk with the Manager, Harold Gardner. It was a rather sticky occasion, and the conversation did not flow easily.

'Have you got many customers?'
'No, can't say we have.'
'How many orders have you got?'
'Not that many, really.'
'How about prospects, then?'
'Nah, there's not much doing.'

And then there didn't seem to be much else to say. 'Shall we go and have a drink, then?' was a question that seemed to offer a way of breaking the impasse and Sir Edward, thinking in terms of a cup of coffee, immediately replied 'Yes'. Instead of which, he was led to a rather sleazy bar in a nearby street. On entering this, they were greeted by the barmaid: 'Oooh, you're late this morning, Mr Gardner!'

Demonstration, incarceration, compensation, 1960s   Albert Brook

Dennis M. was site engineer at the Southern Electricity Board in the Oxford Region, and also a staunch supporter of CND. One weekend there was to be a major demo in Trafalgar Square, so he went off to London with a pal in order to take part. They got separated, and Dennis became convinced that his pal had been arrested (in fact he hadn't; he had lost interest and quietly returned home). Not to be outdone, Dennis became so vigorous that he really did get arrested, and spent a night in custody. Nobody knew about this until SEB rang up half way through Monday morning, saying: 'Where's our engineer?' Then a telegram from Dennis himself arrived, saying simply: 'Detained in London; will be in tomorrow.' Which just proves what a mess you can get into by being too outspoken.

'Yes', said a quietly smiling Dennis, who had been listening to this tale being told against him; 'but at least I got to share a cell with Vanessa Redgrave.'

The floor-lady explains, 1960s   Sandy Walker

In Moscow I was staying at the National Hotel, and one day returned to my room at lunch-time to collect some papers. I asked the usual gigantic floor-lady for my key. Once she had understood the number I was asking for, her face lit up and she produced a piece of paper on which was a message in English, but written phonetically in Cyrillic script so that she could convey it. She intoned: 'At midday, man in room with gun. Take no notice.' Taken a little aback, I asked for some explanation, but she merely chanted again: 'At midday, man in room with gun. Take no notice.' Then she gave me my key.

My door was locked and I opened it cautiously, not without some rattling of the key so as not to surprise my new room-mate. He might, after all, have been of a nervous disposition. Sure enough, by the open window stood a man in uniform holding a sniper's rifle with a telescopic sight. He glanced at me over his shoulder, then returned his gaze to the window, ignoring my attempt at a cheery 'Good morning'. I collected my papers and left quietly.

Later I discovered that Marshal Zhukov, hero of the Great Patriotic War, was being buried that morning under the Kremlin Wall in Red Square. My window had a good view of the square, ideal for potting disturbers of the peace. I only wished I had known beforehand...

Mainframe sizing, 1960s   Michael Brew

In the early days, sizing was not such a precise art as it is today. When arriving outside the factory gates of a new prospect the new ICT recruit asked the salesman: 'How do you know what size of machine to sell them?' To which the salesman replied: 'Well, my lad, you just count the number of chimneys. If there's one then it's a 1901, and if there are four I sell 'em a 1904.' Some might say that was just as accurate as today's methods.

Deep throat, 1960s   Michael Brew

A salesman was having difficulty convincing his Regional Manager that he really did have this multi-million pound deal under control. The forecast date for the order was still some way off. As time went by the Regional Manager grew increasingly impatient and distrustful of the salesman's ability to deliver. Our hero spent much time attempting to convince his manager not to interfere and jeopardise the business.

Eventually the great day came, and the salesman duly presented the Regional Manager with the telex in confirmation of the big order. 'That's great!', was the response; 'Give me that telex, I'm going to stuff it down the throat of the

Regional Director!' To which our hero replied: 'Well, you'll have to get it out of yours first!'

Interruption, 1960s   H.C.

There was an afternoon when *very* little work was done in Putney. The windows of LON11 were thronged with spectators of the zany goings-on below, on the bridge and on the river. It was Michael Bentine again, filming.

What the plot might be we didn't ever decipher, and it probably doesn't matter anyway.

One scene involved Bentine himself, clad in immaculate white ducks, a fraightfully proper Henley striped blazer, and a straw boater, running along the pavement of the bridge as one pursued by fiends, then vaulting the parapet into the river thirty feet beneath. Only they chose to film it at low tide, so that his landing would be dry. But it was a massive distance to fall, and there was great fascination in watching the construction of the shock absorber for his landing. This consisted of empty old cardboard boxes, stacked until they were at least eight feet high, surmounted by a layer of old mattresses to hold the mass together. It didn't look in the least as though it would crumple safely, but when put to the test it jolly well did.

The second scene was easier to understand, though we saw it shot in its component parts; the whole would have to be composed later in the editing room. Up the river towards the arches of Putney Bridge came a real gin palace of a motor cruiser, with two bikinied lovelies sunbathing on the foredeck (gallant of them, really, since this was all taking place on a decidedly chilly late autumn afternoon). Down the river towards the arches of Putney Bridge came a water-skier, towed by a little speedboat. For some reason (fear of hypothermia, perhaps) he was wearing a full frogman's outfit. Out from the arches of Putney Bridge emerged the motor cruiser, with the two startled lovelies emoting like billy-oh, and the frogman water-skier impaled on the prow.

Never did see it on the box. A pity, really, but it couldn't have been more fun than watching it being made.

Punched card horrors: 3 (the transparent ones), c. 1966   Chris Penfold

I was once asked to write a program on the 1004 to cater for stock control in a chain of British Leyland garages. Looking at the specification I could see that in addition to the part number, stock in hand, orders last month, etc., there would be room on the printout to include the part description. 'Oh no', said the customer. 'They don't need that. The Stock Control Clerk knows all the relevant part numbers by heart, and it would just be a waste of your time to include it.' So I didn't.

The printout listed all parts and, where orders for a part in the last quarter exceeded the stock remaining in hand, printed out a number of asterisks to draw the Clerk's attention to the probable need to re-order.

A month or two after the system went live I had a phone call: 'One of the garages has just received 800 badge bars for MGs, and they've only sold two in the past year! But they ordered 800 because the printout said that 800 had been sold.'

The cause of the embarrassment (both to me and to the Stock Control Clerk who clearly didn't know all the relevant part numbers after all) was a piece of transparent material in the punched card which recorded that part's sales in the last quarter. That ill-placed speck of transparency recorded 800 sales when there had actually been none! I never did hear whether they eventually sold all those badge bars.

Universal providers, 1966   ICT House Magazine

Spares and Accessories Division receive many varied and unusual demands, but few as vivid as a recent cable from Overseas: 'Please rush off pair of well-shaped legs for Collatrice'.

By return: L160375 Collator Legs (Queen Anne style), 2 off. How mundane!

The Galactic Storage Device, c. 1966   H.C.

This was undoubtedly the most successful spoof in the history of ICT. It probably originated in the Engineering Training School at Letchworth, but I have been unable to identify an author. Whoever he was, all honour to him!

The principle was simple: first generation magnetic storage media, i.e. magnetic tape, had been essentially one-dimensional; its successor, the magnetic disc, was in effect two-dimensional; what could be more natural than to assume that the next generation would be three-dimensional. The write-up, all absolutely straight-faced, covered the fundamental nature of the storage element: a hollow aluminium spheroid with a ferrite surface, having both polar and equatorial recording tracks; the arrangement of the planetary transport, with 16 large spheroids in an outer orbit and 16 smaller ones in an inner orbit; the combination of four planetary transports into a single Galactic unit; the use of air pressure to load spheroids into the read/write chambers, to rotate them during reading and writing, and to return them to the orbital drive; the capacities and access times; and the programming commands, compatible with other 1900 series storage device software, forming the Galactic Housekeeping System (GASH).

The penny only really dropped when one read the last page of the specification, which included the following list of Console Error Messages:

NOBLS:	No Balls – Runout
GOOLY:	Small Ball in large reading chamber
JAMBL:	Large Ball in small reading chamber
BLAB:	Ball Abraded
BLUP:	Small Balls up in chamber
BBLUP:	Big Balls up in chamber
LOSBL:	Can we have our ball back?
DUMBL:	Dump a ball
CHEWBL:	Remonstration condition
KNOTBL:	Jam on planetary transport
OOOH!:	Ball flattened
ABLDP:	All Balls dropped; end of run
WALOB:	What a lot of Balls! (too many spheroids on planetary transport).

Keeping a straight face, c. 1966   *Bob Millar*

I first came across the Galactic Storage Device when I was a lecturer at the ICL customer training centre at Bradenham Manor. I used to introduce it with a straight face on appropriate all-male courses. The specification was so well-written and plausible that I could usually get 20 minutes into the session before anyone realised the device was just a load of balls.

Local commitments, c. 1966   *David Stafford*

When the specification of the Galactic Storage Device reached Melbourne, some wag leaked a copy of it to *The Age*, the prestigious serious newspaper of the State of Victoria. But in doing so he was careful to remove the give-away last page.

Grateful for the scoop, *The Age* went to town and gave it a glowing write-up in their weekly technology section.

A couple of days later Neil Lamming, then the MD of ICT (Australia), received a phone call from someone frightfully high up in Canberra, explaining that ICT's chances of securing future Government business would be much enhanced by a decision to manufacture this revolutionary new storage device in Australia. Neil never did track down where the leak had come from.

Duff FUD, c. 1966 David Bell

An ICT customer mentioned to the visiting IBM salesman that he was very interested in ICT's Galactic Storage Device. The response was typical, and instant: 'Oh, you don't want to waste time thinking about that! Ours is a much better product and, what's more, it will be out sooner'.

The Van der Merwe effect Fred Skeat

I was giving a standard course on 1900 peripherals in South Africa and, as we all did, tried to liven it up with a session on the Galactic Storage Device. Which was very well received, on the whole, and rather too well in one instance because the man from the insurance company could not be made to understand that the whole thing was a joke. His company would very much like to be the first to have a GSD installed in South Africa. He'd get his boss to sign an order as soon as the course was finished. There was just one problem: their punch girls were a rather strait-laced lot, who would be embarrassed by having to punch some of the specified commands; how much would it cost to have the software modified to include less contentious terminology?

Malapropism? c. 1966 Gordon Collinson

There really was, at one stage, an FU2 project at 1/3 Factory, Letchworth.

Mismatch, c. 1966 H.C.

It must have been about 1966 or 1967, when Corporate Systems (or whatever we called ourselves in them days) were recruiting programmers to work on the ODBS system. Among the candidates who showed up at 113 Upper Richmond Road was one broth of a boy who was the living embodiment of yer cartoon Irishman; tight black curly hair, a triangular face with a pointy chin, twinkling eyes, a voice dripping with honey, the lot! We started talking, and it soon became pretty clear that we were at cross purposes somehow, so I asked him why he thought he was qualified for a job in computer programming. His answer was blissful: 'Well, I've been working on the bottling plant at United Dairies in Fulham, so I'm used to dealing with complicated machinery'. So, at least, the ODBS wasn't his fault!

Perspicacity, c. 1966   *John Deas*

Mike Gifford, MD of ICL (Pacific), was another man with the ability to take one glance at a page of figures and see any mistake or inconsistency. When given a document to sign, if he was in a good mood he would point out the first two or three errors and then hand it back, saying: 'Tell me, when are you going to bring me something that you actually expect me to *sign*?' If feeling less sunny, he would point to the first mistake and say: 'That's wrong; piss off.'

One's great career in the films, Ducky, c. 1967   H.C.

It had been decided that there ought to be a company film to extol the virtues of this great new programming language, COBOL! Mid-60s this must have been, when Grace Hopper was still only a Lieutenant Commander.

It has to be said that there was not a lot of plot. The ICT technical expert was going to expound the message to an ignorant but willing-to-learn customer. That was it.

For the part of the ICT technical expert someone had selected a professional actor. A good-looking chap, well known at that time for appearing in a TV ad for India Tyres, whose extravagant virtues in dispersing road surface water he emphasised by the athletic way in which he jumped into the grooves in the tread of a giant mock-up of said tyres.

For the part of the ignorant but willing-to-learn customer there was volunteered Muggins. Yes, me.

Little action was involved, so rehearsals proved no problem. Except in one crucial particular. Our actor friend could not rid his tongue of the conviction that the product's name was pronounced 'COBBLE'. Round and round we went, but it always came out this way.

At length we surmounted that one, and moved on to the next stage, rehearsals on the set!

This was to be the machine room (associated with the Demo Room) in Bridge House South in Fulham. For the obvious reasons of visual interest, the background was going to be the row of tape decks. 'Expert' and 'Customer' were to be posed with opposite elbows leaning on opposite sides of a conveniently-placed 1933 line printer (why they should choose such a daft place to discuss a programming language was never explained). During the conversation, the camera would track ever closer to our vividly conversing faces, with the circus of a mag tape sort going on visibly behind us. Nothing really wrong with that, just lots of 'clitches' as Ernest Bevin used to call them.

I can't imagine what it was that suggested to me that something was different and wrong, but before we were actually committed to the final takes I glanced away from the camera to the row of tape decks. No, it wasn't normal! On the centremost deck, the one which would have been bang in the middle of the shot, was a card which didn't ought to have been there. I didn't need to move to read it. It would have been equally plain on camera. It was from the engineers. It read: 'DO NOT OPEN THIS DECK IF YOU VALUE YOUR FINGERS'.

The film was never completed. I can't think why.

Twice tides table, 1960s   Richard Banks

Dave Carpenter had a meeting in LON11. He was late, rather portly, and didn't like walking much. He was pleased to find a parking space on the river bank across the road from LON11, behind the Star and Garter. On his return from the meeting he was aghast to find that the tide had been in and out, and the foot well of his company Marina (well-named, eh?) was full of water, not to mention the wet and muddy state of the seats. It was with some difficulty that he got home.

On another occasion he was equally late, and found the same parking space. Having 'learned from his previous mistake', he leant over the wall and decided from the ripples that the tide was going out. He was wrong! On this occasion he returned to LON11 to get a plastic cup to bail out the foot well, and met Ed Mack who had also been in the meeting, and managed to persuade him to help push-start the car.

The Marina later suffered from premature rusting.

Gated! c. 1967   Cecil Kellehar

On one occasion when Lyon Lightstone was manager of the Southern Sales Region, he decided to hold a conference in Worcester College, Oxford, to review and determine sales policy. Among the items debated was whether a Regional Support Team should be set up.

After the business of the day was rounded off with a good dinner in Hall, some of us felt we would like a change of atmosphere and adjourned to the Mitre for coffee and a glass of port.

Absorbed in continuing the discussions of the day, we were surprised to hear 'Time' being called and, when we got back to Worcester, even more surprised to find the gate locked and no-one to respond to our ringing and hammering.

We looked round for a low part of the wall, as no doubt many undergraduates had done before us, but could not find one to scramble over. At length we found a window with a light shining from it about ten feet above the pavement. Throwing pebbles produced no response, so in the end it was decided that I, being lighter, should stand on my Regional Manager's shoulders and bang on the occupant's window for help. This was eventually accomplished, with not a little difficulty, and from my wobbly eminence I saw a colleague with his head buried in a pile of papers. I believe it was John Grover but, whoever it was, he would have been equally aghast to see this disembodied head hovering outside like some foul fiend in the dark. At length he steeled himself to open the window, knocking me backwards in the process, so that I slid down Lyon's back to the ground, grabbing a fistful of his hair on the way. Thankfully, communication was established, and John kindly came down, wrestled with the bolts, and let two apologetic and sheepish characters in.

Next day it was decided that a Regional Support Team *should* be formed to help Area Managers deal with untoward problems.

The filthy evidence, c. 1967 *Ted Evison*

When part of the false floor in the Atlas room had to be taken up, among those present was Robin the administration chappie, an ex-Gurkha officer with the ramrod back and all the trimmings. As the tile came up there was revealed a neat pile of poo. The Sandhurst wallah was shocked and horrified: 'Those foul weekend engineers! Too lazy to take their dog outside to do its business! How perfectly frightful and despicable! You there!! Shovel that lot up, bag it, and bring it to me; I'm sending it off for analysis.' Well, whether it was rat, or squirrel, or fox we never found out. It certainly wasn't dog or we'd have heard more about it.

Guesstimating, c. 1967 *Bert Molsom*

On one occasion, when I was providing sales support for Data Management Software, I had arranged to meet two salesmen in London to devise a system for a prospective customer for whom a quotation was required. Very early in the meeting it became obvious that the salesmen had not done any of their homework, had not carried out any detailed investigation, and had no factual information on which I could judge the suitability of the software for the tasks proposed. I kept repeating that I was quite unable to help until they provided the information I required. Each time they pooh-poohed this and demanded that I give them guesstimates out of the air for them to use, although I would have been responsible for the results. They were a couple of real wide boys (we had a few!). I am normally a very patient person, but under their constant pressure, two to one, I eventually cracked, closed my books with a slam, told them to contact me again, but not until they had acquired some usable information, and stormed out of the room – into a broom cupboard!

GEORGE and the DRAGON, 1968 *Tim Goldingham*

From Dataline International Number 9. A fairy-tale written after reading the GEORGE 3 manual once too often:

Many GENERATIONs ago, in a far-off land, there lived a PERT little maiden named JEAN, who was confined in a dungeon by an evil PERI. One day she managed to SET A FLAG on a TREE-LIKE STRUCTURE with an EXTENDED BRANCH; this was seen by a TRUSTED knight called GEORGE, who happened to be HUNTing on his CHARGEr, after an EARLY MORNING START.

GEORGE boldly approached the castle and demanded to ENTER. 'What is the PASSWORD, PLEASE?', asked the SENTINEL. 'BOOTSTRAPS' was GEORGE's DIRECT RESPONSE. The drawbridge was lowered and GEORGE crossed the moat.

He was puzzled to see so many MONITOR lizards, for he knew that these were supposed to give warning of crocodiles; it was then that he realised he had fallen into a TRAP, for what he had taken to be a LOG IN the STREAM was indeed one of these beasts. He must, however, FIND JEAN and CONSOLE her. At last, after a prolonged SEARCH, he found the dungeon.

'Do not ABANDON hope!', cried GEORGE, to RESTORE her confidence. 'I will soon have you out of this DUMP. I have found the FILE STORE and will cut through your CHAINS.'

'You thrill me to the CORE', cried JEAN; 'I never hoped to meet such a crafty PLOTTER'.

'I, too, long to HOLD you', said GEORGE; 'You are what I call a perfect ESCAPE CHARACTER. Now, I have a PLAN: we will use MOPs to empty the moat, TRANSFER the water into the WELL, and refill it with BUCKETs of GIN. This will ABOLISH the crocodile.'

And so it was that they were able to do a POSTMORTEM on the crocodile and write his EPITaph. After this JEAN could not refuse GEORGE's request for a DATE, PLEASE; and they soon proved to be so COMPATIBLE that you will no longer FIND JEAN'S name in the DIRECTORY, for she has been RENAMED and is happily doing the HOUSEKEEPING.

Bassett Enterprises: In full flight, c. 1968   *Apocryphal*

That year there was a very successful trade in pot plants. Through the credit control network orders were solicited in many parts of the country and, in particular, there was a very healthy demand from West Gorton.

How to get pot plants from Letchworth to Manchester at minimal cost? Obviously, ask the Shipping Department in 1/3 Factory, Blackhorse Road. 'Yes, sure, we've got a 1933 Line Printer going up to West Gorton almost at once'. And there was just room in the crate for the consignment of plants.

It was entirely bad luck that a red alert should come in at that moment from Lagos, saying that there was a desperate need for a replacement printer. In answer to which the first available 1933 went straight to Stansted Airport to be collected by Air Nigeria.

There were two consequences: people at West Gorton got understandably shirty at the non-delivery of what they had ordered, and ICL Nigeria got into terrible trouble for importing prohibited vegetable material.

The middle watch, c. 1968   *Anon (for obvious reasons)*

The trainee was a charming girl, very pretty and very sweet, and I was delighted when she was assigned to my team. Being already well smitten, I was even more thrilled when I found we were scheduled to do a night testing session together on the 1900 service at ICL House, Letchworth.

So, late in the appointed afternoon, we drove up from Putney, handed over our programs, data, and instructions to the operators of the night shift, and went off for a Chinese meal. When that was over we returned to the fray, checking results, making corrections, resubmitting various jobs, until we could do no more, and retired.

Now the operators must have divined something of my feelings towards her, because they set off the fire alarm at 5.30 in the morning, and then rampaged upstairs to see if they could find us in compromising circumstances. They found me, all right, asleep on some cushions on the floor of the office where we had been working, but of her there was no sign. Sensible girl, she had long ago locked herself into the nurse's sick bay, several floors higher up.

The operators were really disappointed; they had been so sure their trap would work. What they didn't know was what she had told me over supper of the giant size, appalling ferocity, and jealous temperament of her rugger-playing boyfriend. And I'm only a little fellow.

Jobs in the night, c. 1968 A.J. Adams

Back in the good old days of the 1900 series there operated in London a fearless gang of fellows called the Night Maintenance Team. It was their job to carry out maintenance on large systems during the night, when they naturally tended to be more available for engineering work.

One night the schedule was: Mullins (Merchant Bankers) 23.00 to 02.30, Bank of England 02.30 to 05.30, Eastern Gas 05.30 to end of shift.

On this particular night Fred Atkins and Peter Florence, on emerging from Mullins, were confronted by the Law, two constables from the City Police. ' 'allo, 'allo, 'allo' said the Law in the approved manner, 'where have you lot been?' 'We've been inside doing a job', said Fred Atkins. The Law was *not* amused. 'And where are you going now?', said the Law. 'Across to the Bank of England', said Fred; after all, the Bank was only a short walk away. 'And what are you going to do when you get there?', asked the Law. Fred could barely keep a straight face as he said: 'We're going to do another job.'

Humour eventually prevailed, and our boys were saved from spending the rest of the night in the cells.

Imposture, c. 1968 Robert Moscrop et al

'Can I speak to the Company Secretary, please?' said the ICT salesman on a cold call. 'Certainly, Sir,' said the receptionist, 'you'll find him through that door.' Surprised at the implied informality, the salesman knocked lightly on the indicated door, opened it, and went in. Oh Lord, it was the Board Room and a Board Meeting was obviously in progress. All faces swivelled towards him in a mixture of surprise and annoyance. 'May I ask which of you gentlemen is the Company Secretary?' 'I am', said a particularly stern figure, 'and who the heck are you?' 'I beg your pardon, Sir. I'm from IBM. I'd better call another time.' Never was retreat more hasty.

Civil war at Putney, 1968 David Marwood

The creation of ICL in 1968 resulted in five major shareholders, English Electric, Plessey, HM Government, Vickers and Ferranti. Together they held over half the company's issued share capital and all, of course, were represented on the Board. In the early autumn of 1968 Plessey made a hostile bid for English Electric. For the next few months, while that bid was being contested, neither the Plessey nor the English Electric representatives were willing to attend ICL Main Board meetings. This meant that, until English Electric escaped Plessey's clutches by merging itself with GEC, our Main Board meetings lacked the presence of our two largest shareholders. That was tiresome, for there were many key matters on which the views of the absentees were absolutely essential.

Sweet clarity, 1968   *Arthur Humphreys*

Just before the English Electric merger there was a spot of trouble with Ferranti and Vickers, because one of the consequences would be their demotion to minority shareholder status, and they weren't happy about it. So a meeting was called to thrash it out. Then the preliminary question arose: who should ask the first question? Ferranti or Vickers? Eventually Sebastian started, and his question was: 'Is Arthur going to be the boss and, Terence, when are you going to resign?'

A big con, c. 1969   *Michael Brew*

Some would say that Dataskil always had that cowboy outfit image. At an internal sales review of Dataskil's business in ICL Government (Civil) Region, the Dataskil salesman referred to a flip chart on which he had prepared a list of the year's successes. Against each item was an abbreviation indicating business type, the meaning of which we, the audience, were left to infer. There was 'devel' for development, 'con' for consultancy, 's/w' for software, etc. As most entries were labelled 'con', one wag from the audience asked the chap from Dataskil: 'Is 'con' short for anything or not?'

Down and up, c. 1969   *Sally Rosebery*

There was a benchmark demonstration at a customer site near Redhill. The 1904A was running a simulator, and about half a dozen teletype terminals were chattering merrily away when their Chief Programmer accidentally leant against the big red emergency stop button which had been installed at a very convenient shoulder height on the wall. There was that horrid sound of fans slowing down and gradually the terminals fell silent. We looked around for the cause. The salesman's eyes were popping out and his face turned bright red as he struggled for words. Then the cause was found and the machine started up again. Imagine our amazement and delight when the machine just carried on as if nothing had happened. The terminals started chattering again and our mouths fell open in surprise. Southern Region subsequently adopted this demonstration of the capabilities of GEORGE in other benchmarks.

Now you see it... c. 1969   *Sally Rosebery*

We also had the case of the disappearing paper tape. This was on a 1904A at Hawker Siddeley at Kingston. The tape was read into the machine and vanished into thin air. We found it three weeks later under the false floor. The air conditioning had sucked it down a grill!

Chastened at Cheadle Hulme, 1969   *Roger Catto*

One morning as duty programmer it was my duty to go and collect the trolley of overnight test results for the whole team. The computer room was very cramped as they were just removing the old EMIDEC 1100 tape decks and I had to squeeze through a small gap behind one of the decks. As I did so my shoulder brushed against the emergency stop button, and that horrid silence fell on the whole room. Seconds later my other shoulder encountered the back panel of another tape deck, which fell off and, in that silence, made one hell of a noise. I just wanted to disappear into the false floor. Unfortunately there was something wrong with the emergency stop procedure and it took us around four days to recover. The good news was that if this had not been discovered until we had gone live it would have been a *real* disaster, with 60,000 people not being paid. The next morning, the office wall sported a cartoon of a computer blowing up, over the caption: 'CATTOSTROPHE!'

With a little bit of luck, 1969   *Roger Catto*

I was a programmer with the MoD Industrial Pay & Records System in Cheadle Hulme, when we encountered the saga of the 'dropping bit' on the then new 1904E. Nobody would believe me, but we had a truly random error. So every night when I put my work in for testing I added a simple count routine. Sure enough, one night – eureka! – the dumb computer went 1, 2, 3, 4, 4, 6... You wouldn't believe how quickly the site became infested with senior ICL and CCA officials until they nailed down the problem and isolated the defective part.

High-level training, the low-level solution   *H.C.*

It was certainly before 1970 that we developed the first on-line system for some of the Directors in Putney to use in their own offices. There were two stimuli behind this development:

First, if we made information available on-line, then everybody would get access to it equally fast. There was continual dissatisfaction around that time that person A, asking questions on the basis of a print-out he'd just received, say a Weekly Summary of Orders, couldn't get satisfactory answers from person B, because B hadn't yet received his copy of the same printout.

Second, it was already company doctrine that management ought to have direct access to relevant information and ICT's Directors felt that they should set an example.

So we built a very simple application based on the principles that information could be organised into 'topics'. Each topic had a number of pre-set screens through which the user could move Up and Down. The Current screens coexisted with Past screens, showing the same information from previous reporting periods, and with Future screens showing the corresponding forecast information. Commands consisted of single letters U, D, C, P, F, etc. Technically it worked OK. In the event it wasn't of much practical use, because the first generation VDUs, with only 1200 character screens, were far too small to display enough information to make them convenient.

So, the system was simple, the end user interface was simple, but how could we train the Directors in how to drive it? The problem was put in the hands of a highly glamorous red-headed American lady, who evolved a training technique of striking effectiveness. Positioning the trainee Director at the keyboard, she knelt on the floor at his side, and issued her instructions. Every time he got something right, he got a congratulatory pat on the knee. They loved it, and it worked a treat!

On the receiving end, 1969 *Arthur Humphreys*

When making the appointments, she used her academic title. Thus when my secretary said: 'At eleven o'clock Dr Tyler is coming to give you some training' it sounded quite daunting. When the door actually opened and this gorgeous girl came in it was quite a relief.

Tales of the turf, c. 1970 *Bill Foote*

A fairly senior manager moved into a 'new' office in Carlton Drive (LON15) and found that it was fitted with vivid grass-green carpet tiles. He promptly 'planted' some plastic daffodils into a tile or two to liven it up.

An ICT song, 1960s   *John Carter*

Tune:

> *obvious*

Chorus:

> *All things bright and beautiful,*
> *Computers great and small;*
> *All things quite unusable*
> *ICT makes them all.*

Verse:

> *Each little gate that opens,*
> *Each little wheel that spins,*
> *They gave us shiny covers*
> *To cover up our sins.*

Performance monitoring, timeless   *David Bell*

The three girls happened to go out with three computer salesmen, one from ICT, one from Honeywell, and one from IBM. Next day they compared notes. Said the girl with the Honeywell experience: 'Mine performed as was to be expected, he did what was necessary and nothing more. I give him seven out of ten'. And the ICT expert: 'Mine did a bit better than that. I give him eight out of ten'. The girl who'd been out with IBM said: 'I don't think I can give mine a score like that. He just sat on the end of the bed and spent all night telling me how good it would be when I got it.'

Four Elliott Automation

Early days at Elliott   *Philip Sugden*

I was recruited by Elliott Automation in 1960 to be the first full time operator in the computer bureau that was run at their factory site at Borehamwood. Prior to that the responsibility for running programs was given to the programmers who wrote them (often for good reason) as a degree of hand cranking could be needed to get them to run through to completion.

At that time Elliott Automation had an agreement with NCR whereby NCR marketed Elliott computers for commercial applications and Elliotts marketed their systems directly to the technical and scientific market. The same type of system could be known as an Elliott, an NCR-Elliott, or an NCR depending on who the customer was.

In 1960 the bureau consisted of:

2 × type 405	large commercial systems
2 × type 402 (or 403)	medium sized scientific systems
1 × type 802	small sized scientific system
1 × type 803	small sized scientific system

The 402, 403, and 405 were all valve systems dating from the mid 1950s and were coming to the end of their production runs. The 802, which dated from the late 1950s, was mostly transistor-based but still used some valves; and the 803, which followed a year or two after the 802, had a very similar order code to the 802 but was an all-transistor system. I believe it was claimed to be the world's first all-transistor computer system; it was certainly the first Elliott system to sell in volume.

Although I was recruited to be an operator on the 405, the first thing that happened was that I was put on a programming course for the 803. I had only the vaguest idea of what operating a computer system was supposed to involve; I had not the slightest idea what programming was about. I spent the first morning in a total daze. Because of all the 'day 1' formalities, I joined the course late and missed the introduction to the basic concepts of the 803 system and its Autocode programming language. The lecturer embarked on a long sequence of instructions that began 'a = a + b'. As this seemed to be in total conflict with all the algebra I had learned on the way to A levels in Pure and Applied Mathematics, it did not take me long to lose the thread of what was going on. As the rest of the course seemed to be taking things in their stride I decided to keep quiet. I was more than grateful when the course came to an end and I was able to escape back to the bureau.

The 405 was massive. It was shaped like a shallow letter U and occupied an area roughly 30 × 20 feet, though no two were ever exactly the same. The console, which was fully worthy of the name, was between the two upright arms of the U. Main store (of about 256 words) was provided by nickel delay lines and backing store was on an oxide coated disc. Data input and output was by 5-channel papertape and magnetic file (tape). Bulk output first went onto magnetic file and then on to four papertape punches, each working simultaneously at 25 cps, and then on to a bank of teleprinters working at about 6 cps. Line printers (except in prototype form) had not quite arrived and punched cards were virtually unknown.

The magnetic file was an Elliott unique. It was 35 mm cinema film coated with a magnetic oxide. The instantaneous data transfer rate was, I believe, about 4 kch/sec. The effective rate was only half of that because data was recorded in alternate blocks. Data was written as the film travelled from the start up to the end and also in the reverse direction. The data blocks in one direction were the inter-block gaps in the reverse direction. Magnetic tape housekeeping software was limited. 'Scratching' a magnetic file was a physical exercise: the reel was placed over a strong electro-magnet and rotated slowly in both directions. This job could be bad news for your watch if you forgot to remove it before scratching.

The 405 used to get an exhaustive maintenance of about $1^1/2$ hours every morning. Even this would not guarantee that you would get through the day without a breakdown of some sort. If the breakdown was a long one there was the exciting prospect of overtime at 6s. 8d. (33p) per hour, and gross pay for the week might even exceed £10. 0s. 0d.!

Some things in the bureau were remarkably casual. Although people were not supposed to smoke, the rule was not enforced unless there were visitors; and even then was not applied to visitors. On more than one occasion cigarette ash or an end was idly flipped into a bin of loose papertape with spectacular results. The fire would be over very quickly but the ash would float around for ages and it was not easy to remove the scorch marks from the ceiling.

Another casual area was that of the computer room environment. Elliotts insisted that their customers install their computers in an air conditioned environment, but did not feel the need to follow their own advice. The bureau had floor to ceiling glass along the front and was not sealed off from the rest of the building. Consequently it had a tendency to heat up, and it would become a race to see if the work could be completed before the thermostats on each of the computers would power down the system. On one occasion the thermostats on one of the 405s failed to shut it down, and the first warning that anyone received that something was amiss was when they detected the smell of the read/write heads ploughing furrows into the surface of the disc. That took the system off the air for nearly two days.

After about eight months I 'graduated' to programming, and that was a very different world.

Minutes of the 33rd meeting
of the 803/503 User Group, 16 June 1976 *Seppo Torvinen*

304, Discussion of User Problems: The Chairman stated that the noughts and crosses program will not allow the user to win. He was requested to send data to Mr Williams.

The cleverness of ordinary people, 1960s *Peter King*

Input programs and data for our Elliott computer were punched up on paper tape by a small group of cheerful girls in a typical punch room. Among the tapes so produced there were a number that enabled the 'hooter', via a suitable music generator, to play a variety of tunes. Every processor had one in those days and the sound they made was very agreeable.

Come the Christmas party, the punch girls arrived with an unexpected sheaf of unpredicted tapes which proceeded to play a number of Christmas carols. They knew nothing of the spec. of the music generator but, simply by analysing backwards from the other tapes they had created, they had deduced exactly how it worked and how to drive it; and they made the party a roaring success.

Ever since then, degrees, doctorates and professorships notwithstanding, I have had a very healthy regard for the cleverness of ordinary people.

Five Ferranti

Requiem for Ferranti   *Frank Taylor*

Abridged from the BCS Computer Bulletin *for June 1994*

Today's digital computers only really began to take shape some two to three years after the first successful running of the Manchester University MADAM machine in 1948, more or less concurrently with the first machine at Cambridge University, known as EDSAC. Go-ahead companies, which included Ferranti, rapidly saw the potential of the new technology. In those days the National Research and Development Corporation (NRDC) had the rights to all innovations resulting from research and development pursued using Government money. In due course, in 1950 51, Ferranti negotiated the commercial rights to take over, adopt and utilise the technology of the early computers.

The company's contribution to the development of computing as a profession and as a technology during the 1950s was outstanding. During that decade Stanley Gill was credited with the invention of the subroutine [*though that might be disputed: some would say they go back as far as Ada, Lady Lovelace. H.C.*], while a software team produced PEGASUS and MERCURY Autocode, the first true user interface to a computer system specifically designed for scientific users rather than programmers. Concurrently the foundations were laid for NEBULA (a Natural Electronic Business User LAnguage) which was a superb innovation, but less widely marketed than COBOL, which eventually overtook it.

The company's links with Manchester University were strengthened during the 1950s. Ferranti negotiated the rights to manufacture machines researched, designed and developed by that university with co-operation from seconded Ferranti staff. They then modified the design to accord with production needs and methods, subsequently supplying the first production example to the university for ongoing use, testing, and enhancement of development. Machines which started life in this way included: MARK I, MARK I*, MERCURY, ATLAS, TITAN (also known as ATLAS II).

The proliferation of machines designed in those early days was almost unbelievable. Ferranti had two parallel ranges of machines: one in the field of defence which has never been publicised but from which there was a spin-off into the complementary range of machines for the civilian environment. Many Ferranti civilian sector machines were named after constellations, and can be grouped into three broad user sectors: Scientific, Data Processing, and Process Control.

In those days of relatively slow hardware and highly expensive delay line memory (core store was just emerging), hardware was designed around the user requirements, hence many variants. Scientific machines, especially MERCURY and ATLAS, had powerful arithmetic units for number crunching. The design team supremo was always the designer of the adder, because it controlled the system's performance. Data Processing machines had relatively slow arithmetic but facilities to block transfer DP data to and from backing drums (equivalent to today's discs). Process Control machines were made down to a price and size, with modest arithmetic and storage.

In the Scientific sector one had machines such as MERCURY, ATLAS, and PEGASUS I. One early PEGASUS machine has been preserved at the Science Museum, and is now restored to working order. ATLAS pioneered virtual memory, including real/virtual paging and automated page transfer. IBM were to adopt and harness this technology (at least in principle) but not until ten years later. Their main contribution was to roll it out in the form of VM to make, it available on thousands of their contemporary mainframes. This contrasts with the total of five ATLAS Is made by Ferranti. But then it is well known that one academic did a study of UK computing needs in the late 1950s, and concluded that five ATLASs would satisfy *all* the country's scientific computer requirements.

In the Data Processing sector there were machines such as PEGASUS II, PERSEUS, and the ORION range. It is remarkable that the total working storage of most PEGASUS machines was a delay line store with a capacity of 330K words of 39 user bits, which could be structured as seven five-bit characters. This equates to 2.31 Mbytes of modern store, if each character were mapped into a byte. PERSEUS was a particularly interesting computer using a mixed radix approach. It had a series of accumulators which could be used for different amounts of differing currencies being manipulated: for example, to handle pounds sterling took three accumulators, one each for pounds, shillings, and pence.

In the Process Control field the smaller ARGUS machines emerged. The first of these (the ARGUS 200) required hardware skill in order to program it. Programming was literally done by inserting a ferrite peg in every hole which had to register '1'; all unpegged positions at the intersection of orthogonal conductors represented zeros. In 1964, ARGUS became the keystone of another Ferranti first: the successful development of direct digital control of a complete plant, replacing many separate and less reliable analogue controllers. The first joint installation by Ferranti and ICI was at ICI Fleetwood.

The ORION project to create a state-of-the-art data processing machine in 1958 was typical of the forward-looking attitude in Ferranti. ORION I was based on neuron logic using the principles of electronic balloting, sometimes termed 'ballot box logic'. It was not an easy technology to use and the project was considerably slowed by the technological problems encountered.

Consequently the ORION II project was initiated to produce a machine to satisfy immediate customer requirements. This project really showed what Ferranti could do: within eighteen months from start to finish a complete large mainframe computer was designed, developed, built, prototyped and sold to the first customer, the Prudential Assurance Company. The design team and development team, including the author, literally sweated blood round the clock. Everyone was really dedicated to the job, but every now and then one of the development staff would quickly take a few minutes off to nip round to the oven provided at Ferranti's Development Laboratories at Lily Hill House, Bracknell, to cook a few frozen meals. Working midnight meals were really the order of the day.

This project was an outstanding success. Ultimately the Pru acquired three of the four ORION IIs built, one of their cluster being acquired secondhand from another customer. The first prototype was delivered in 1964 and ORION II served them well as a workhorse until 1976.

The problems with the delayed development of ORION I created cashflow problems for Ferranti and consequently the Large Machines Division was merged into ICT on 26 September 1963. This apparent cloud literally had a silver lining for both companies. Ferranti UK had rights to the Canadian Ferranti-Packard FP 6000 machine which was a state-of-the-art medium size mainframe. ICT urgently needed a replacement for their ageing 1301 machine, for which they had a tremendous market. After combination the two organisations immediately launched the rebadged FP 6000 as the ICT 1904 and, with an added floating point unit, as the 1905. These were an outstanding success. Many 1900 series variants including the 2903/2904 have served many customers through to the 1990s.

A long way South, c. 1960   *Conway Berners-Lee*

We were trying to sell a PERSEUS to South African Railways. One of the first questions they asked was: 'Does your printer print in Afrikaans?'

Le Mot Absolument Juste, 1960s   Frank Taylor

It had been a typically jolly and enjoyable Christmas lunch at Lily Hill House, and the festivities were far from officially over when it was observed that two people were missing from the party: the porter/gardener/factotum and one of the girls from the typing pool.

A search was made and, not to your surprise, they were discovered taking strenuous physical exercise in the garage. Reshevelled, and summoned before Authority, they received a stern example of what in other circumstances might be called a dressing down. Disgraceful behaviour... spoiling the occasion for others... letting the side down... abuse of company property (I shouldn't wonder)... deserve severest treatment... make an example... however, since it's the Christmas lunch, perhaps justify unusual lenience... don't do it again... dismiss.

'I suppose', said Authority, turning to his Assistant, 'in engineering parlance that's what you'd call a 'grubscrew'.

Qui va la? 1960s   Frank Taylor

The culture was not totally dedicated to work. Lighter moments involved particular members of staff. One (who must remain nameless) arrived in Paris one day, without his diary. He had quite forgotten where he was going so telexed his secretary from the airport asking where he was going, what time the meeting was and who he was seeing. She telexed back the necessary details and added, rather tersely, at the end: 'and, don't forget, your name is XYZ'.

Quick thinking, 1960s   Bill Foote

There was the engineer who, seeing a transistor literally burn out inside the printer he was working on, doused it with the cup of tea he was drinking at the time.

Nicotiniana, 1960s   Bill Foote

It is said that a certain prototype machine located in the clean room at West Gorton was equipped with a pair of ashtrays built into the console desk because one senior designer was a chain smoker and refused to work without smoking at the same time.

I meet my first 'ICL' product, 1960s   *Chris Cheetham*

Early mainframe computers were expensive and not very powerful. Their time was accordingly so valuable that they were operated 24 hours a day and 365 or more days a year. At Oxford, operation was delegated to licensed, but not always very well-trained, end-users. The Christmas and Easter shifts were in the hands of Australians and others too far away from home to travel in those days before cheap international air flights.

The basic skill required to operate the Ferranti Mercury was to load a paper tape containing the program, then punch a sequence of buttons which caused the tape to be read and obeyed. The computer then cogitated before punching out its reply on another paper tape. All this took place within the 1 Kbyte memory, backed up by an exceedingly noisy High Speed Drum. Among tricks known to experienced operators was how to deal with the drum 'losing synchronisation' by jumping up and down on the springy floor of the Victorian house which held the computer.

That, however, was a highly developed skill. Late one Sunday afternoon in the autumn, I handed over operation of the Mercury to a stranger new to such tasks and it became apparent to me that his skills were in no way so advanced. He put the tape in the reader and pressed the buttons. The tape moved with great speed but to no effect. 'You have it the wrong way round in the reader', I explained. This was true: paper tapes were asymmetric and, if loaded the wrong way, the holes effectively became invisible to the reader. My colleague painstakingly wound up his tape and put it the other way round in the reader and punched the button sequence.

It was at precisely this point in the Clarendon Physics laboratory, half a mile away, that a friend of mine started up a 2 megawatt electricity generator, which had once powered the tram system of some northern city. It was now used to create strong magnetic fields but, while idling, it fed spare power into the university's electricity grid. On this occasion, the start sequence misfired sending a jet of burning hot oil 50 feet into the air. This much alarmed my friend but fortunately did no harm. It also put a massive 'spike' on the electricity supply which tripped circuit breakers all over the university.

And so, in the computer room, when my companion pressed the button, instead of reading the paper tape the computer died. Not only the computer but the fast drum, the air conditioning system and even the lighting system all failed. Instead of noise and light and activity there was silence and the gathering gloom of a November afternoon in which I heard a little voice ask nervously: 'Are you sure the tape goes in this way round?'

His own phone, 1960s   *Brian Russell*

One of the de Ferranti brothers was somewhere on the West Gorton site and picked up a telephone to ask for an outside line. The telephone operator, following instructions, asked if the call was necessary and who was making the call. A short discussion ended with her saying: 'Sir, if you had been using your own telephone, I would have known who was calling' to which de Ferranti replied: 'Actually, my dear, these are all my own telephones.'

Ferranti culture, 1960s   *Frank Taylor*

Most business operations run the business as an administrative machine operating a service or manufacturing capability with the aim of generating a profit. This was not the case with Ferranti. As a private company run by a family who were enthusiastic about future achievements, Ferranti reversed this philosophy and simply used cash as a resource to make better technology and to make faster, better or higher performing computers. In Ferranti the engineer was king! Subject only to approval from one's devolved manager (since there was no centralised management), one simply thought up an idea and, once approval was given, got on with its implementation.

This was not without its problems and, in the mid-1960s, two separate divisions of Ferranti found themselves competing for the same marketplace with two different ranges of machines: the ARGUS range developed in Manchester and the HERMES range developed in Bracknell. Nevertheless, both were highly successful.

Another classic story is that of NEWT: the Neuron Electronic Working Testbed, alias SIRIUS. It was designed to produce correct results when the (changeable) ORION cards within it worked correctly. One day, a West Gorton engineer showed such a testbed to one of the sales staff and demonstrated its capability as a simple computer. Two weeks later the salesman proudly reappeared to announce that he had sold a NEWT to a customer. Rapid production followed as the internal NEWT hook-up was converted to a presentable computer. The sting in the tail came later when one of the costing staff proved that the (guessed) selling price was around one half of the total production cost.

Unfreezing the freon, 1960s   *Gordon Hobbs*

The Harwell site is very exposed and the computer room which housed the Mercury was particularly vulnerable to cold weather. The Mercury ran 24 hours a day for five days a week with no problems but was always closed down at the weekend, along with all the attendant services such as the air conditioning system (without which the Mercury would overheat in no more than 30 minutes). A vital valve in the cooling circuit lived outside, in a small square pit dug into the surrounding concrete, and in cold weather its tap could be guaranteed to freeze solid. So the Monday morning instructions for switching on the Mercury service began:

'Step 1: Boil a kettle'.

What the eye can't actually notice, 1960s   *Ben Gunn*

Powers Samas and Ferranti had a joint project which involved the Samastronic printer being used with the Ferranti Perseus. The full Samastronic was an electro-mechanical monster which proved notoriously unreliable but the actual print mechanism was quite successful and, sold on its own, would have made a tidy revenue. So two printers were prepared for a Swedish contract and another two for a site in South Africa. These had to match the shining and glistening Perseus computers, which had covers made by Molyneux at great expense (including some 14 coats of paint, all hand-polished).

I was project manager at the time when these printers were built in what we called the 'cow sheds': in fact, Whyteleafe was built on the site of an old swimming pool and these had been the old dressing-rooms. Just before the completion date, one of the engineers (Paul Lambert) upset a can of paint thinners over the control panel and covers of one of the printers. In desperation, we stripped the machine down and took the panels to the local garage, asking if he could match the colours well enough for us not to be found out. The garage returned them in *perfect* condition and, when the inspectors came from Ferranti to pass the equipment, no mention was made of the paintwork finish. If only Ferranti had used our garage on a regular basis they might have saved enough on the paint job to stave off being drawn into ICT.

AN ICL ANTHOLOGY

Six LEO

'*Down memory lane*'   *John Pinkerton*

Recollections of the early days of LEO abridged from the BCS Computer Bulletin *for September 1986*

LEO (the Lyons Electronic Office) was conceived within the offices of J. Lyons & Company, though the name itself was not invented (by John Simmons) until the project was well under way. At that time (the late forties) office management, as taught and practised in Lyons offices by J.R.M. Simmons and T.R. Thompson, both Cambridge wranglers, was a long way ahead of that in most other British or foreign businesses. Looking back, this is what gave the project its unique character. They believed, and by the mid-thirties had demonstrated, that highly efficient ways to organise everyday clerical work could be found by taking analytical thought.

In 1947, having discovered (while on a visit to the USA as it happened) what Maurice Wilkes was planning to do at their university and knowing just what they wanted to achieve (the automation of the routine aspects of clerical work), they saw it as just a matter of correctly applying technology to achieve that ambition. As we now know, their concepts have been realised to an extent and in a variety of ways then unimaginable.

Programming was seen as a system rather than a coding problem. To take charge of it Lyons chose David Caminer. He had been in charge of the so-called Systems Research Office (nowadays we would call it the O & M Department) and had worked for them since before the war. My good luck was that I happened to know Maurice Wilkes (through a common interest in radio and radar) and to have seen their advert in 1948 for someone to take charge of the hardware development. Following broadly the design and techniques already proved by Maurice in EDSAC I, and with the creative help of Ernest Lenaerts (who had worked in Lyons' offices and had become an electronic engineer in the RAF during the war) Ernest Kay (ex-GEC Labs) and several others, we constructed LEO I.

Lyons did not see much virtue in publicly claiming technological firsts: they thought others would only copy them. Lyons' chief interest was first to find, and then to demonstrate, effective ways of applying computers to clerical jobs. However, many important technological innovations were made: for example, multiple buffered input and output channels, and convert and reconvert instructions for decimal as well as sterling whole numbers were both introduced with LEO I. And LEO III, following Wilkes' lead, was the first commercially designed machine to exploit micro-programming.

LEO I was physically enormous, but of very low performance by the standards of today (it executed about 700 instructions per second). It employed some 8,000 valves, drew 30 kW of power and occupied most of a room 45 feet square. Despite its low speed, it could run a sophisticated payroll, including cash dissection and departmental totals, at the rate of fifty persons per minute, printing two or three-line payslips two copies at once on a line printer. The buffered input and output channels meant that processing seldom had to wait for input data or for output results to be cleared. Also there was no operating system to absorb large amounts of processing power. Checkpointing was found to be essential and was adopted from the beginning (we called it 'bringing out restart totals'). Operating, or data, errors merely caused the system to stop, quoting a stoppage number: the reason for the stoppage and how to clear it had to be looked up in a book by the operator off-line.

Although its MTBF (Mean Time Between Failures) was measured in hours rather than days, after LEO I was fully committed to regular work early in 1954 it never failed to complete its scheduled tasks within the week. It ran on a three-shift, and finally a two-shift, basis until it was closed down and dismantled in January 1965.

The working atmosphere was in fact extraordinarily creative, though at the time no-one felt this to be in any way remarkable. If, say, David Caminer felt the need for some new program instruction, Ernest Lenaerts would first work out the appropriate logic, then design the circuit and have it all wired up, tested and working in a few days. Individual schemes were invented for connecting the widest range of peripherals to LEO I and later to LEO II, ranging from paper tape readers from Ferranti, or card readers, punches and tabulators from British Tabulating Machine Company, to magnetic drums from Ferranti and magnetic tape drives from Decca. A notable achievement was the linking of the Powers Samas Samastronic printer to LEO II, using a high power valve circuit invented by John Sylvester.

Much of the inspiration for hardware development as well as for that of software, came from Raymond Thompson, known invariably by his initials, TRT. He had the quickest intellect of anyone I ever met: on occasion he could become almost incoherent as his ideas struggled to find expression. Sometimes, when trying to persuade him of the value of some new approach, one would meet a momentary resistance but, if you were right, then in a second or two his attitude would switch, your idea was seized on and elaborated in ways beyond anything that had occurred to you, and it became a strain to keep up with his fresh thinking. He maintained the enthusiasm and management tone of the LEO project from its beginnings to the merger in 1963 with the English Electric computer department.

Hearing the weather, c. 1960   Brian Russell

The engineer switched on the radio in his hotel room. 'That's a LEO hooter', he thought, 'and it's got a store fault'. The newscaster's voice came on, announcing: 'That is the voice of the new LEO computer at the Meteorological Office, as it works out tomorrow's weather forecast'.

Hello sailor! 1960s   D.J. Russell

Prince Phillip once visited the LEO 3 site at CAV in Acton. Many machines in those days emitted sounds when certain instructions were obeyed and this fact could be exploited to develop music generators. The LEO 3 had a good one. The visit was a great success, and as the party was leaving the processor gave a spirited performance of the Sailor's Hornpipe. Himself turned back to the assembled group, showed that his hearing was in good fettle by raising two fingers in a certain manner, and then departed.

Hard cheese, 1950s   Peter Hermon

At the end of the LEO training course, one of the prospective programmers was told that his services would no longer be required. He protested; the things that had gone wrong hadn't been his fault; it had just been his bad luck that they had affected his trial programs. 'Yes, yes', said David Caminer, 'I'm not firing you because you're incompetent; I'm firing you because you're unlucky'.

Ignis fatuus (fire is a waste of time), 1967   Pete Towndrow

As an eighteen-year old, with basic training behind me, I set off for work as normal one morning in 1967. I was due to start at 07.30, preparing LEOs III/7 and 3/26 for the normal 08.00 start of operations (III/7 was a LEO 3S, serial number 7, 'S' for Slow as it had a 13 μsec store cycle time; 3/26 was a LEO 3F, serial number 26, 'F' for Fast because of its 2.6 μsec cycle time).

Normally I would collect the key from Security and unlock the computer suite. This day I was told: 'It's already open'.

As I entered I was amazed to see my manager and his manager involved in maintenance duties in the console area of 3/26. But the 'maintenance duty' involved a bucket of soapy water and a couple of sponges; this was something in which I had not been trained. My first thought was that I had not been doing my maintenance correctly and they were in some way making good my deficiencies. At this point I was told: 'Pop next door and run the Verification Suite on the other machine'.

Dutifully, I went and (this is the part I will never forget) entered the second computer room which was quite dark. I looked to see why and was amazed to see the light diffusers from the fluorescent units hanging in a strange distorted way from the ceiling. I took another few steps and saw that *everything* was covered in black soot.

Now I was waking up fast! There had obviously been a catastrophic fire overnight. I was just realising this when a voice suddenly echoed through the eerily quiet room (no air conditioning was running): 'Ooooooh... what have you done?' I turned to see my bosses silhouetted in the doorway and one set of whitish footprints (mine) on the blackened floor. My heart jumped. Surely this was too serious an incident to joke about and, for what seemed like ages, they both kept seriously straight faces until they both burst out laughing. My face must have been a picture. I wonder whether they remember that morning as well as I do.

The culprit was an early XEROX printer, a pioneer of the selenium drum and carbon toner technology but using CRTs instead of a laser. It had a 9 kW heater in the fuser pad and this had ignited paper trimmings from the roll-fed stationery. The wax which was used as an insulator filling the cable trunkings had caused the extensive soot deposits.

There followed frantic efforts to get the computer operations up and running. XEROX had a new printer installed later that day (its 1967 price was about £90,000) and operating the following day after we had got one of the AMPEX TM4 tape decks overhauled. The 3/26 was also rapidly patched up.

III/7 required a production line method of disassembly–clean–reassembly, using an army of programmers, operators, engineers and other factory staff brought urgently down from Kidsgrove. After that it was a case of fault-finding our way through dozens of hardware faults on the early transistor-based logic of the mainframe and its peripherals. I had the opportunity of working, sleeves rolled up, alongside people who had been involved in the design and construction of LEO III prototypes and so had a marvellous opportunity to learn the machine inside out. So some good came of it after all.

Seven English Electric

Prelude to Budget Day, 1954   *George Davis*

Transcribed from State Service,
the Journal of the Institution of Professional Civil Servants, April 1955

'Tax tables? Nothing to do with us! This is the Mathematics Division' they said with a capital M (you could hear it). I thought this was rather a pity, so I went and asked the Inland Revenue what they wanted.

They explained at great length. 'It takes us a fortnight usually', they said, 'on a Hollerith tabulator, working all night. More', they said, 'if you allow for mistakes. And the terrifying thing is: *People have to know in advance*. How long would it take you?' they wanted to know 'on your Electronic Brain?'

'Ooh' I said airily, 'about forty minutes.' They were incredulous. 'Well, say half a day', I compromised.

Two quite separate computers were to do the job in parallel on the day, 'in view', as the Inland Revenue delicately put it, 'of the present stage of development of these machines'. Early on, I had been put in touch with our rivals, who co-operated by sending me a succession of flow charts, setting out in broad terms how they would tackle the calculation of the various individual tax tables. These were large documents, suitable for papering a small office, and this, in fact, was the only convenient way I found of studying them.

Their methods seemed rather uneconomical. I asked them about it. 'Oh, that isn't how we actually do it', they said, 'that's just the flow chart'. I turned the charts over and tried writing on the back, but they were too big to be really useful.

To put a job on a computer, one must first write down a program of the elementary operations which the machine can do, in the order in which they need to be done, or rather in the order in which one thought they needed to be done. It is quite fascinating, by the way, to sit in front of a computer which is doing precisely what you have told it to do, and not to have the slightest idea what it is doing.

By now the programs for the PAYE tables were beginning to take shape and were showing the usual esoteric series of errors. They had passed the first stage of producing no answers at all and the second stage of producing complete gibberish. Now they would work perfectly except that a man with zero taxable pay was always required to pay tax of £10. 13s. 0d.; or that for a short patch in the middle of the table the taxable pay was wrong while the tax remained correct; or that the last entry in just one or two of the tables was printed away in a separate column by itself; or that the expense allowance made to senior seamen caused an increase rather than a decrease in the tax demanded.

In the midst of one precious program testing session on the machine, a very senior member of the laboratory looked in. 'What's the job?' he enquired. 'Tax tables? But isn't that child's play? I had to use tax tables once', he continued, 'Terrible things! Horizontal lines all over the place, and vertical ones, and that abominable type, and why do they group entries by fours instead of by fives? Never be accepted by any self-respecting table maker. Someone must tell them about it. Who should we get?' I mentioned the most self-respecting table maker I could think of. The next visit of the Inland Revenue concluded with a shattering homily delivered more in sorrow than in anger. They wrote afterwards thanking us for our advice.

Answers always came from the Pilot ACE punched on Hollerith cards. A tabulator was needed to produce the printed tables. Also a man who knew how to operate the tabulator. This man worked to a regular schedule. The day after hearing the requirements he would come back and offer additional facilities; two days later he would prove with a wealth of technical detail that the thing was impossible; and finally on the next day would produce a perfect specimen tabulation and say: 'Oh, is that what you wanted? Why didn't you say so in the first place?'

Inland Revenue wisely insisted on a rehearsal. This was a day of great joy for those who favour the re-introduction of the abacus. The trivial job of preparing the tax information in the form required by the programs, I had left to be done on desk calculating machines. It took two of the best computers (human) in the Mathematics Division two hours to do no more than half of them. After this, I reverted to the cards I had punched previously for the purpose of testing the programs. A previously punched card got in with the new ones fed to the Pilot ACE output and caused chaos. The last program, which I had finally got to work in the small hours of the morning, had been left in a state more suitable for testing it than using it. I had to correct this on the spot by the light of nature, having left all my detailed notes in another building. 'I don't know how you tell which instruction is which,' they said, leaning over my shoulder, 'it must be very difficult'.

Afterwards, they wrote and said that one of the tables showed an error of one shilling for multiples of £18 taxable pay in the weekly version and for multiples of £9 in the seven-shilling tax range of even months in the monthly version. I wrote back that this was exactly what I had been expecting and got down to work again.

Came the great day. I spent the afternoon finalising my extra program to do what the two computers did at the rehearsal. The engineers were meanwhile giving the machine a special overhaul (fortunately not including any parts that would be used on the job, though I didn't tell them this). The program was that a man would arrive from Inland Revenue at about 4.30 p.m. with an envelope containing the Details. As soon as the Chancellor had sat down, he would be told by telephone to open it. We would then start, working all night if necessary. The man duly arrived, clutching his envelope in his innermost pocket. 'Of course, I don't know what's in this myself', he said, looking at me sideways. At 5.15 p.m., the Chancellor sat and the man was telephoned.

That year there were *no* changes to Income Tax, so the existing tables remained valid.

Inland Revenue wrote afterwards, thanking us for all we had been going to do.

But the most frantic part was trying to cancel the gallon of coffee and the large quantity of sandwiches which the NPL canteen were preparing for the night shift that wasn't needed.

Budget Day: After the event, 1955   *George Davis*

Transcribed from NPL NEWS, *May 1955.*
© *Crown Copyright, National Physical Laboratory*

'And now,' she said, 'what about an account for the NEWS?'

'But I've written it up already', I said, 'I can't do it again, it'll look silly'.

'Oh, it must have been quite different actually doing it', she said, 'after all that waiting. Such a thrill!'

'Oh yes', I agreed, 'of course. Naturally. But nothing happened, really... it all went just exactly according to plan'.

'You must have it all very well organised'.

'Well', I said, 'nearly according to plan... well, more or less... well, we got through it in the end... well, most of it'.

'You must tell us all about it', she insisted, 'because not everyone will have seen the other write-up'.

'But they did', I said. 'They kept coming and asking if the little man with the envelope had arrived yet. We said "No"... It never seemed to occur to them to ask about a little woman'.

I had been up to Somerset House to fetch her, with her familiar brief case that had been in and out of Maths Division so often. She had done most of the extra programming needed this year. On the way down, I predicted the contents of the brief case. Inland Revenue had been as cagey as ever, but I had managed to put two and two together. Obviously, 'Minimum Earned Income Relief' would come in: they had made us alter all the programs to take it and it would be a good election point, giving away very little but reducing a lot of people's tax). And probably a little 'Extended Earned Income Relief': this would pull in a few votes at the top of the scale. These would be the main changes.

The phone call telling us to start came at 5.05 p.m. We pretended it hadn't because we were still busy getting the tables together, for the people who cut up the results and stick them together, and collecting sandwiches and coffee. At 5.30 p.m. we opened the envelope. Most of the information had already been punched on Hollerith cards at Somerset House during the morning so there wasn't much preliminary work. I checked some of the cards: one was wrong. I marked the changes on it and then forgot to punch them in. This led later to some hasty reshuffling of result cards before sending them over from the Pilot ACE to the tabulator. Another error escaped detection, which had the effect that the first results produced were blank cards. We postponed this issue and pressed on with the rest of the work.

Some of the new data wouldn't fit the old layout. We phoned Inland Revenue for instructions. This took about twenty minutes. It later transpired that our rivals had not been able to spare the time to obtain this information. I realised only a little too late that the scheme we had hastily agreed would produce about two hundred unwanted cards in the middle of the run. These were successfully withdrawn from the output.

Coffee and sandwiches were taken on the run. Fortunately, none of the corned beef crumbs landed exactly in any of the holes in the cards. We came off the Pilot ACE at about a quarter to ten with the last batch of results and adjourned to the tabulator room. The computer was kept desultorily running on routine work till all the results had been tabulated and found superficially correct.

We found things easier now since other people were doing the work. I played a game of chess and discovered a gambit of remarkable originality and unsoundness (BxKBP at move five). There was conversation. I reminded the little woman of the chap we had tripped over when trying to get into the Duplex building on our last late-night program testing session. This, I informed her, had turned out to be the NPL Security Forces, and more would undoubtedly be heard of it (it was).

The tabulator worked disappointingly smoothly, apart from a tendency to ease the paper gently out of the way and print on the platen. The last line was printed at about a quarter past eleven. We packed the rolls of paper and the little woman into the car and set off into the night.

The ghost in the machine, 1956 *John Deas*

The English Electric DEUCE had two rows of electronics with an access bay between them. At the Blackheath Lane site during the cold winter of 1956 the temperature in the labs was barely adequate and one of the development engineers was in the habit of taking a chair and his papers inside the prototype where it was warmer. There he would sit happily winding the handle of his Brunsviga mechanical calculator. One day a party of VIPs came round, and their guide showed them the glossy outside panels of the machine and gave them the standard spiel, 'electronic brains' and all that. 'Can you tell us how it actually works?', asked one visitor. 'Well', said the guide, 'It will be easiest to explain if I open this door...'

For want of a..., c. 1958 *Sally Rosebery*

My first computer was an English Electric DEUCE, a valve machine that occupied an enormous amount of space. One day it wouldn't work because a piece of string broke. The piece in question was attached to a metal plate at one end, went over a pulley, and terminated in a heavy weight at the other end. There were two of them, of course, one for each end of the metal plate. Their function was to hold the program cards in the card reader. No string; no program input.

Another time we couldn't get it to work only to find that an engineer had gone to coffee with a valve in his pocket.

On a third occasion it was a broken rubber band in the air conditioning that prevented us using it.

DEUCEd clever, c. 1958 *Sally Rosebery*

Of course one operated the DEUCE oneself. The console had switches and a telephone dial, as well as two cathode ray oscilloscopes. The CRTs displayed the binary digits of the instructions that the computer was obeying. This was useful in solving converging mathematical equations because if the solution did not want to converge one could stop the calculation, use the hand keys to change the program, and then continue. What was the telephone dial for? One could stop the machine, dial the number of instructions one wanted it to obey, continue, and then look at the results (in binary) on the CRTs; obvious, really.

Into the unknown, 1960s   *Chris Horrobin*

English Electric's Computer Bureau also had a second generation KDF8 computer. It was the last machine that actually looked like a computer, with a 2 metre horizontal console bank filled with an impressive array of illuminated buttons, looking like some Star Trek prop. Virtuoso operators used these buttons to control the beast's operation.

Programs could take several hours to run so the male and female staff on the night shift amused themselves in various imaginative ways. There were chariot races in the wheeled console chairs, amorous activities behind the massive tape decks and... the famous rubber band fights. The rubber bands were actually part of the magnetic tape containers and were exceedingly heavy duty. During one such battle a rubber band hit the 'general reset' button in the middle of the payroll run. It was attributed in the log to one of the many 'unknown failures' to which such machines were prone.

No, not those sockets! 1960s   *Chris Horrobin*

The English Electric Bureau's DEUCE computer was a real work of art, with lots of glowing valves in big cabinets. One of the memory components was in the form of mercury delay lines, looking like big mushrooms dotted around the room. However, they were problematical as they had to be kept at a constant temperature. Accordingly each one had a fat heater cable terminating in a 13 amp socket on the floor beside it. It took some time to persuade the office cleaners *not* to unplug the heaters in order to substitute their vacuum cleaners.

Willpower, c. 1960   *George Davis*

The early English Electric system at the research labs in Stafford apparently went psychic. There was one pack of cards which the operator couldn't get to load properly. He called an engineer, who took the cards, loaded them, and the job ran perfectly. The operator tried again, and they wouldn't load. The engineer tried again, and the job ran. They tried this several times, and were completely puzzled. Others gathered to join in the fun. After a while the mathematician who had been watching from the sidelines approached the reader and took the cards. 'I am an operator', he told the machine, and the job failed. 'I am an engineer', he then told it, and the job ran. He had observed that the operator, being properly trained, always joggled the cards against a left hand edge before loading them, whereas the engineer didn't bother with such niceties. In the middle of the pack there was one card which was fractionally short of a full length, and joggling shifted the holes in that card just enough to baffle the reader.

Hartree services, 1960s   Chris Horrobin

In these days of all-year-round availability of exotic products in supermarkets, it is hard to remember that not so very long ago it wasn't like that. Hartree House in Queensway was fortunately surrounded by a variety of little shops which sported exotic produce at appropriate fleeting moments of the calendar. Once a year great excitement awaited the arrival of the internal mail with certain 'urgent' jobs at the Kidsgrove bureau. Several 80-column card boxes would arrive, bearing fresh lychees in individually ordered paper bags, each bag marked with the recipient's name.

Who needs friends? 1960s   Peter Byford

We were doing a massive customer job at Hartree House, working all the hours known to man, plus some others. I did at least one 96 hour week. In the course of this I went to sleep one night in the operators' rest room. When I awoke, there were two problems: the door wouldn't open, I could just see that it was blocked by a massive stack of print-out boxes; and I had no trousers. Actually, there was a third, because some of the operators were girls. When the blighters eventually moved the print-out I sheepishly emerged and found my trousers, stuffed with paper tape chads and taped to the door. It is from that moment that I really date the rupture in my friendship with Toby, the shift leader.

Transformation scene, 1960s   Chris Horrobin

A Scottish steel company waited many months for their English Electric System 4-10 computer. It was the smallest model in an ambitious range that went from 4-10, 4-20, 4-30 all the way to 4-70, based through a licensing agreement on the Spectra 70 architecture used by RCA in the United States. As time passed the delivery kept being adjusted to match the reality of development times and the reduction of models in the range.

Finally they had their order fulfilled by the delivery of an RCA Spectra 70/45, specially imported from the USA. This was effectively the 4-50 model, so they were overjoyed with such a bargain. The machine was commissioned on site and it was then left to the customer's electricians to tidy up the mains wiring. Unfortunately, the large 110 volt transformer supplied with this American machine was inadvertently reversed in the process.

Widdershins at Kidsgrove, 1960s   Chris Horrobin

There was a problem with the two prototype System 4-70 computers being unable to read each other's exchangeable discs. The penny finally dropped when it was noticed that one machine's discs were spinning the wrong way. Kidsgrove Systems Test was famous for having its 3-phase wiring colours mixed up, which the visiting disc engineers did not know.

The fitness program, c. 1960   Chris Horrobin

There was another very early English Electric computer, housed in a large aircraft hangar, or was it the giant hall containing a wind tunnel? There were no operators as everyone ran their own programs. A holiday student had the unexpectedly energetic experience of running a program which produced a graph on a continuous piece of paper from a pen plotter. The computer only controlled the movement of the pen, not the movement of the paper through the plotter. The student therefore had to start the plotter and then start the print program. Unfortunately this involved sprinting down the length of the hangar in a desperate race against the limited supply of paper which was spewing forth at great speed.

An English Electric song (a fragment) c. 1965   Trevor Mills

Tune:

> She'll be coming round the mountain

Verse:

> Oh we've got a new machine
>   System 4;
> Yes, we've got a new machine
>   System 4;
> We've got models made of wood,
> And they're very very good;
> We'd make real ones if we could
>   System 4.

The wooden models were made for the launch presentations. The song itself became so popular, and was thought to be so contrary to good order and corporate discipline, that it was decreed that singing it, humming it, whistling it or repeating the words were all to be dismissible offences.

The ghost in the machine: 2, c. 1965   *Guy Haworth*

Prince Phillip was touring Kidsgrove, and was about to peer into the innards of the System 4 Fast Drum, a huge device in its own walk-in cabinetry. Just as the company spokesman got to: 'and this, Sir, is our new advanced memory device' a white-coated engineer peered through the service window... from the inside.

'Oh, see ye not yon narrow road
sae thick beset with thorn and briars?' 1967–68   *Harvey Brown*

I joined English Electric in September 1967 and, after a period of initial training, was assigned to the Post Office Giro project at Docos House in Commercial Road, London, there to work on the development of the GIRO software.

In those early days, before discs were commercially available, we worked on an RCA SPECTRA 70/45, the predecessor of English Electric's own series of mainframes, which had very many banks of magnetic tapes.

Program compilation and consolidation was a fraught process involving around six tapes, including four worktapes, with plenty of scope for misoperation. The process was affectionately known as 'CACTUS', which I took to be an allusion to its prickly nature: i.e. inherently difficult and prone to failure.

GIRO was a good project to work on, both personally and for the company. In its day it was the largest commercial computer project undertaken anywhere in Europe, and we brought it in on time.

It must have been around a year later, after our move to Bootle to implement GIRO, that I discovered the real meaning of 'CACTUS': a 'Completely Arbitrary Collection of Totally Useless Software'. A brilliant acronym and one I've never forgotten.

Spoilsports, 1967   *Colin Clayton*

When I joined English Electric Leo Marconi Computers in 1967 I was sent on a System 4 course. The disc drive element was given by an elderly gentleman who had been in the company since ACE and DEUCE days. He bemoaned our rotten luck: how unfortunate it was that we were learning these new systems (the first to use integrated circuits). 'It's taken all the fun out of it, and the engineers can no longer get close to the machines'.

DEUCE: 1, 1967 *William Eyre*

The Staffordshire College of Technology boasted an English Electric DEUCE computer. On one occasion, soon after starting to learn programming, I was in the computer room on my own (the operator having popped out) and fed my program in through the paper tape reader. To my alarm, instead of getting out another paper tape with the answer to a calculation punched in it, reams and reams of completely blank tape spewed forth, with nothing at all punched in it. With no apparent end to it, and lights flashing all over the console, I became quite worried as to what to do. Fortunately the operator returned and, of course, he was easily able to abort the program. Obtaining the lecturer's assistance to diagnose the problem, it transpired that because of the figures I had happened to use in my test data, the program was trying to calculate the square root of a negative number which, of course, is a mathematical impossibility, and this had caused the machine to go berserk.

DEUCE: 2, 1967 *William Eyre*

The Staffordshire College of Technology again:

There was a queue of about eight students in the computer room, waiting to load their paper tape programs. One of them, in the middle of the queue and presumably bored with the waiting, burst out with: 'I wonder what this button does?' and simultaneously pressed the large red button on the console to which he was referring. It turned out, of course, to be the emergency stop which brought everything to a complete halt and rendered the machine so useless that the operator could not restart it and the engineer had to be called. Naturally, the culprit's tendency to cause calamities, together with the fact that his level of articulation lay somewhere between a Birmingham accent and Stanley Unwinism, did not exactly endear him to his fellow students or to the staff.

We have lift-off, c. 1967 *Gordon Cumming*

David Caminer, who had lost a leg in the war, headed for the lift in Hartree House, Queensway. The doors opened, revealing Mike Gross (renowned for his considerable size and with the *gravitas* to go with it). As David moved forward, Mike stabbed at the 'Open Door' button. Unfortunately, he hit the wrong one and the doors closed sharply, trapping David between them. Overbalancing, he slumped to the floor. The doors opened and he staggered to his feet. Once again Mike stabbed the button, only to hit the wrong one a second time, and David once more collapsed on the floor. He looked up at Mike. Mike said: 'Try again and I'll really get you next time'. Earning David's respect was not straightforward, but this did the trick for Mike.

Splash, splat, 1960s   Conway Berners-Lee

Another Caminer story:

We were at a hotel in the United States. It was hot. The hotel had a very inviting pool. Before diving in, David took off his leg. The pool attendant fainted.

Pause for thought, 1968–70   Colin Clayton

During program development, source code was entered from punched cards for compilation and, as compilation runs took a long time, they were usually left for the night shift operators. Apart from their having to re-punch the occasional damaged or mis-read card, this was a nice quiet job and appreciated as such. One such program progressed thus through the development and testing processes and, eventually, went live. The language was System 4 UserCode which had a PAUSE instruction: this caused the program to send some text (which was a parameter to the instruction) to the operator's console, suspend, and await reactivation.

Several years went by and the program's live overnight runs became routine. However, late one night as the operators were dozing, feet comfortably up, the console burst into life clattering out an unexpected message. Not expecting any such interruption, the operators were more than startled to find the program suspended and the console reading: 'F*** my giddy Aunt!'

Panic stricken and not knowing what else to do, they called out the standby programmer. He, not wanting to abandon the run and thereby waste several hours' work, delved into dusty source listings, and called out several more programmers. About breakfast time they found the error message in the code, realised that it was a harmless prank by their predecessors, and that all they had to do was to press SEND to allow the program to continue. They suffered a serious sense of humour failure.

Well, it seemed a good idea at the time, 1968   Colin Clayton

In 1968 I went to my first customer site as an engineer, and found the customer was using computers for the first time to control a client's stock and ordering procedures. One of the runs generated mailshots for prospective customers. A splendid machine was purchased which would take the printout produced by a line printer, decollate it, split it, put it into window envelopes, and pop these into a basket for posting. It had two inputs: the paper from the line printer and a stream of continuous envelopes. The line printer ran at 2,000 lines per minute (which was pretty fast for those days) and it was quite a job to keep up with the decollator, carrying each completed box of printed paper to it and setting it up. It kept the two operators of the evening shift very busy indeed.

But just across the road from the computer room was a pub whose welcoming lights were really very tempting.

The crucial observation was that the printer printed and the decollator decollated at exactly the same speed, so they had the bright idea of feeding the output from the printer straight into the decollator. And, to prevent the printer running out of paper and the decollator running out of envelopes, they lined up several boxes of each, taping the last sheet of each box to the first of the next. Satisfied that it was all working, and would last half an hour or more, they crossed the road.

On their return, the printer was still printing and the decollator was still decollating, *but,* about two minutes after they left everything had got horribly out of synch. So the guillotine on the decollator was cutting the paper at the wrong place and this caused each envelope to tear during the insertion process. Each crumpled result was added to an ever increasing mountain of paper which they viewed with horror. To compound the error, the decollator had also franked all of the envelopes. I can't remember if they lost their jobs.

Te Deum Laudamus, 1968   Colin Clayton

When the Yorkshire Computer Services Bureau became operational the local newspaper and the Lord Mayor visited for a formal opening. During the commissioning period I had written a program for fun which allowed a 'conversation' to take place with the computer via the teletype console (there were no VDUs then). The computer's responses were selected at random from a database comprising the operators' responses in previous interchanges. Nothing very sophisticated but it was decided that the program should be run so that the Lord Mayor could ask the computer a question.

He typed in: 'Who is God?' No-one knew he was going to do this but, selecting the answer completely at random from the, by now, large database, the computer responded: 'You were, but I am now.' The assembled gathering was most impressed.

Unfair! Unfair! 1968   Colin Clayton

He was quite a good operator, as operators go, and his ingenuity enabled him to devise a system of winning on the pub's fruit machine. Then, as operators go, he went, but not before paying for his leaving do out of his winnings. The landlord, with dark suspicion, was convinced he had been using 'this new-fangled computer thing' to do him down.

The letter of the lease, 1980s   Chris Horrobin

When ICL finally vacated the warren of offices known as Hartree House, Queensway, there was one difficulty in conforming to the requirement that we should restore the building to the state it was in when our occupancy commenced: nobody could identify a supplier of rats.

Overheard in Oxford   George Davis

'This KDF9, it needs nine inches of headroom to run the cables underneath.'
'You keep your head in a funny place!'

Eight ICL: The Nineteen-Seventies

The water-cooled 1906A, c. 1970   *Brian Russell*

Some inspired architect designed the West Gorton R & D block with the boilerhouse on the roof, and it was the custom to turn the boiler off over Christmas. One year the pipes froze. When the boiler was turned on for the New Year, the prototype 1906A was underneath and took a real soaking. It was covered in plastic sheeting for weeks, but was eventually dried out and made to work again.

A tall story, c, 1970   *Mark Saxon*

The building of the tower block at West Gorton was a godsend to harassed programmers, and improved productivity significantly.

It happened thus: For those old enough to remember, the worst thing that could happen to a programmer was to drop a pack of cards or drop the middle out of a large reel of paper tape. In West Gorton we were one of the last bastions of paper tape usage. When you dropped the middle out of a reel, there was only one way of clearing up the mess. The work of the office would come to a halt while people were placed at strategic positions with their arms held up to act as a feed for the tape. One person would then begin to wind while the people around the room acted as knot-spotters. If a knot was detected they would have to shout to the man on the winder to stop before the knot hit it and the tape broke. The knot would then be disentangled and the process would continue.

Once the new tower block was built, the tape was taken to the twelfth floor, a tape winder was attached to the banisters, and the tape was dropped down the stairwell. Only two other people were then needed, strategically placed at the sixth and ninth floors, to give early warning of knots and to disentangle them.

Bangers and the Oxford benchmark, 1970   *John Deas*

A large 1900 order for universities was dependent on a benchmark set by Oxford University, based on a real university workload. This was extremely demanding and exercised the prototype 1906A hardware much more strenuously than the engineers' test programs had done. After many mods, both to the hardware and to the GEORGE 3 operating system, the benchmark ran inside the stipulated 90 minutes, and the customer representatives were invited to see it.

On the day, the benchmark ran beautifully for the first hour or so, and then the system crashed. A second and a third try had the same result. So we took the customers out to dinner and left the engineers struggling. When we came back the atmosphere was transformed: broad grins all round and the benchmark had already run well past the failure point. The customers had it re-started so that they could see it right through but all was well and, some time after midnight, everybody staggered happily but wearily off to bed.

Only later did I hear what had happened while we were at dinner. One of the engineers had concluded that there was no more that he could do and had been told that he could go home. As he was driving through the Manchester suburbs, his thoughts turned to supper: he had bought a packet of sausages at lunch-time. With a pang he remembered that he had left them in the machine room. It wasn't worth going back but, as he drove on, his thoughts played around the sausages, and the shelf he had left them on, and then wandered to the processor cabinet nearby, and in a flash of inspiration he realised what was crashing the benchmark. Screeching to a halt by the next phone-box, he rang West Gorton and passed on his suggestion, and it worked!

History does not relate what he had for supper.

The Oxford benchmark, 1970   *Chris Cheetham*

In 1968, ICL was formed with the full and high profile support of the then Minister for Industry, one Anthony Wedgwood Benn. An integral part of the plan was the launching of a new range of mainframes to replace the existing 1900 and System 4 computers, but ICL decided to complete the well-advanced development of the 1906A as an interim top-end mainframe. It became necessary to convince a then prestigious and influential (but very unsympathetic) group of government-funded universities and other research bodies that the 1906A would be powerful enough. Oxford University was scheduled to take the first 1906A but was determined not to be palmed off with something inadequate. Thus it came about that ICL undertook to prove, using a 1906A still in development in West Gorton, that it could perform, in under 90 minutes, a benchmark test which I had devised.

The first trial was cancelled without troubling the university's representatives, who comprised my then boss at Oxford (John Rollett) and myself. A second trial was held late one night in West Gorton and the machine, alas, took one minute too long. John would have pronounced the test failed if it went over by one second. With some difficulty ICL prevailed on him to allow a last chance to prove its case and a third trial was scheduled.

And so once again, late one night, the two Oxford representatives settled down for 90 minutes (or hopefully less) to time the Oxford benchmark on the prototype 1906A. To while away the time (surely for no other purpose), Gordon Haley the brilliant senior engineer from West Gorton, engaged John in a game of shove ha'penny. The game was not notably exciting but a computer running for 90 minutes provides little competition and it absorbed the attention of both players.

Now the 1906A suffered from a problem called 'loss of prepulse'. As I understood it, it would appear to die but could be raised from the dead as if nothing amiss had occurred simply by touching the right nerve; if only one knew which and where. During the trial, the 1906A performed true to form, which is to say that after about 68 minutes it lost prepulse. But the ICL engineers took a chance and successfully guessed which was the right nerve to bring the 1906A back to life. As the benchmark came to completion, the game of shove ha'penny came to an end, and many anxious eyes were turned on clocks and stop watches because it would surely be a close run thing.

Finally a message appeared marking the finish of the run. John looked at his watch and said: 'Well, we started at 9.23 and it is now 10.55, so I make that 92 minutes but let's be precise: *what does the computer clock say?*' And the computer clock, which had of course been stopped for three minutes, along with everything else, said 89 minutes. 'Funny', said John; 'I could have sworn it was more than that. Still, the computer can't be wrong.' And so the Oxford benchmark was pronounced passed.

For the record, the final target was for the 1906A to achieve 45 minutes when delivered and, in fact, it achieved 38 minutes, so arguably the right result was indeed obtained. But at the time I was more concerned with avoiding the necessity for a third visit within a month to West Gorton. The 1906A long retained, however, its amiable characteristic of suddenly stopping. The computer operators at Oxford swiftly learned that one could often restart a dead machine merely by touching a particular circuit board at the right point with one's finger.

Incidentally, if any computer deserves to be preserved as a memorial to the dinosaurs of the computer age, it should be the 1906A. Designed so that nine multi-layer circuit boards could be held in exact juxtaposition, it was constructed out of iron beams more appropriate to bearing the load of a multi-story building, and weighed many tons. Needless to say, when it finally arrived at Oxford just a wee bit later than ICL had promised, the floor duly gave way under its weight.

New Range planning: 1, 1970 — Gordon Cumming

George Felton, as head of Software for New Range Planning, was also responsible for issuing the first full set of manuals, bringing together all the work done by the Planning team. This amounted to some eight or ten four-ring binders of material and it was distributed to a significant number of people around the company for evaluation and comment. The production task was large enough in itself and, once the copying was completed, the insertion into the binders was no mean task. Unfortunately, the settings of the hole punch did not match the ring binders, requiring the whole job to be redone.

Some two or three years later, George moved to Bracknell, and initiated a set of standards for software development. The very first document concerned the standards for four-ring binder hole punching. A short while later, Issue 2 was distributed.

New Range planning: 2, 1970 — Gordon Cumming

David Caminer was chairing a New Range Planning meeting on the tenth floor of ICL House, Putney. It was approaching one o'clock, and some early lunchers from the canteen on the fifteenth floor were already leaving the building. Another of these was waiting for the lift. As he stood there (and that building is woefully short of lifts) his fingers played, as they do, across the glass of the fire alarm button. But there wasn't any glass over the button and only the lightest of touches was needed to set off the alarm.

As the building was evacuated and as fire engines soon appeared in force from the nearby Putney station, the lifts were of course disabled as part of standard fire procedure. David Caminer who, with his artificial leg, would never have contemplated the stairs, up or down, in any circumstances, turned to his meeting and said: 'Well, I presume you are all prepared to burn with me'. With no further hesitation he carried on. Nobody dared to move.

What's in a name? 1970s — David Sutherland

There was a user (was it the Atomic Energy Authority?) whose IT manager decreed that all usernames should start with 'ICL'. It wasn't long before he acquired an 'ICLAUDIUS'.

On demand, 1970s — Sarah Hamilton

Of course, some customers are always more demanding than others. In Egypt there was a time when ICL would provide servicing for our most important customers out of normal working hours – but very unofficially you understand. One evening, a certain engineer received a very late call at home from a customer, asking him to come *now* to service an urgent problem. The engineer apologised and refused. Half an hour later the peremptory knocking at his door announced a policeman, insisting on his immediate presence at the company. The customer was so furious, or maybe just so desperate, that he had rung the police and told them to fetch the engineer *PRONTO!*

Consequences, c. 1970 *Arthur Humphreys*

Lord Weinstock was talking to the Industry Minister, on whether the country should spend money to develop a native UK microelectronics industry. 'We're all losing money at present, but it's absolutely vital'. 'But do we need it?' 'Not really, if you don't want radio, TV, aircraft engines and other advanced industries. Then your only problem would be to export forty million people'.

Communication and non-communication, c. 1970 *Chris Cheetham*

Many were the meetings at which ICL's unfortunate sales force had to cope with their reluctant customer at Oxford. All too rarely were these home games on ICL premises but the first, memorably, was at Letchworth which we visited, ostensibly, to view communications equipment but, in practice, to acquire a life-long hatred of factory visits and a life-long love of good burgundy. Many ICL salesmen in those days were gentlemen and some had been officers, but it was Pamela Stone-Jenkins (who had missed out on the visit) who unwittingly set off the mine: 'Have you thought about your options', she said, 'now that ICL has cancelled the 7902 system?' Alas, Gwyn Harper had shown us both the replacement choices and had plied us with ample measure of good burgundy, but it had somehow slipped his mind to deliver the news that lay behind ICL's generosity on this occasion. And, to be fair, it was not until Pamela spoke that it occurred to us that we had been all the way to Letchworth without seeing the 7902 that we thought we were going to buy.

New Range casts some shadows before, c. 1970 *Chris Cheetham*

Early work for New Range was done on 1900 systems and ICL was particularly coy about the machine-independent software technology used. Once while using the Putney 1900 computer (which, rather oddly, was used to provide service both to ICL's senior management and to customers), I happened to spot some computer output which I thought I recognised and realised that it meant ICL was using a particular technology. Unfortunately I was discovered reading it before I could verify my conclusions, an event which for ever damaged my reputation and caused all computer output for internal use thereafter to be segregated in a secure area. I was made to swear that I would keep secret anything I had learned about New Range. I wasn't asked but I did also keep to myself the information it contained about ICL's annual financial results, due to be released about a week later.

The badness of George 3, c. 1970 — Chris Cheetham

A fellow user of the Putney service was Peter Nutter, then commanding a secretive MoD establishment where his office was a very attractive summer-house in the garden. I met him one day as I was going in to do some work at Putney. 'Will you be long?' he asked, 'because you won't get any work done after five o'clock'. He had been utterly failing to convince ICL that George 3 was insecure and had taken steps to demonstrate the fact in the most vivid way possible. Unfortunately I was still there when it happened. Although, eventually, all the evidence pointed to my being innocent, I did learn how a criminal feels when the police have 'felt his collar'.

A nose for it, c. 1971 — Ted Evison

The Bryant discs on the 1906A at Harwell were horrors. The trouble-shooting team were there all weekend, every weekend. One engineer claimed afterwards that he had furnished his house on the overtime these discs necessitated. The starting up procedure alone took about four hours and there was always the risk that, at the very last minute, something would cause a head crash. There was even a sniffer unit under the floor which was supposed to be able to detect the smell of something going wrong and to whip the heads out of the way before they crashed. One engineer went one better: at the very end of the startup procedure he would open the little spring-loaded lid of an inspection opening and bend down close to it. His nose, he claimed, was more sensitive than the sniffer, and he could whip the heads out faster.

Drum majors, c. 1971 — Ted Evison

At one stage there was a small marquee in the middle of the West Gorton site, which housed two engineers who did nothing but commission drum systems (poor souls!). Their names really were Bill and Ben.

Feeling foolish, c. 1971   *David Bell*

The two-man George III course started on 1 April. 'Good morning', said the instructor, 'and welcome to the George II implementation course.' No reaction. But at coffee-break, the shy one said tentatively: 'Excuse me, I think I'm on the wrong course.'

Tongue Goulashing, c. 1971   *Sandy Walker*

I once arranged for the Hungarian Ambassador to visit Arthur Humphreys in his office at 5 p.m. The Ambassador, after the regulation gins and tonic, obviously felt very much at ease and talked on and on until nearly 8 p.m. despite the best endeavours of Arthur and myself to bring the meeting to a close. When, at last, the Ambassador and his side-kick got up to go, Arthur solemnly shook hands with both of them, and then shook me also by the hand saying, in a loud voice: 'Thank you, Sandy my boy, and take the rest of the day off'. The Ambassador had the grace to laugh.

Close business relationship, c. 1971   *Mike Forrest*

During the New Range planning phase, I was once booked into a Westbury hotel in the States with Arthur Humphreys, but the arrangements had gone wrong and we were allocated a single room with only a single bed. 'OK, we'll have to share it', he said. 'Does duty and discipline take one this far?', I wondered. It turned out he meant time-share.

Hertz to Hertz, c. 1971   *Mike Forrest*

I collected a car from Hertz at the airport and parked it in the car-park opposite the Westbury Hotel. Next morning it had vanished. I rang Hertz. 'No problem,' they said, 'have a replacement'. It was when I was parking this one that I realised these were the spaces reserved for returned Hertz cars and the first car had simply been re-rented to someone else.

Spotting the hotspots, c. 1971   *Chris Cheetham*

A common early problem was that the cost of hardware made almost every resource a potential bottleneck to cause poor performance of the computer as a whole, but the software provided nothing to help the computer manager determine how best to deploy that resource. At an early stage in providing a service from the 1906A, Oxford University knew that performance was affected

115

by overload of one high speed drum, while another remained almost idle. We lacked any way, however, to identify what information was being accessed, and therefore to even out use of the two drums.

Having failed to provoke ICL into providing suitable software (we had not yet learned that it takes ICL years rather than days to produce software), or even temporary hardware to monitor the situation, one morning Robin Atherton, the Operations Manager at Oxford, had an idea of how performance could be measured. He realised that, by chance, the key information was so laid out on the busy drum as to lie at very different locations. While providing no software, ICL had provided copious signal lights which lit up to show the location, actually the target address, of each information transfer.

The same day, at lunch-time, Robin visited his former colleagues at the Oxford Nuclear Physics department and came back carrying some photo-sensors and an electronic counter. By three o'clock that same afternoon, we knew exactly which information was being most heavily accessed, and were able to even out the drum accesses overnight.

Beyond the call of duty, 1971   Chris Cheetham

It was at the time when ICL was supplying, with each major release of software, a human chaperone whose job was to fix any problems that arose, if he could, and to mobilise other ICL resources if he couldn't. Thus it was, that at one o'clock one Saturday morning, Dick Hodges and I realised that there was no way we were going to succeed even in loading the new software he had brought, let alone trying it out. Now Dick was not a software expert, but a Project Manager, which meant that his job description was to achieve the impossible.

First we sought to take two EDS 8 discs from Oxford to Bracknell to load a standard system. Failure: it was not possible to get two people and two exchangeable discs into Dick's Lotus Elan. Then we decided that we could achieve the result a different way by taking only one disc and loading the right program onto it. Problem: which ICL location had the program and the hardware and the software to use that particular type of exchangeable disc? By trial and error we found three sites still at work at three o'clock on Saturday morning. One (Lily Hill House) had the program, another (Friar Street, I think) could handle EDS 8, and a third had the software to handle the disc. Eventually all three elements were brought together on one site and a working disc was taken back to Oxford. The 1906A was initialised from the disc and, at eight o'clock on Saturday morning, we handed over a working computer and went to get our breakfast.

Before political correctness, c. 1971   *Mark Saxon*

At a meeting of the 'New Range Upper Sub-Range Primitive Interface Interpretive Committee', chaired by John Bowthorpe, there was a lengthy debate one day about the proposed implementation of the SWEQ (Scan While Equal) and SWNE (Scan While Not Equal) instructions. Near the end of the meeting, one of the engineers got up and said that he was happy with the implementation but unhappy with the names of the instructions. He explained that he came from Oldham and that in parts of Lancashire 'while' meant 'until', so that any Lancastrian engineers and programmers would interpret the instructions in exactly the opposite way to that intended. An action was duly placed for the Architects to rule on this.

At the next meeting the chairman came to this action and solemnly declared that the matter had been duly considered and the instruction names would remain as they were. It was felt that 'ICL specifications could not be written to cater for ethnic minorities'.

The phantom password changer of Oxford, 1971   *Chris Cheetham*

We tried of course to maintain a service to our users but my ideas of customer care seem, in retrospect, a bit harsh. A constant problem was a tendency for people to just walk away from their teletypes, leaving them logged in free for anyone else to use. This was not just dangerous to the user, since anyone else could use the teletype, inspect and destroy files, and so on, but actively anti-social, since there was a limit on the number of active users and others were thereby prevented from using the service at all.

Whenever I noticed this, I used to change the person's password and log out, arguably sparing the user a worse fate but causing him considerable annoyance through inability to use the system until he had found the new password from us (payment for which was a standard lecture on good housekeeping). I knew the message was getting round when people from other sites started asking me about the 'phantom password changer of Oxford'. Eventually, of course, we solved the problem properly by getting the software to auto-logout. Until that happened, my biggest problem was to convince our own customers that the problem of changed passwords was not a software fault without disclosing my own role.

Post-ERNIE, pre-CAMELOT, 1971   *Anthony Lucas-Smith*

When in training I used to teach disc programming, including a randomising technique known as the 'Berners-Lee algorithm'. It was a useful time-filler because it worked and was just complex enough to impress the customers without confusing them. One day in 1971, I received an unexpected call:

'Is that Anthony Lucas-Smith?'

'Yes?'

'My name is um, er...' long pause, has the caller forgotten his own name? '...Conway Berners-Lee. I hear you are teaching a disc record randomising algorithm attributed to me. Could you please outline it to me as I've forgotten what it is?'

I explained the algorithm to its originator... another long pause.

'Mmmmm. It's not very good, is it? I'll work out something better and send it to you.'

And, in due course, a long memo arrived with a more detailed algorithm. But I could never quite follow the argument, so continued to use the first version.

The Bryant rotating, vibrating, and frustrating fixed disc, c. 1972   *Chris Cheetham*

I'm sure many people have this as their favourite white elephant. It contained about 740 Mbytes of information, an enormous amount for those days. This was held on 52 disc surfaces, so 26 discs in two blocks mounted horizontally either side of a central drive unit. The physical dimensions were impressive: discs nearly four feet in diameter in a cabinet six feet long. The entire head assembly of (I think) six heads on each of the 52 surfaces weighed a few hundredweight, moved as one, and was positioned by oil pressure. One oil pipe equated to 1, a second to 2, a third to 4, another to 8, and so on. The functioning of the mechanism could be seen to best effect when the entire surface was scanned. As the heads moved from track 127 to track 128, pressure came off the 1, 2, 4, 8, 16, 32 and 64 pipes and went on to the 128 pipe. You could see that it happened in that sequence because the whole head assembly fell back as though exhausted and then moved forward again.

In 'normal' use, which was a rare event, tracks were addressed randomly, and the heads were moved in small and big leaps across the entire surface. The effect of a few hundredweight lurching to and fro was enough to shift the entire disc unit along the floor. I once saw a disc with a glass of milk on it: some wag wanted to see if it would turn into butter. As a fact, the disc at that site had been measured to have moved six inches. Functionally, the discs were of little use, even when working, because the access time was fearsomely slow, and George 3 was optimised for 4 Mbyte discs, not 740.

More commonly, the disc was not working but being thoroughly cleaned: part of the four hour recovery procedure from any incident, however small, and most of them were not small. Cleaning was done by inserting a long vacuum cleaner pipe wrapped in gauze moistened with cleaning fluid between each pair of surfaces in turn, while the discs were rotated manually. One way or another, pressure was the problem. The main difficulty was that the head engineering was just too close to the edge: the heads 'flew' on air pressure but, in fact, they were constantly crashing, often damaging the disc surface beyond repair. The damaged discs made good coffee table tops. More rare, but an impressive event, was when pressure caused a burst in a pipe, spilling oil everywhere. The discs were usually installed with large drip trays under the false floor.

They had to go, of course. Geoff Cross made a round trip one day to RAOC Bicester, then Oxford, and finally the Atlas Laboratory, Chilton. The big disc was top of my list of problems and it was obvious, as soon as I mentioned it, that I had hit a raw nerve. This was not a surprise. Mike Killeen and the other ICL Engineers at Oxford were in cahoots with their colleagues at Bicester and Chilton, and made darned sure that we all complained about the discs. Not that we needed prompting, but you could see their point: the idea of maintenance is that the beast should work if well maintained but constant and fruitless repair of the fixed disc was a heart-breaking and Sisyphean task. Evidently Cross was convinced, because the recall order came the next day.

Sounds like a case for Will Hay, 1972   Dick Hodge

At the Putney System Centre we had a night cook who came in to cook the night shift lads a hot meal in the canteen on the second floor (the one with the large balcony outside overlooking the river).

One night there was a fire in the cinema on the lower ground floor. It was about 01.00 and some of the lads, including the Shift Leader, were eating their egg and chips in the canteen when the fire alarms sounded. The Shift Leader looked up and saw smoke curling up over the edge of the balcony. Knowing that he was in charge, he opened one of the 6 foot windows (they had centre hinges top and bottom), ran to the railings and peered over the edge of the balcony. He saw at once that the smoke was indeed coming from our building and raced back to deal with the fire. Unfortunately the window he returned through was not the one he had opened: he went straight through the plate glass and, though he only suffered a few cuts and bruises, he was thoroughly dazed and unable to retain command.

Number two took over. His first task was to call the fire brigade, and the only usable phone was with the security guard at the lower ground floor car park entrance. There he had a little glass booth with his desk and phone, and immediately above the desk was one of the fire bells. My man arrived, having rushed down the stairs, and shouted at the guard to call the brigade. The reply was: 'How can I call the brigade when I can't even hear myself think! How can we stop this bell ringing?' The solution was a pullover rammed between the bell and its clapper.

The cause of the fire was never certain: it may have been a cigarette end thrown from the pathway outside through a window left open accidentally. The fire was restricted to the cinema but that was gutted and was never restored. The early smoke had been sucked into the computer air conditioning system, whose inbuilt smoke alarms triggered the main alarms, so that worked OK.

My only embarrassment was that they had been so busy that no-one had telephoned me (the System Centre Manager) and I arrived at work on the next day at the normal time, only to find that Geoff Cross had been there half an hour earlier, had asked for me, and I wasn't around!

The Hutchins cost-effective approach. 1972 *Chris Cheetham*

As use of the Oxford 1906A increased, performance deteriorated, especially when the machine was being used interactively by many different people, and it became apparent that George 3 was spending 50% of its time on its own internal operations rather than supporting useful work.

This problem was very considerably ameliorated when Rob Hutchins correctly diagnosed a problem in the way memory was used. By changing a single byte in the operating system he was able to improve the performance of the Oxford machine by a measured 27% and of other machines by lesser but useful amounts. This must rank as one of the most cost-effective changes ever made.

It had a lasting effect not only on machine performance but also on Rob Hutchins, who thereafter devoted himself to seeking changes which produced even greater effect but required even less effort on his part.

Thunderstruck in PNG, c. 1972 *Rosie Dean et al*

The work force at the mines near Port Moresby were locals, but they had learned to drive dump trucks and graders and bulldozers with some panache.

Then from somebody, probably an Australian, they picked up the concept of strikes, and decided that they ought to have one. So, one fine day, they drove their dump trucks and graders and bulldozers through the administrative compound, flattening everything in sight, including the Portakabin offices, and especially flattening the one that contained the computer, a 2903 probably or it might have been an ME29. A good time was had by all.

The following day they were all back at work as normal. And, as normal on a Thursday, they turned up for the midday pay parade. Only to be told, of course, that there was no pay because they had flattened the hut containing the pay machine. The lesson slowly sank in.

The next industrial dispute proved this: mere offices and stores were again ruthlessly flattened, but the huts containing the generator and the replacement computer were inviolate.

Not enough tonic? 1972   *Robert Dimmick*

I was responsible at one time for developing and maintaining the assembler for GIN, a dialect of the 1900 PLAN assembly language specially written so that the GEORGE 3 operating system could be written in it. I'm not sure who originated GIN. By the time I took it over, the GIN assembler was itself written in GIN.

After several months of development I had produced a new, improved and faster version of the assembler. There was one bug still in it, but I knew the solution to that and I was ready for the final test.

There was only one possible final test for the GEORGE 3 assembler: to actually assemble GEORGE 3. It contained several hundred thousand source records held on two magnetic tapes. Because of the considerable speed improvements I had achieved, the job would now only take two hours on the 1907F. Because of the bulk, we only ever listed the full source when issuing a new GEORGE version. At all other times (such as this) we produced a much more compact compilation listing which identified any compilation errors, plus a couple of lines for each of the hundreds of 'chapters' or program modules.

So on this particular night I set up a batch job. First, the old GIN assembler would compile a new version of itself (the bug I knew about didn't affect that compilation). Then the new version would load itself and compile GEORGE 3. Expected time: about 2 hours 10 minutes.

Next morning I came to work in confident mood. However, this was soon destroyed when I found myself unable to reach my desk because of the trolley-load of printout in the way. On top was a plaintive note from the operators, saying something like:

'Your job took twelve hours, not two. Where would you like the second trolley-load?'

Also on the trolley was a long roll of console log with the time printed out at one minute intervals for twelve hours, terminating in the rather contradictory messages:

```
0#GIN5:     NUMBER OF ERRORS IN THIS RUN: 363000
0#GIN5:     DELETED OK
```

I forget the last three digits; I'm horribly certain of the first three.

So what had happened? Simple. A mistake in the bug correction meant that every line of source which generated object code was treated as a compilation error. Why twelve hours? It took that long to print with the printer going flat out.

In those days, when we were reliant on overnight runs, it was tempting to get as much achieved in each run as possible. It would have wasted a day, I reasoned, to put in a simple test the first night and run the full compilation the next. We'd never do things like that now; would we?

Meanwhile, unless anyone cares to contest the claim, I hold the record for the most spectacularly unsuccessful program compilation of all time.

Inventiveness, c. 1972 *Dave Kelson*

In my early days as an ICL Customer I was invited down to Bracknell by an ICL Sales Manager who was keen to sell me an all-powerful 1900 series computer.

At the end of a long day and evening of being force-fed highly technical information (much of it way beyond me) the meeting finally concluded at about 8.30 p.m. Wearily trudging down the stairs, I finally arrived in the main reception, only to find that the front door was locked. Looking round in desperation, my eyes locked onto a smart, but weird, white-haired gentleman who had also arrived in reception.

'Excuse me, Sir', I asked, 'but can you please tell me how I can get out of the building?'

'Smash the window!' he abruptly replied.

'How do I do that?'

'Don't ask me', was his response, 'I'm an ideas man, not an implementor.'

I related this to my ICL Sales Manager some days later and the questionable saviour was identified, of course, as Ed Mack, ICL's Development Director.

A *waiting game, 1973* *Chris Cheetham*

While still an ICL customer, I was called in by the company to help improve the performance of the 1900 computers on which ICL was developing the New

122

Range. I thus became privy to the awfulness that was ICL's New Range while still in the crawling stage, before it transformed itself over the years into the butterfly that is Series 39.

I therefore wish to claim the credit, on behalf of John Grogan and myself, for a simple performance change made very early in the life of New Range. At that stage it was taking its instructions directly from a card reader, but so slowly that the reader usually switched off between cards. In fact, a third of the time disappeared while the card reader warmed up again. By lengthening the time to switch off from 15 to just over 20 seconds, we achieved 50% speed up in overall computer performance.

Dim drums throbbing, c. 1971   *Chris Cheetham*

John Grogan was the author of an even more minimalist strategy for High Speed Drums: he switched them off because he swore the computer went faster with the operating system *not* on drums (Ron Bailey immediately wanted to know how fast it went with just cards). Maybe John had a valid point, because ICL ended up a few years later with over a hundred drums in an expensive dry store in the Nevada Desert. Innumerable people told Peter Ellis to cut his losses and dump them in the ocean but it went against the grain. One day, shortly after I had joined ICL, he rang and asked my advice on how best to use them. My only original thought concerned who ought to be tied to them before they were dumped, but I chickened out of saying it.

Pent up in Poona: Feelings and managers, 1973   *David Marwood*

Geoff Cross and I visited India, mainly to negotiate with the Indian Government in Delhi for import licences for components to enable ICIM (International Computers Indian Manufacture Ltd) in Poona to manufacture new products. We also visited ICL India's sales offices in Delhi and Bombay. Geoff Cross insisted on a brief visit to ICIM in Poona on our last day; the return flight was due to leave Bombay at 2 p.m.

Accompanied by Utam Singh, the Indian Managing Director, we flew by private plane to Poona (a half-hour trip) arriving about 9 a.m. The Works Manager, Vasant Kher, met us and said that ICIM's employees had struck the previous evening for a 20% increase in their bonus rate. He advised us not to visit the ICIM factory as the mood was uncertain. Instead he took us to a nearby hotel where we listened to presentations from the Indian trade union leaders arguing for the 20% higher bonus.

Geoff's patience ended with him saying that he had not come all the way from England to settle a local industrial dispute. He instructed Utam Singh to sort it out and telex London to that effect by the end of the week. Then, with a glance at his watch, Geoff said: 'We've still just time to visit the factory. Let's go!' Despite protestations from Vasant Kher, we drove to the factory and found most of its 400 employees parading outside with banners demanding the 20% increase and displaying black crosses.

We walked through the chanting, jostling crowd, entered the factory and inspected its silent production floor and machines. On returning to the front hall, we found the doors locked. We had been 'Gherao'd', an Indian industrial dispute tactic of locking the management in until they give in and concede the claim. Retreating to Vasant Kher's office, we tried the window as a means of escape. But no joy, the chanting mob was right outside.

They then entered the corridor and began banging on the office door and chanting '20% boonus, 20% boonus', accompanied by shouts and yells. The strikers then switched off the air conditioning system and we got hotter still. Vasant Kher tried his phone and luckily it still worked, and he got through to the Chief of Police in Poona, who promised help if he could spare it.

Some twenty to thirty minutes later (though it seemed much longer, with the noises outside getting ever louder) a commotion occurred in the yard outside. In came three three-ton lorries out of which poured some thirty armed Indian police under a dapper little Lieutenant swishing his swagger cane. With their lathis they cleared a way through the mob, the Lieutenant entered the office and told us to follow him quickly and silently. He led us through the still-shouting crowd, guarded by his policemen, to our cars.

Thankfully, we drove off to Poona airfield and got back to Bombay just in time to catch the afternoon flight to London. It was a close-run thing!

A couple of days later, Utam Singh telexed Geoff Cross to say that the dispute had been settled by a 3% increase in the bonus rate.

Taking (out) the Chair, 1972–73   *David Marwood*

The Board Room in ICL House, Putney was refurbished and the work included fitting new circular plastic covers, about 14 inches in diameter, over the ceiling lights. At a rather stressful point during a Board meeting the Chairman, Col. Terence Maxwell, thumped the table to emphasise a point. This caused the plastic cover immediately above him to spring loose and fall sharply upon his balding head. Fortunately there was no serious injury, but the sudden shock put the Chairman out of action until he recovered. During that long long pause all eyes were turned upon the embarrassed and apologetic Secretary, whose administration responsibilities included all building services.

Not seeing the belaiti joke, 1972–73   David Marwood

A telex was sent from Putney to Alan Richford, the Managing Director of ICIM, to wish him well on his retirement after many years of distinguished service. It included the lighthearted words: 'Congratulations on 40 years of undetected crime!'

The Indian Customs authorities had been examining some ICIM papers for evidence of imports on which duty had not been paid. They came across this telex. The immediate result was the confiscation of all of ICIM's records and the start of the celebrated 'Customs Case', one of the biggest events in ICIM's history. It lasted for years, with claims and counter-claims dragging their way through the Indian courts. The eventual settlement was reasonably moderate, but Oh what a cost for a tiny bit of friendly flippancy.

The hair of the dog, 1973   Charlie Barker

I joined the Dataskil staff manning the Computer Aided Design Centre, the offshoot of Cambridge based first at West Gorton and later in St Helens.

Having just bought a house I decided I needed a dog, so acquired a rather scruffy six-month old mongrel from the dogs' home. She didn't take kindly to being left shut up in the kitchen all day and did a lot of damage to the lino and skirting boards. I mentioned this to my manager and he, kind fellow, said why didn't I bring the dog to work. So I did and she used to spend most of the day on a chair in my office, with intervals of barking at the window cleaners.

Anyway, after she had been there a while we had a problem with the keyboard of a Termiprinter, some of whose keys would not work. When the engineer came to fix it he found these hairs were preventing proper contact with some of the keys. He told us that hairs quite often caused this sort of problem but, when he removed one, he found that not only was it half black and half white, but it had a right angled kink in it. He couldn't work out what sort of person this had come from and we hadn't the heart to tell him there was a dog in the office.

Inspiration, 1973   Dick Emery

My knowledge of New Range in development caused me to be selected for the New Range launch team in 1973. For a year, I shared an office in Computer House at Euston with Ninian Eadie who was in charge of the small team. I was responsible for the presentation of the technicalities. We judged that the way to do this was to prepare a film which explained the 'architecture' of the new series and I was the technical consultant to the agency chosen to make the film.

It was hard work trying to explain to script writers, visual artists and film directors what this new computer series had going for it. I tried analogies of mirrors and prisms to explain 'virtual storage', but it was all an image too far for them. I was despairing of ever getting the act together till, one day, the phone rang and I was invited to rush down to the studio in Bloomsbury where they had something to show me. I was ushered in and stood before a table on which there was something mysteriously covered by a cloth. They explained that the visual artist, who had until then been the most obdurate in failing to understand what I wanted, had become inspired. They drew back the cloth and there was a glass ball with ground facets all over it. Impatiently they asked whether this was what I meant. I enthused and asked the artist where it had come from. He said that he had been sitting on the toilet and noticed this glass ball on the end of a chain next to his head.

Few people knew that the glass ball, which we later saw around the world on the silver screen, had started life as a humble toilet chain pull. Indeed, the imagery used in all the advertising material and standard presentations derived from the same glass ball. We even presented customers with memento glass balls which were vastly more expensive than the original and lacked the eyelet for attaching the chain.

Kilocycle, 1973   *Chris Horrobin*

In 1973 the use of Remote Job Entry via a telephone line was very prestigious and state-of-the-art. The ICL 7020 RJE station gave 80-column card input with printer listings as output. A certain African government department accordingly invested in a connection between the computer room and the programmers' office, a distance of about one kilometer. The system worked OK, but the modem speed and poor telephone lines were unable to match the speed of the computer processing, leading to huge bottlenecks with completed jobs.

The surprising thing was that the office seemed to get through a lot more jobs in a day than the connection could theoretically handle. It was discovered that most of them were still despatched using the previous communication medium: a large baker's basket attached to the handlebars of an elderly bicycle. The rider pedalled leisurely between the two locations throughout the day. He took great delight in beating the RJE system that had threatened to make him redundant.

The finger of suspicion, c. 1973   David Marwood

In the mid-1970s, when Col. Maxwell was Chairman, the vast amounts of waste paper generated by the eleven ICL buildings in the Putney/Wandsworth area were collected for disposal once a week by a contractor's lorry.

One morning, a Metropolitan Police Sergeant appeared at reception in LON11, asking for an interview with a Col. A.T. Maxwell whose address was at ICL House, Putney. The Chairman was in his office and willing to see the Sergeant, who proceeded to interrogate him on his whereabouts between certain times on the previous Saturday. On being satisfied that the Colonel was no criminal, the Sergeant displayed the reason for the enquiry: a large brown envelope addressed to Col. A.T. Maxwell at ICL House. This had been found inside an otherwise empty sack lying on the floor of an empty lorry, stolen from our waste paper contractor, which had been used in the robbery of some electrical goods from a warehouse in another part of London on the previous Saturday. So the first clue naturally led straight to the company Chairman.

How do you do, what do you do? c. 1973   Chris Cheetham

John Pinkerton and Conway Berners-Lee visited me at Oxford, and sought information on how we used the computer. They were tasked with projecting New Range workloads but ICL had no idea what people actually did on interactive terminals and, apparently, no other way of finding out. I had to admit that I too had no useful information, but I did offer a way in which it could be gathered. We all used teletypes, devices that produced a hard copy of everything the user did. Of course, an interactive user normally had no use for this when he had achieved success and simply threw the paper away. Thus it was that Conway and I, to the curiosity and surprise of our customers at Oxford, spent the afternoon going round every teletype terminal and removing from the waste bins the discarded paper logging the day's activities. After they had been more or less smoothed out, Conway departed happy with a briefcase of crumpled but usable raw information for John and himself to peruse at leisure.

Windy in Windhoek, c. 1973   Chris Horrobin

On a site in Namibia it was found that the ICL System 4-50 computer room air conditioning was unable to keep the room cool over long periods. The environment calculations were re-checked and seemed OK but the deficiency persisted. An extra cooling unit was supplied and all was well.

On a subsequent visit the software support team were impressed by the very welcome refreshment of cold beer and cold watermelon. The operators' fridge was apparently cavernous and very well stocked. The key to the fridge turned out to be a floor-tile lifting tool. Down below were the nicely chilled supplies, snuggled against the underfloor output of one of the air conditioners.

...and roses, probably, c. 1973   *Roger Daw*

Cedric Dickens laid on one of his high level sessions for the CCTA in Norwich and arranged to stay the previous night in a very old and traditional hotel in the city. Taking care that everything would be all right on the morrow, I called in during the evening to confirm that he had arrived successfully. A very old and traditional hotel retainer, overhearing my conversation at reception, tottered up and quavered to me: 'Is that right, Sir? Are you with Mr Dickens, Sir?' 'Yes, I am.' 'Ah what a pleasure, Sir, to serve a gentleman who orders champagne for breakfast.'

A hardy perennial, 1973   *Atypical customer*

Invoicing of Hand Punches and Verifiers

I have written, telephoned and requested during face to face discussions with your representatives that the invoicing for the maintenance of hand punches and verifiers be cancelled.

I have returned previous quarters' invoices to you with notes to the effect that the invoicing was to be cancelled.

You have had formal notice of this requirement on company headed paper.

I realise that you use a computer to produce your invoices. We also have one of your computers and I know how difficult they can be to control. If you are unable to halt the invoicing process, may I suggest you do one of the following:

(a) Remove the invoices after they have been printed but before despatching through the postal system;

(b) Modify your computer system so that output not required is not printed.

If neither of the foregoing is possible, I would suggest either:

(a) You call in the IRA, blow it up, and ask IBM to supply you with a new machine and a new system; or

(b) You offer the thing to Esther Rantzen of the BBC as the 'Heap of the Week', again asking IBM to supply you with a new machine and a new system.

Yours faithfully

PS My consultancy fees, should you be interested in producing a new system, are quite reasonable.

Avoidance of high jinks, c. 1973   H.C.

The flight was from Vienna to Sofia and, because British Airways didn't go to Bulgaria in those days, the airline was TAROM. And the aircraft was a Tupolev 154 (the one with the clear plastic nose-cone which was always supposed to make it easier to take out the radar and replace it with a bomb-aimer). It wasn't a long trip, but we got up to about 30,000 feet.

I had an aisle seat on the port side. In the row immediately in front of me were three Cuban students. They must have been rewarded for exemplary ideological orthodoxy by a trip to the glorious Eastern Europe in order to study the marvels of communism at first hand. They were in extremely high spirits, having a wonderful time.

Alongside them, on their left, was an over-wing emergency exit door, operated by a simply massive metal lever. Idly glancing round the cabin, as one does, my eye strayed over the instructions for operating this door, in Cyrillic letters, of course. It took some time to realise that the lever was at the position marked 'OPEN', but no time at all after that for feelings of panic to set in. But what to do?

Asking Cuban students in their condition of hilarity to do something about it didn't look a very safe option. Eventually I had to be content with tightening my seat belt as never before and crossing every finger and toe I could move.

When we landed I pointed out the condition of the door to the Romanian air hostess. She went as white as a sheet. I flew back on Lufthansa.

The case of the Bulgarian miniskirt, c. 1973   H.C.

In the early 1970s, ICL supported a Management Training Centre on the outskirts of Sofia, the capital of Bulgaria, and I was asked to read a paper on ICL's own internal approach to computerised management information at a seminar which the local ICL operation was sponsoring.

Having by this stage visited several of the East European countries and having met several East European delegations at the Demo Room in Bridge House South, Putney, I was reasonably accustomed to working through an interpreter, with either simultaneous or interleaved translation. However, on this occasion, a different approach was to be followed: my paper would be translated into Bulgarian and read by a native Bulgarian speaker. So we spent two or three interesting days turning my script into the local language. My role was going to be reduced to putting each slide in turn onto the overhead projector and pointing to each significant item on the slide when the script called for it. This was in fact extremely challenging because it required me to follow the unfamiliar Cyrillic letters with the closest concentration, while listening carefully to the speaker.

Nevertheless, it turned out to be one of the most successful presentations I have ever given, for the following reason:

In the centre of the stage of the lecture theatre was an extremely simple lectern, consisting of four slender vertical metal rods, one at each corner, joined by a plain metal shelf at a comfortable reading level. The person chosen to read my paper was an announcer on Bulgarian television and the simplest thing to say is that she was just *gorgeous*. Moreover, the miniskirt had by then arrived in Bulgaria, and her legs were *superb*. And the structure of the lectern gave everybody a *magnificent* view. If she had simply recited a table of logarithms the audience would have approved and, by the end of forty minutes, the party dignitaries in the front rows were utterly convinced that management information was the best thing they had ever heard of.

As I say, it went well: but not a success that's been easy to repeat.

The realist's problem =
the optimist's opportunity, c. 1974   *Peter Woodhouse*

I was doing a Project Manager's job at AZLK in Moscow, where two System 4s (of unique specification in order to comply with COCOM restrictions) were installed as the forerunners of a total of 13 systems which were to completely automate an entire car factory. There were, as usual, plenty of problems and the penalty clauses in the contract were very tough (who the heck had agreed to them?): in effect, they stated that if the hardware, the operating system, the database management software and the application software didn't all perform perfectly we would lose the follow-up orders, be kicked out of the initial site and have to pay heavily for the privilege. Having been asked to assess the viability of the project, in my memo to Sandy Walker I covered all these points and, in summary, said: 'This raises the question of whether we ought to be doing business in Russia at all.' I later saw the version of that memo which had been passed upward to the Board. Arnold Jewitt had altered it to read: 'This raises the question of two P3s': i.e. solve the problems by an upgrade.

Also spracht der Minister, 1974 *An engineer*

Tony Benn, as Minister of Technology, was invited to switch on one of the earliest New Range systems, for whose development he could really take a lot of the credit. It had all been well rehearsed and the ceremony passed off with admirable smoothness. Then, displaying a shrewd appreciation of the possible artificiality of the occasion, he likened it to the day when Her Majesty the Queen inaugurated Subscriber Trunk Dialling. It had been decided that she would make a call from Post Office Headquarters to the Lord Mayor of Bristol and there were telephone engineers posted at every link in the line to make sure that the call succeeded. Just before the call was initiated, by one of those flukes that technology likes to play, the sound of the private lines on which the engineers were talking to each other got hooked up with the sound of the television and the whole party heard:

Voice A: 'But what if she dials the wrong number?'

Voice B: 'It doesn't matter what she ****** dials; she'll still get the Lord Mayor of Bristol.'

Bulgarian blues, c. 1974 *David Bell*

Jim was giving a training course on his first visit to Sofia and, at the weekend, went drinking at a lodge in the mountains with a couple of the local ICL people. It was quite a spree. When they staggered out into the cold the car wouldn't start. The other two got in and Jim pushed. When the engine fired he slipped and fell face down in the snow, where he passed out. The other two, drunk as owls, drove off down the mountain. Jim was found about an hour later by an Austrian lady diplomat who took care of him. Apart from a blinding headache, he found out the next day that he had slight frostbite on both hands. At the end of the course he flew back to UK and went to Paddington Hospital for continued treatment to his bandaged hands. England was basking in an unusually early heatwave. 'What's the matter with you, then?', said the extremely cheerful Nigerian doctor, who didn't believe him when he said 'Frostbite'.

The rule of four, 1974 *Chris Cheetham*

The computer hall at Bracknell had a viewing gallery. In the early days of New Range when reliability was, shall we say?, less than perfect, people would gather round the errant machines to discuss what should be done. From the gallery I was able to formulate the 'rule of four': the optimum size for a group of people discussing a problem is four. Larger groups always split into fours; smaller groups get nothing decided until they become four. On one occasion I

131

counted no fewer than 63 people on the floor discussing malfunctions of one sort or another, including the Director of Software Development, Mike Forrest, and his boss, Ed Mack. And in accordance with the theory they were indeed grouped into fifteen clumps of four people. Who were the unattached three? I'm not saying.

More secrets, 1974   Chris Cheetham

ICL was naturally very secretive about the New Range, especially about its technical features, and the actual *name* was extremely hush-hush. Heard on the Bracknell Tannoy at about this time: 'Would a P3 Engineer please go to the Twenty-Nine-Seventy'.

Hot stuff, c. 1974   Chris Horrobin

In the 2903, all the mechanics of the peripherals were controlled by programming in the central processor rather than by their own electronics. Of particular note was the pair of instructions to switch the card reader's 'picker' solenoid on and off. The solenoid was rated for dissipating heat on the basis of only being 'on' for extremely short periods. This led to the famous software failure known as 'select card reader and catch fire'.

The size of the 2903, 1974   Chris Maslen

The design of 2903 started in 1971, the first prototype was switched on in August 1972 and it was launched at the Hanover Fair in April 1973. By the time it was into full production, and we in Product Development had a chance to look up, it must have been early 1974.

During that gestation period, enormous developments had taken place in the integrated circuit field while the most complex chip in the 2903 was a four-bit arithmetic unit. So, having lived and breathed and redesigned parts of 2903 several times in the three years I'd worked on it, I felt I knew the system well enough to totally redesign the logic using the new LSI chips which were by then available.

Thinking I had quite a good idea (to re-engineer an existing design so that a room-sized office system would become small enough to fit under someone's desk) I disclosed my thoughts to a fairly influential member of the company's development organisation. He responded, rather snootily I thought, that it was not in line with the company's image to produce such small boxes.

Memorable Arnieisms: 1, c. 1974   *Tom Rothwell*

There was a user who was well-known as a critic of our services (we called him a moaning old sod, actually) and, when he got on the telephone, he just would not stop talking. I was sharing an office with Arnold Shaw when such a call came in. He waited until the caller had got into his stride, dropped the receiver gently into the waste bin and went to make a cup of coffee. I could hear the critic's voice droning on but now with a wasplike buzzing quality to it. Arnold returned with his coffee, picked the phone out of the bin and continued as if nothing had happened.

Memorable Arnieisms: 2, c. 1974   *Tom Rothwell*

He complained bitterly about that bloody woman from Training Division at Beaumont, who always started the phone conversation with 'Hello Arnold, How are you?' only to continue without registering any response that might have been made. Her next line was always: 'Good, good; what I'm ringing about is...'
To prove it, one morning it started:
'Hello Arnold, How are you?'
'Two of the kids died last week'.
'Good, good; what I'm ringing about is...'

Memorable Arnieisms: 3, c. 1974   *Tom Rothwell*

The Senior Manager came up from Putney. Knowing we would be summoned to meet him we had all practised our best salutes (longest way up, shortest way down). Six of us assembled, and he went along the line asking for names and ranks (well, it felt like that). The sixth response was: 'My name is Arnold Shaw and I am a harmless drudge'.

Peace, imperfect peace, c. 1974   *Tom Rothwell*

We always seemed to be working late and, particularly when you were on your own, some things didn't receive the required attention and anyway, three in the morning is not the best time for thinking things through. Pericles was looking after every user this side of the Berlin Wall and was naturally the focus of great attention but at the time yours truly (and yes it was really me) was unaware of any of the technicalities of the great God. I was on support duty, terribly late and terribly urgent and terribly short of disc space. I pored over the List_Volume and my own God led me out of the land of nowt and presented me with DUF FILE 1 and DUF FILE 2. Everybody in the western hemisphere knows that 'duff' means 'useless' so I thought things through for all of five milliseconds and deallocated them and went home a tired and happy man. I arrived late the next morning and I can still recall the unhealthy peace and silence which hung in the air. I was questioned briefly and surprisingly calmly by one of the visiting managers from down south about Pericles failing to come up that morning because of some missing Delayed Update Files. And I can still remember Arnold's stifled laughter.

Acronyms, c. 1974   *David Sutherland*

DALKEITH = Defies All Logic – Kidsgrove Exits Into The Highlands
ALICE =   A Language I Can't Explain

Half way off the back of a lorry, c. 1974   *Colin Hunt*

I was computer manager for a brewery in southern England and purchased some EDS60 disc drives. When these were being delivered, the driver approached me and asked if I wanted any more, cheap! If not, did I want any other type of ICL equipment, also cheap! And for cash! Playing along with his suggestion, I said that I would think about it. Immediately afterwards I informed both my own management and the local ICL management. ICL internal security contacted me very quickly and it was agreed that I would try to get more information about the 'offer' with its implication of fraudulent dealing by ICL staff. Unaccounted stock losses from at least one factory were mentioned. A sequence of scripted and recorded telephone calls then followed between myself and the driver, concluding with my agreeing to buy some equipment for cash and that we would meet at night in a car-park in Southampton to conclude the deal. This was all getting to be very cloak-and-dagger and, as I drove to the rendezvous, bundles of marked notes at the ready, the adrenaline was certainly flowing. But he never showed. Whether he spotted security staking out the car-park, or whether something in the phone calls had aroused his suspicion, I will never know. Nor do I know what action was taken within ICL, though I gather it was effective.

The 2900 press launch: 1, October 1974   *H.C.*

There were lots of press there on the day, young and old, male and female. One of them was decidedly young, deliciously female and devotedly courted throughout the day by one of the American directors whom we had in those days. So much so (and no-one had been counting the glasses of wine as they flitted by) that she rashly accepted a desperate wager: a successful landing in the moon-landing game *or* hey for the nearest bed!

Do you remember that moon-landing game? A primitive precursor of so many others. It told you, chattering on the teletype, the height of your module above the lunar surface, your current rate of descent and your reserves of fuel. You told it at what rate you wanted to burn fuel for the next ten seconds. Then you got another status report. And so on. A few people landed successfully, but not many of us had NASA training.

Anyway, full of confidence, this lovely lass essayed a descent, giving her commands with initial confidence which rapidly tapered through mounting doubt into squeaking dismay. When she got the final response: 'WE'LL NAME THE CRATER AFTER YOU', and realised the implicit consequences, her shriek could be heard from one end of Bracknell to the other!

The 2900 press launch: 2, October 1974   H.C.

Apart from the formal presentations, in the Bracknell Lecture Theatre, the day was marked by a number of exhibition items and demonstrations, laid out in the demonstration area which, at that time, was on the first floor of BRA01, conveniently outside the theatre.

One of the items which it was particularly desired to show to the press was the process of teleloading the 7502 Communications Controller. It seemed at the time such an exceedingly advanced use of technology because it meant that the user didn't have to boot his machine from a local papertape reader every time it was switched on (how fast things have developed, to be sure!)

Unfortunately, nay even *very* unfortunately, the process still wasn't quite robust enough to demonstrate for real on the day. But the invitations had stressed that it would be shown. What to do?

In the corner of the demonstration room where the 7502 and its disc controller (those prodigious hernia generators) were to be on display, there was a tiny square office. Into this were squeezed, on the morning of the great day, a papertape reader, a silent-ringing telephone, two chairs and two engineers. Then the door was locked from the outside and more or less concealed behind some giant shrub.

When each party of visitors needed to be shown the wonders of teleloading, the phone on top of the 7502 would be lifted, there would be some ostentatious dialling, the demonstrator would say into the mouthpiece, with heavy emphasis: 'Dalkeith? We're ready to teleload the 7502 now'. Twenty feet away, behind closed doors, the cheese of papertape went into the reader and everything powered up OK. It was terrifically successful.

The engineers had not, however, correctly predicted how long the press would remain on the premises, which turned out to be an extremely long time. And it had been their own idea entirely to take a crate of lager into their caboosh with them. Had the cabin not also contained a sound metal waste paper basket their condition would have been *dire*.

The 2900 press launch: 3, October 1974   H.C.

The programme for the visiting journalists naturally incorporated a tour of the Bracknell site including, of course, the dramatically large central machine hall itself. Pride of place in the middle of this was accorded to a 1906S, possibly it was a dual: anyway it was the largest manifestation of the equipment now to be superseded by the New Range.

For the purposes of the demonstration to press visitors, the engineers had disabled the safety micro-switches on two of the doors of the central processor cabinet of this massive beast, so that the doors could be opened and so that the journalists could watch the electrons buzzing about their business inside (it's always difficult, isn't it, to find something suitably *visual* to catch the attention).

One of the groups into which the assembled journalists had been separated duly reached this point in its tour of the facilities. Their host and guide (who should have known better) led them to this focal point at the very centre of this extremely impressive temple of electronic processing, explained what was going on, stressed the power, speed and importance of the 1906S and then opened the wrong pair of doors.

As all stood agog, there came that dreadful sound of power failing throughout the system, that dirge of all the fans slowing down, that trauma of all the lights going out, that... 'Oh well, the next thing we want to show you is...'

The 2900 press launch: 4, October 1974   H.C.

The centre of the presentation material was a film (this was probably before the advent of video) with a theme of the wonderful advances embodied in the 2900 Series. These were symbolised partly by the white gymnastic-suited silhouette figure of an athlete starting with simple floor exercises and then performing ever more advanced, dramatic, picturesque and daring manoeuvres on a variety of equipment. He represented *power*, and *flexibility*, and *speed*, and *responsiveness* and every other marketing desideratum.

The film also had somehow to show the magnificently advanced electronic technology on which the 2900 series was based and this obviously led to a major difficulty: electronic activity simply isn't visual! You can't make it visual. The electrons always do their thing out of sight. Too bad!

So you can only symbolise their activity. Which you do by showing lights, in rows, flashing on and off, as fast as you like, with an appropriate voice-over. Make them slightly out of focus, as well, and you emphasise that these things are not happening on any human level.

Well, it was a long time since the Royal Navy had taught me to read Morse from flashing lights, and the Service tends to send Morse, as you might say, a bit at a time, rather than a letter at a time. But it seemed pretty clear to me, as I watched this film several times over, that one little patch of the screen, about seven lines down on the left hand side, was repeatedly flashing dot-dot-dot, which is 'S'; followed by dot-dot-dot-dot, which is 'H'; followed by dot-dot, which is 'I'; followed by dash, which is... need I go on? And I think someone in the company producing the film was taking the dot-dash-dash-dot dot-dot dot-dot-dot dot-dot-dot out of ICL.

Over my shoulder...1974   *Chris Cheetham*

I was sent once at the request of SPARC (I forget the rest of the acronym but I'm pretty sure the 'A' was for Action) to West Gorton to solve some problem with New Range development. I soon found that there was ample resource in the development team slaving away methodically and thoroughly to identify the source of the problem. My natural brilliance failed to find a more instant solution but I did discover that there were already two people from SPARC involved in the same task. The first had failed to solve the problem and the second had been sent to look over his shoulder, exactly as I had been sent to look over theirs. And on the fourth day SPARC sent Bill Littlejohn to look over mine. Bill, in effect, won the game by being the last person sent by SPARC before the original team solved the problem.

Why I never became a Director, c. 1975   *Michael Brew*

In the mid-1970s, the high profile director sometimes known as 'Hero Nobrain' was interviewed by *Computing* and was asked what would happen if, having promised to take his wife out for the evening on her birthday, he was faced with a critical problem on an urgent project. He replied: 'That's no problem, I would send her present home in a taxi.'

My wife said: 'If *you* did that to *me* I would send it straight back again!'

Tales from Holborn Bar, c. 1975 — *Vernon Hardman*

Bureau West was one of the first 2900 installations and a prime MoD site. Consequently it was in the spotlight on many occasions and received a good deal of attention from top management. On one occasion, a review was scheduled which was to be attended by the company's then Managing Director, Geoff Cross. On the day before this great event, there was a great coming together of senior management representatives from sales, support, customer engineering, product development, etc., etc., plus their lieutenants, plus their lieutenants' lieutenants, plus anyone else who might remotely be required. All foregathered on site for an internal review and a rehearsal of the presentations which were to be given on the following day.

After a long and (for some of the minions, at least) a harrowing day, the senior management repaired to their hotel for some R&R (a technical Defence term signifying Rest and Relaxation). On the whole, all went extremely well. But unfortunately, at some point in the proceedings, one of the players (R.G. 'Spud' Taylor) left his jacket and his room key in his room and closed the door behind him. At the end of a long and successful evening, tiredness set in. Courtesy, however, was not exhausted. Considering the lateness of the hour it was deemed inappropriate to disturb the hotel staff with a request for a master key. But the exile gratefully accepted the offer of another (Mike Sorenson) to occupy the spare bed in his room, particularly since this included the loan of a razor and a clean shirt in the morning.

At about 8.15 on the following morning, the lone secretary on site was considerably surprised to be confronted by a powerful-looking person who introduced himself as the Managing Director. This was at least an hour in advance of the arrival time according to the officially announced schedule. With admirable resource she made him welcome, provided coffee and introduced him to some of the workers on site. As soon as there was a chance, she made her excuses, slipped away to the phone and rang the hotel where the management team had been ensconced.

At that hotel, most of the management team were in the middle of a pianissimo breakfast consisting, for many of them, of no more than black coffee. The senior man present (Dr Peter Aylett) was handed a written message informing him of the great man's premature arrival on site. He immediately told the others and all of them, including Spud who had not yet recovered the key to his room and who was therefore still minus his jacket, made the speediest of exits. Reception were told, over a fleeing shoulder, that someone would come along later to sort out the bills. Cramming into several cars, they made their way back to the site at top speed.

In due course, with no visible fuss and exactly according to the timetable, the review got under way. After about three quarters of an hour (and presumably during a less than riveting passage in one of the presentations) a written note was passed fom the MD to the jacketless manager. 'Where is your jacket?', it demanded. The offender hesitated, and then scribbled a brief reply on the foot of the note. Presumably, given the sexual mores of some top members of the company at that time, it was deemed to be acceptable. It was certainly less embarrassing than the truth and the matter was never raised again. The response read: 'Sorry. Her husband came back unexpectedly'.

But it's all standard, innit? 1975   *John Booth*

Shortly after ICT and English Electric merged to form ICL, Special Systems Division was set up to develop special products not covered by the standard ranges, particularly in the field of data communications and peripherals. It became better known as the Letchworth Development Centre, 'LDC', under Jack Houldsworth.

While the main development divisions were concentrating on the New Range, LDC was responsible for continued development of communications processors for the old ICT 1900 systems. To replace the 7903 Front End Processor, a new system called the 7905 was designed, based on a CTL Modular One mini-processor. The unit connecting it to the 6-bit wide 1900 Standard Interface was called a Local Processor Link to Nineteen Hundred, 'LPLN' for short. The communications interfaces were handled by a Command Chain Unit, 'CCU', which buffered the Modular One from most time-critical events.

The Post Office were major users of English Electric System 4 computers. Faced with the requirement to attach these to a large network, it was found that the standard communications multiplexers supplied with System 4 could not cope with the speeds and the number of interfaces required. LDC were given the task of adapting the 7905 to connect to the 8-bit wide System 4 Standard Interface. Code conversion between 8-bit EBCDIC on System 4 and 6-bit 1900 code on 7905 was performed by hardware in the Local Processor Link to System 4, 'LPLS'.

At the same time as the 7905s were being installed at PO Harmondsworth, LDC were involved in another 7905-based network at Liverpool University. This led to a clash of priorities, and the following correspondence:

To:	J. Houldsworth	From:	G. Cuttle
	LET06		PDG 7905 Programme Mgr
			BRA01

16.9.75

PO TOLD

I understand that a special was done for PO Told involving code generation, and that a number of problems were encountered. Could you please let me know why the problems arose and whether there is any possibility of the situation recurring.

To:	G. Cuttle	From:	J.L.D. Booth
	PDG 7905 Programme Manager		Systems
	BRA01		LDC, LET06

19.9.75

PO TOLD CODE CONVERSION

It is a little difficult to explain why so much trouble has been experienced with LPLS code conversion. Both LPLN and LPLS had originally used a Company Standard ISO-EBCDIC code convertor and the conversion was detailed in the design specifications. Test programs used these tables to check the hardware and so no problems arose until a real System 4 customer tried to use converted data. It was found that the control codes and some of the graphic characters were incorrectly received at the System 4.

Apparently the standard convertor, in the form of a number of ROMs, was designed for New Range EBCDIC, which differs markedly from System 4 EBCDIC. Mr Rowley programmed a new set of ROMs for 7905 ISO to System 4 EBCDIC and vice versa, which were to be pin-compatible with the existing ROMs. Unfortunately the original designer had confused engineers' and programmers' conventions for bit order and had used inverted outputs.

It took a little while to sort out why the convertor was producing gibberish, by which time Mr Rowley was due to go on a fortnight's leave. To save the time it would take to re-program the ROMs he disconnected inputs and outputs by cutting the tracks, reversed them end for end, removed or inserted inverters where necessary, despatched the board to TOLD to be tested, and went on leave, leaving a pile of conversion tables, program tapes and print-outs describing what he had done. Unfortunately he did not have time to document the temporary changes he had made to the board, expecting that nothing would need to be done until he returned.

As it happened there was a single error on the program tapes (besides the lack of inversion and rectification). This was quickly spotted by TOLD who sent another, unmodified, convertor board back to LDC to be modified correctly. Mr Chick picked up the file and managed to deduce that half the codes on the tape were wrong, not realising the difference between NR EBCDIC and S4 EBCDIC. In the middle of negotiations with TOLD over what constituted an error in code conversion, he was sent to Liverpool to assist with CCU problems.

I then took up the problem and within a day or so discovered that EBCDIC was not always EBCDIC. With this revelation I was able to pinpoint the single bit in error, get a set of ROMs programmed, and have the second board despatched to TOLD to be tested. The result was complete chaos. Suspecting that the ROMs might be faulty I requested a detailed printout of the results but was then, in turn, sent to Liverpool.

Fortunately, at this point Mr Roake returned from Liverpool and was able to devote a fresh mind to the problem. He was still puzzling over the matter when Mr Rowley returned from leave. Between entering LDC and departing for Liverpool, Mr Rowley just had time to mention problems with inversion. Mr Roake then made up conversion tables for 7905 ISO to inverted S4 EBCDIC and S4 EBCDIC to inverted 7905 ISO, and punched up the necessary 640 lines of code on a teletype.

At this stage I returned and, being suspicious that the problem could not be solved so easily, checked through the logic diagrams and discovered that the inputs to the EBCDIC ISO convertor were reversed end to end, but failed to notice that the outputs were likewise reversed.

Mr Roake then produced a revised set of tables for reversed S4 EBCDIC to inverted 7905 ISO and proceeded to punch up a new set of tapes. As a final check we took the TOLD results and checked that the errors could be explained by the lack of inversion and reversion. Imagine our horror when after the first few characters came out correctly the conversion obstinately produced much the same rubbish as before.

After looking at these results the penny dropped that where the conversion was correct the characters were palindromic. The final conversion table, reversed S4 EBCDIC to inverted-reversed 7905 ISO, was produced, I was ordered once more to Liverpool, and Mr Roake repeated his virtuoso performance on the keyboard. A set of ROMs was programmed from the new tapes and the board despatched to TOLD before Mr Roake went on leave. It is possible that a note of sarcasm entered the proceedings when they informed us that there was only one error in the coding this time.

The board was returned once more and Mr Rowley, having returned from Liverpool, found the fault was due to a component failure. This was replaced and, the matter now being urgent, the board was immediately despatched to TOLD for testing. It may surprise you to learn that it worked.

As to the possibility of such an occurrence in the future, I can only say that the day-to-day switching of resources, even on such a straightforward job as specifying a code conversion, can always lead to complications. But such eventualities are, presumably, always weighed in the balance when priorities are being defined.

Oh Horrible! Horrible! Most horrible! 1975   Colin Clayton

After eight faithful years, tirelessly doing its work 24 hours a day, the old System 4 was to be replaced by a UNIVAC machine. On the morning when it was to be removed it did its final run. It had been lovingly cared for by the client and in fact was probably in better condition than when it was new. It, and the whole computer room, shone like a new pin. However, nobody wants a computer when it's old, so it was sold for scrap. At the end of its run it was switched off and I sadly disconnected the power and the many interface cables. The fork lift truck came in and lifted in turn the various tape decks, disc drives, printers, etc. and loaded them onto the lorry. The tines wouldn't fit underneath the central processor cabinet so, without a moment's hesitation, the driver backed off a couple of yards, lifted the tines about four feet, and drove forward full speed. The tines went straight through the CPU, logic boards, main memory and all and came out the other side. You could almost see the blood. Everybody gasped with horror. It was as if an old friend had been murdered.

But O'Heron is an Irish name, c. 1975   Peter Woodhouse

Brian came over to Dublin to meet the people and to do a bit of what might be called morale boosting. His first mistake was to time the meeting for 5.30 p.m. on a Friday, by when even the most diligent were liable to be elsewhere or well on their way there: John Daly had to issue the sternest ever three-line whip to ensure even a token attendance. His second mistake was to misread the Irish situation: at that stage the largest machine in the island was a 1902A. His third mistake was to misjudge what impresses the Irish: he was going on about his important experiences in UNIVAC, major online systems, rocket control systems for NASA, nationwide banking systems. Up went a tentative hand in the front row: 'Why now are you telling us all this? It doesn't seem to be relevant to our market, at all, at all.' Unidentified voice from the back row: 'He's not telling us annything; he's applying for a fecking job'.

Apt but inappropriate, c. 1975   *Mike Forrest*

Geoff Cross summoned Ed Mack in the middle of Ed's staff meeting. When Ed returned I was telling the others about my recent trip to the USA and, as he opened the door, I was actually quoting the words of Balfour: 'I return empty-handed from the country of the long-winded and the short-sighted'. Ed always thought I meant it personally.

Press on regardless, 1975   *Chris Horrobin*

The ICL BARIC demonstration of the INTERACT 75 service was always going to be particularly difficult. The venue was Barclay's Lombard House in London; the computer centre was at Winsford in Cheshire. INTERACT 75 was going to be a state-of-the-art terminal service for commercial business users. The night before the occasion, the GPO engineers were still trying to get the telegraph lines connected. In Winsford everyone was painfully aware that the demo had never yet been run without crashing at some point.

The terminal operator was instructed that she must not deviate by one keystroke from the set script, no matter what the press or enthusiastic sales people said. This is prudent in any demo but, in this case, there was a secondary motive. The terminals in use were slow mechanical teletypes, which also had papertape reader/punch attachments. In the event of catastrophic failure, 'plan B' involved substituting another teletype for the remote computer system, so that it became a simple back to back dialogue between two human operators. The Winsford terminal had a roll of papertape with all the matching responses to the demo script's commands.

On the day the computer system unexpectedly worked perfectly. It did crash, though, immediately after the press conference, and wouldn't work again for several weeks.

A bevy of beauty, c. 1975   *Arnold Shaw*

I once asked Leo Spillane why it was that his programmers in the Exec testing area at West Gorton were nearly all young ladies with extremely pretty faces.

He explained that since interviewing is such an imprecise art, he had decided that if he chose for the looks he would get at least the same ability. I never knew if he was pulling my leg.

Timeliness, c. 1975   *Arnold Shaw*

Leo related with huge delight a conversation at a social event with Mike K's wife. She remarked to him that she could not understand Mike's reputation for always being late for work since she always woke him at 8.30 a.m. He had to tell her that work was supposed to start at 8.20 a.m. sharp.

Mid-Atlantic yak yak, c. 1975   *Tom Rothwell*

This was the strange tongue spoken by one of the weird visitors from south of Walsall who came up to impart wisdom. He would constantly urge us to 'Put a peg in the ground' and 'Get our ducks in a row' and 'Put the man behind the eight ball', etc. One local sycophant adopted the habit with such keenness and ineptitude that we ended up with 'Ducks in the ground', 'Pegs in a row', and 'One behind the egg ball'. We didn't have the heart to tell him – it was far too much fun.

A lament, c. 1975   *Anon*

The Rime of the Ancient Programmer

Oh early in the morning, as I walked in Reading Town,
I met an ancient programmer, worn out and broken down,
And he spied me as I passed him, though I stepped across the way,
And he caught me by the coatsleeve, and thus to me did say:

'I remember, I remember, the days that used to be,
When there was only ENIAC and MANIAC and me,
And I've worked on 1300, 1900, System 4,
But now the times are changing, and I'm going to work no more.

'In the old days, Ah the old days, when I did first begin,
I had a little card-box to keep my programs in;
And when I found an error, well I just bodged in a chad
To make a LOAD a MULTIPLY, or a DIVIDE an ADD.

144

'Then they invented source code, which seemed a shame to me,
And yet I grew quite happy with old XPLG,
And still I had my card-box, until to my dismay
They said: 'We've thought of COSY, and here's XPMA'.

'Ah, of my happy memories is certainly not least
How the whole team lost its programs when five mag tapes got creased,
Yet I learned to live with COSY, and I quelled my rising gorge.
Till oh, Till oh, God help us, some fool invented GEORGE.

'So I would wait for MOP lines, and sit to get logged in,
An hour or two if lucky, to see the fun begin:
'SORRY BUT THAT FILE IS LOST; AFRAID RESPONSE IS SLOW.
AND OH, WE'VE HAD A RESTORE FROM SEVEN WEEKS AGO'.

'And now you wrote two programs for the one you wrote before:
The program and a macro, to guide it through the store.
And when it came to testing, the honest truth to tell,
The programs weren't much trouble but the macros gave us hell.

'And still the times are changing, and now I'm on New Range,
And nothing's where you think it is, and I find it rather strange,
And they say core doesn't matter, and they have hysteric fits
When I spend an afternoon or two to save myself twelve bits.

'And I often fall to thinking as I sit and drink my tea
Of all the craftsmen I have known, and now there's only me;
And people keep on asking me what things are going to cost,
And it's time that I was going, for I'm old and tired and lost.

'So I'm heading for that round-up, the last of all they say,
And the mercury delay tubes shall light me on my way
To that greater Installation where the System never fails,
And the programs sweetly working make a noise like nightingales.

'And there there's waiting for me a little attic room,
Where the ghosts of old computers shall be round me in the gloom,
With a desk to put my feet on, and some cocoa in a mug,
And a lovely pile of core-prints I can sit down and debug.

'And St Peter, when he comes along to get an estimate
And I tell him: 'Oh, ten thousand years, but I may be a bit late',

He'll say to me: 'Don't push yourself, you take it nice and slow;
There are no managers up here, for they're all Down Below.

'And though we let the users in (they've had enough of Hell),
They're perfectly contented in a little padded cell
With all the latest disc drives, and a terminal or two,
And a New Range coming soon, so they won't be troubling you.'

That was all he ever said to me, for then I made a dash,
But later over Reading Bridge was heard a sudden splash,
Yet though they dredged the river there was nothing ever found
Except ten tons of printout and a note: 'I'm homeward bound'.

A long, long time before Camelot, c. 1975 — Alan Trangmar

As a junior programmer, I discovered that Pericles could be used for gambling: use of a certain new option caused a reference to a word one beyond the last word of defined store. Since 1900s rounded allocated store up to a multiple of 64 words this did not usually matter. However, every time you amended any module and consolidated them altogether (a process which took about two hours even for a test environment) you had a precisely 1 in 64 chance that the total store would be an exact multiple of 64 and that, therefore, the program would crash when you tried to use it. However, almost any alteration to any module (even those not involved in the function in question) then had a 63 out of 64 chance of appearing to solve the problem.

The secrets of the confessional, c. 1975 — Absolutely anonymous

During somebody's time as Operations Systems Manager at STE01, servicing the manufacturing community up north and the development communities at Stevenage and Putney, services were always being moved about between the three DME machines, the so-called A B and C services.

On one occasion, when some Putney development work had been moved from one machine to another, it quickly became apparent that the move had not been a good one: everything was going slower than before.

'OK, let's move it all back again', we said, and that's when things went from bad to worse.

Remember that old friend, George 3's Tape-To-Tape-Processing of filestore? Well, during all this palaver of moving from one machine, then deciding to move back and then actually moving back, TTTP didn't stop. The first machine said: 'These files have been deleted, so don't process them any more'. The second machine decided it didn't know about those files anyway.

The result was that Putney lost about 200 COBOL source files, covering live systems as well as systems in development. A mammoth key punch exercise had to be mounted to get them back.

Oh well, *forsan et haec olim meminisse juvabit.*

VME/K, c. 1975   *John Deas*

This alternative 2900 Series operating system was Ed Mack's special baby. It was going to be marvellous and do anything but actual details were hard to come by. The initial designer was one Ypsilanti, whose name was rumoured to be an acronym: Your Program Specification Is Long And Not Terribly Informative. There came a time, about 1975, when senior management were pressing very hard for VME/K to be proposed to customers, but the middle rank technical staff who had to sign off the Blue Border risk appraisal documents felt that there was still not nearly enough information about the nature and capabilities of the product.

At a meeting in Putney called to explain to sales representatives why S&TS would still not approve any VME/K Blue Borders, the S&TS spokesman said: 'We simply don't know whether it's a square object or a spherical one.'

Voice from the back: 'It sounds to me like two spherical objects!'

Speak to me, Nadia! c. 1975   *George Brodie*

The Voice-Operated Calculator at the Research and Advanced Development Centre in Stevenage was super for demonstrations. Go up to it and say: 'Four plus four equals' and it would faithfully answer 'Eight'. And so on for other numbers and other operations (no, this is not Alan Beer's French counting pig joke, that might come elsewhere).

Came the time when a highly important delegation from the USSR was to be entertained. The recognition and encoding process was essentially language-independent so, in preparation for the day, it was educated in Russian numerals and arithmetic operators. And in due course, after appropriate exposition through the interpreter, the leader of the visiting delegation was invited to challenge this great western machine. Advancing to the microphone he uttered the Russian equivalent of 'Four plus four equals' and awaited enlightenment. None came. He was asked to try again and did so. Again an embarrassing lack of response. He tried for a third time, with the same result.

'I'm very sorry', said the machine's developer, 'but it doesn't seem to recognise the gentleman's Russian.' Straight-faced, the interpreter duly interpreted this. Whereupon two things happened: the face of the leader of the delegation became empurpled with rage and embarrassment, and all his colleagues nearly fell about with laughter. It transpired that he was a Georgian, and spoke extremely bad Russian with an accent so thick that it was almost impenetrable.

The parameter-driven speech synthesiser, c. 1975   H.C.

One of Mike Underwood's RADO demos showed brilliantly how much additional information is carried in the human world by inflection, tone, timing and other characteristics of speech that are so natural to us that we never think about them. But we do immediately notice their absence when a synthetic voice (as in the response to a Directory Enquiry) repeats a series of numbers in an undifferentiated monotone.

Mike's PDSS played on this. Give it the string of digits '1234567' and tell it to speak those as an integral number and it would emit '1, 234, 567', with the million digit clearly, and humanly, distinguished from the thousands, and those in their turn separated from the three final figures, and with all the phrasing, the rises and falls in pitch, the variations in emphasis, that we would expect.

Tell it to speak the same sequence as a telephone number, and out would come '123, 4567' with the exchange triplet equally naturally distinguished from the line quadruplet.

Partly as a joke, but partly to re-emphasise the point, tell it to pronounce the string as a hymn number and it would chant them in an unbroken string on the notes FFFFFDE with '5' on the final 'F' drawn out, and the volume suitably dropping to a long '6' on the 'D', and a properly clerical note of apology for the shorter final '7' on the 'E'.

A shock in Moscow, 1975   H.C.

It was December 1975, just a fortnight before Christmas, when a party set off to educate the Muscovites at a seminar on databases and management information. There were David Berry, Harry Ellis, Tim Bourne and myself, plus Jim Beer, the Financial Director of the city of Leeds, and Martin Francis, Jim's ICL minder and an expert on LAMIS.

It was doomed from the start because of an unbridgeable mental gap between what we meant by 'Management Information' and what they understood by it.

We were thinking about the problems of providing information for management. But they already had the right information, it was all set out in the five-year plan. Their problem was how to manage the data so that it agreed with the information. But we didn't know that when we went.

It was a cold, still and misty Monday morning when we made our separate ways to Heathrow and checked in for a Japan Airlines flight due to depart in the early afternoon. From the windows of the departure lounge we could see the visibility steadily decreasing; on the screens the list of flights 'Delayed' or 'Cancelled' grew ominously longer; but we sat on and on, there was nothing else to do. Eventually Japan Airlines conceded defeat, called us together and shepherded us onto a coach which proceeded at five mph, through the thickest freezing fog that the UK had seen for years, as far as the Post House Hotel just off the M4. But, of course, our suitcases were irretrievably 'airside', so no pyjamas, no clean clothes, nothing of that sort at all. JAL did kindly issue us with emergency toilet kits, which were jolly useful. Mine subsequently went several times round the world with me.

Tuesday started equally cold and murky but we were bussed back to the terminal in hope of a change in the weather. Eventually, in the early evening, it cleared just enough for the JAL flight to take off. But the late start and the change of time-zones meant that it was nearly midnight before we landed at Sheremetyevo Airport outside Moscow. And, of course, all the baggage-handlers had baggaged off home. So no suitcases were unloaded. So no pyjamas, no clean clothes, nothing of that sort at all. They all went on their way to Tokyo. We went to a party organised by Tony Neville. Roger Houbert managed to sneak into the country without being intercepted by Intourist.

Wednesday morning, and starting to smell a bit. I locked the door of my room and went off in search of breakfast. But just before handing my key to the babushka sitting by the lift I realised that I'd forgotten something, so went back to the door and put the key in the lock. But it wouldn't turn. I tried again with the same result. I took it out and looked at it, re-inserted it in the lock and tried very carefully to find exactly the right position. At the fourth attempt the key turned as easily as anything, I opened the door and found the light was on, though I had switched it firmly off not two minutes earlier. Later I found that the lining of my suitcase had been slit. I never found how the searchers had got into the room but there was obviously another door concealed somewhere.

Thursday morning, and wishing I could stand upwind from my socks. There was a knock at the bedroom door. Outside was a smartly-uniformed JAL steward, with a trolley-load of suitcases, a deferential bow, and an explosive 'Hai!' on his lips. Oh joy! I pounced on the suitcase, stripped off Monday's underwear, and eagerly donned the replacements. But! (and colleagues on the trip later confirmed that they had all had the same experience) when one's suitcase, returned at last from Japan, has spent twelve hours at Sheremetyevo standing in the open at -30°C, the underpants it contains are cold to a degree for which one's tender underparts are totally unprepared.

And the seminar? It went much as expected. For lunch, the local ICL team had laid on a buffet in a separate building. But no-one had prepared the delegates for a stand-up meal. They didn't know the form and hung back in embarrassment. The ICL team ate well. By the second day, the Party had clearly issued the requisite instructions, for the delegates attacked the tables with great gusto. The ICL team ate the scraps.

One of the Russian speakers had some 35mm slides, and asked if he could use our carousel projector. Delighted! But his slides were in flimsy thin cardboard mounts, which jammed in the exchange mechanism, and threatened to catch fire. This was clearly a case of western conspiracy to embarrass him.

But we did get to the Bolshoi for 'Eugene Onegin': we did get a tour of the public parts of the Kremlin, we did get to see the interior of the Cathedral of Saint Michael the Archangel, with its array of royal tombs from as early as 1350 (looking at these, our Intourist girl guide sneered: 'Even in death those people demanded the warmest corner of the church').

The return journey was uneventful. It had been an interesting week. But if I go back there again it won't be in December.

Diminutive organs, c. 1976   H.C.

I sat at one time on a committee of the British Standards Institution concerned with the standardisation of the representation of data elements for interchange between systems, the early days of EDI in fact. It was one of the most boring jobs I have ever been involved in since the bureaucratic procedures of the standardisation world are of mind-numbing tedium.

Surprisingly, a lot of the earliest work in this field was concerned with the standardisation of medical information: blood groups, disease names, drug codification, etc. Now I admit it was before my time, and the story may have acquired embellishments along the way, but it is said that one fine day the world's standardisation experts began to consider the best form of representation (oh, purely for purposes of data interchange, you understand) of human sex.

Some gallant country, after prolonged gestation, as you might say, produced a draft-for-consideration proposed standard in which, among the usual bureaucratic waffle, the operative text read something like this:

'Human sex will be represented, for purposes of data transmission and interchange only, by a single digit numeric character code having the following values:

1*   Male
2*   Female

*Footnote: There is no implication of priority or superiority in this arbitrary allocation of values.'

This went round the world, to all the participating standards authorities, for the usual prolonged business of consideration and comment.

After a suitable number of months, the comments were collated and reviewed. The most imaginative came from I'm not sure where; it may have been Japan, but at least it displayed considerable wit. It said, in essence:

'We have no objection to the form of the standard as originally proposed, nor to the values hitherto allocated, but we would like to suggest the following extensions:

0   Not Known
3   Asexual
4   Bisexual
5   Transsexual
6   Hermaphrodite'

And I can't remember all of the others, except that they managed to keep going all the way up to:

9   Not Applicable'

This in turn was circulated worldwide for comment, of which not much was forthcoming except from the Canadian standardisation authority. They said:

'We have no objection to the form of representation proposed in the original draft standard, nor to the values originally proposed, nor to the additional values now proposed by the ... authority. However, we think the standard would now be improved by pictures.'

But by the time I became involved, the committee had moved on to *much* more serious matters.

Buying the poke and poking the pig, 1976   *David Marwood*

In March 1976, ICL and Singer drew up a 4-page 1,200-word memorandum of understanding on the sale by Singer and the purchase by ICL of Singer's international computer business with direct operations in 17 countries and dealerships in 20 more. The remarkable thing is that they got so much of it right.

Continued losses by Singer Business Machines (SBM) had already reduced its credibility in the eyes of both customers and prospects. The uncertainty caused by Singer's announcement of its intention to sell SBM made things much worse. Unless this was resolved quickly, there would be less and less for anyone to buy.

Delay might not have mattered so much to a prospective buyer interested only in enlarging the customer base for its own hardware. But a crucial part of ICL's plan was the continued loyalty of SBM customers to SBM hardware. The object of an ICL acquisition would be to improve and develop the existing operation, not simply to devour it. Singer shared this interest in preventing a complete collapse of confidence.

The orthodox way would have been to prepare heads of agreement, then develop them into a comprehensive acquisition agreement including a final purchase price. This process would have taken some months to complete in view of the complexity and geographical dispersion of the SBM business. Until such an agreement was signed, ICL would not have been able to enter into the firm commitment that was urgently needed to restore the confidence of SBM customers or at least prevent its further erosion.

The impasse was broken by putting forward a concept unusual in the field of business mergers and acquisitions. ICL would commit itself to legally taking over SBM International after a period of six months and, until then, would assume full responsibility for managing the business for Singer's account and risk.

Both parties would benefit from any success achieved during that phase, Singer in terms of enhanced revenues and profits, and ICL in terms of the enhanced prospects for the business. Moreover, during its six months management period, ICL would have unique opportunities to weigh up problems and assess the value of the business from the inside, not, as is usually the case, from the outside.

A great deal of hard work and effort ensued. Agreement on the final, adjusted purchase price was not reached until 1 June 1977. The final figure came out at about $25,000,000.

Christmas Eve, 1976   *Brian Russell*

The P4 prototype, later to be sold as the 2980, had an Engineer's Hooter. It was intended, and was indeed useful, as an audible overview of what was happening in the machine. Like its predecessors on 1900 series processors, the P4 hooter was originally connected to the Jump instructions. Unfortunately for the engineers (though fortunately from the machine performance point of view) the jump rate was so great that the hooter was ultrasonic, totally inaudible. Then it was connected to the Call instruction, which made it audible.

Also like its predecessors, it was realised that, by a suitable choice of program, one could use the hooter to play tunes. Someone wrote 'Good King Wenceslas' and 'We Wish You A Merry Christmas' and brought them in for the morning shift at 06.00 a.m. on Christmas Eve. The program was built round an inner loop whose frequency would have to be tuned experimentally. The engineer's handkeys were used to select either 'play a tune' or 'sound middle C', nominally 440 Hz. The loop was modified until middle C sounded reasonable, but the tunes were not quite right.

Another engineer arrived, and was asked: 'Does this sound like middle C?' 'No', he answered, 'It sounds a bit low'. The loop constant was decreased, but the tunes were still no better. As each engineer arrived he was asked the same question, and the loop constant was increased or decreased when he said 'Too high' or 'Too low'. This continued until Dave Potts arrived and was asked: 'Does this sound like Middle C?' 'No', he replied, 'It's more like B Flat. It's a very good B Flat'.

A quick calculation was made to raise the pitch by two semi-tones, 2×12th root of 2, and... spot on, perfect pitch!

To this day I do not understand why a bunch of engineers didn't connect an oscilloscope and measure the frequency.

Virtual reality, c. 1976   *John Deas*

The conditions insisted on for a 2970 order from a customer in Australia were so onerous that it was not clear that HQ in Putney would agree to them. The project manager designate was fully occupied in London fighting the internal battle for approval but the customer (who thought he had placed an order and was unaware of the problem) kept asking when the implementation project would start. So I was given the job of 'Virtual Project Manager', with the instructions: 'Go down to the customer's building, ask for an office, put up a large sign saying 'ICL PROJECT MANAGER', and sit there looking busy. In fact, you might as well actually start planning the implementation, just in case'. Unfortunately the sale never did get approval and in due course we had to take down the sign and just tiptoe away.

Fragments of an Old Testament, 1976   *David Barron*

Transcribed from the BCS Computer Bulletin

In the beginning was the FP6000, which was made by Ferranti-Packard in a distant land.

And there were in another country divers International Computers and Tabulators and though they did tabulate as their fathers before them yet could they not compute.

And they said unto one another: Let us even go unto West Gorton to see this marvel that is come to pass, and they beheld the FP6000, and saw that it was good.

And they said: Let us offer many shekels, that the FP6000 may be ours; and Ferranti said: Lo, here are men who will pay for that which loseth us much money. Praise be!

Then the International Computers and Tabulators did take the FP6000, clothed it in panels of blue, and did call it the 1905. Thus was accomplished the birth of the 1900 series.

And on the next day they created the 1904, which was in the image of the 1905 but lacked a floating point unit. Next did they fashion the 1902 which was slower, and the 1903 that was the same but with a floating point unit.

Finally did they fashion the 1907, a mighty engine for the crunching of numbers, and the 1906 that lacked a floating point unit. And the unbelievers asked: Who shall purchase a scientific computer that hath no floating point unit? And none could answer.

Yet another time, the salesmen said: Behold the great multitude that clamour, crying out: Lo, we have mighty programs yet the 1905 hath not sufficient core to hold them. So there was created the 1905E, with much store, and the 1905F, whereof some did buy believing the F to signify Fast though none did know for a certainty.

And they did yoke together two 1905s like unto a pair of oxen, to make the 1907F; And no man could comprehend the reason therefor.

Then the salesmen said: Verily, we have so many machines that we know not what we sell, neither do the customers know what they buy. And the engineers said: A new technology hath been revealed to us in platters of many layers; let us make a new series called the 'A' series, and let there be the 1901A, 1902A, 1903A and 1904A, and the company saw that it was good.

And the Devil taketh the company to a high place, and showeth them the IBM 195 and the CDC 6600, and they said: Let us fashion a mighty engine like unto the walls of Jericho, and call it the 1906A. And let there be set up a graven image called George 3, that the heathen may worship, and it was accomplished.

Now the time was come when there should be fulfilled the prophecy that was written: In that time they shall travail and bring forth a New Range.

And it came to pass that although the time was long passed that the New Range should be delivered yet did it not appear, and there was much wailing and gnashing of teeth in the land.

And there arose instead a false prophet who did privily sell semiconductor stores, wherewith were made the 1903S and 1904S, that the people might forget the New Range in wonder at a store so fast that the processor could not keep pace with it.

Then there came forth in succession the 1903T and the 1901T, and the heathen were confused, knowing not which machine was which.

In that season they did call together a monstrous gathering of the press, and there appeared a spokesman of the company saying: Behold, I bring you tidings of great joy, for unto you is available the 2970 and, if peradventure you are willing to wait, the 2980. And there is System B, that controlleth both their going out and their coming in.

But certain unbelievers gathered together privily and murmured among themselves saying, truly the mills of System B grind fine, but they grind exceeding slow.

And the spokesman replied: O ye of little faith, is it not written in your contract that all shall be accomplished, even unto the fourth benchmark? And the unbelievers answered: How can these things be?

A further fragment, c. 1976 • *Dave White*

And it came to pass that the multitude began to murmur among themselves saying: What shall it profit us if we gain 2900 architecture but lose compatibility with our software libraries which our forefathers have built throughout many ages of toil and sweat, yea even of tears? And some began to rend their garments and cry with a loud voice, saying: Not only do the mills of VME/B grind exceeding slow but too often, yea by far, do they fall silent and grind not at all. And in those times no man can reveal wherefore they grind not. And mockery and derision shall descend upon us and upon all our houses, but to our enemies it shall bring mirth and feasting.

Then spake a man of the tribe of Mack, which is also called Peedeegee, who addressed the multitude boldly, saying: Be of good cheer, ye with whom 1900 hath found favour and rejoice, ye followers of George 3, for it is written in DP 116 that behold, a 2960 shall be transfigured and shall take unto itself the form and likeness of a 1900 clad in orange raiment. And its name shall be called 2960T. And after a little time it shall be called DNO. And again after another little time it shall be called DME, which shall bring salvation also to the disciples of Jay, yea even to them that dwell within the gates of System 4.

And all who heard these tidings were amazed and marvelled at them, saying: Verily, wonderful are the ways of this generation of system designers, who can fashion a silk purse out of the ear of a she-swine. But some did believe and went

155

their ways rejoicing, for the days were not yet accomplished wherein they should be converted.

Deliveries in Deutschland, c. 1976 *Chris Sundt*

When the building for the European Space Agency in Darmstadt was being designed, the size of the lifts was determined by the size of the largest piece of equipment which would have to be installed in the building. This turned out to be half of a 2970 processor. The processor was built with two chassis, deliberately to make it easier to transport. Unfortunately, the need to keep the two halves separate for transport was in direct conflict with the need to wire them comprehensively together for system testing. Therefore, when the time came to ship the processor, there were myriads of backplane wires leading direct from solder on one side to solder on the other.

The next problem was how to lift both halves simultaneously and smoothly, when the only thing holding them together was the backplane wiring. The solution was to embed them in probably the largest and heaviest wooden crate that ICL ever manufactured. It was, indeed, so large that some wag suggested that when the delivery had been made the crate should be brought back full of illegal immigrants. It would hold about 140 of them, and at £1,000 a head that would constitute quite a good piece of business.

So in due course this massive piece of equipment was shipped from West Gorton, in one of a fleet of lorries containing the masses of associated peripherals, cables, spares required. In the dead of winter they trundled across England, successfully negotiated the ferry crossing, and set off into Germany. Sadly, the drivers reached the limit of their permitted driving hours while they were still some tens of kilometres short of their destination. They had to stop for the night.

In the morning, none of the wagons would start. People hadn't considered that it gets extremely cold in Germany during midwinter, and no provision had been made for keeping the diesel fuel warm enough to prevent it jellifying. However, after various improvisations they got going, one by one, and straggled into Darmstadt to the waiting site, arriving at various intervals instead of as a simultaneous and impressive convoy. Except, that is, for the truck carrying the giant processor. It failed to arrive at all.

Search parties were sent out, and the driver was eventually located in the hotel where he and his colleagues had spent the previous night. 'Where's the processor?', he was asked. He explained that he hadn't been able to get started at all, and eventually had had to give up and leave the lorry on the autobahn. 'Which autobahn?', he was asked. He wasn't sure. And, of course, in that part of Germany the autobahn network is at its most spaghetti-like; there are autobahnen running in all directions.

By now the commissioning team were in a state of high nervous alarm, at the thought of their millions of pounds worth of processor abandoned, lost, and (of course) deeply frozen. But after the searchers had driven for many many miles, up one autobahn and down the next, eventually it was found, the recalcitrant engine was kicked into life, and the mighty cargo arrived on site. Where, of course, it was far too big to be taken up in the lifts. So a complete section of wall, windows, cladding and all, had to be removed, and a giant crane was organised to hoist the machine to its destined floor. Then came the next problem. In order to spread the lifting strain evenly, and to prevent the giant crate from either hogging or sagging, there was quite a complex cradle hanging from the crane's hook. Although the reception party could lasso the end of the crate and pull it towards them through the opening in the wall, the cradle started to foul the upper part of the wall long before the load's centre of gravity had been pulled inboard. Impasse!

But not for long. The crane driver (let's call him Helmut) saw the problem, used his initiative and devised his own solution. Having assured himself that the load was at exactly the right height, with only a few inches between its base and the level of the floor, he began to swing his jib gently from side to side. To their horror, the installation crew saw their giant processor, in its giant crate, all multi-million pounds worth of it, starting to oscillate like a giant fairground toy. With each cycle, the end nearest the building came further and further through the gap in the wall. Finally, when the load had gained enough momentum, and was at the extreme end of its inward swing, with positively exquisite timing Helmut released the brake on the cable drum, the crate grounded, and *slid* to a safe halt inside. People then remembered to breathe.

The slotted line, c. 1976   *Arnold Shaw*

Corporate Systems decided at one stage that Operations Staff were the real kings and had all the authority. They decided that the big George machines could handle six streams of this kind and three streams of that. The figures were plucked out of the air, as was their style, with no research worth the name. And no, there could be no overnight development slots. I found myself pleading at 2 a.m., over the phone to his home, with some buffoon who hardly knew the difference between an EDS cartridge and a dustbin lid. No, I could not have a development slot to mend whatever the crisis was. Then I heard my good friend Tom Rothwell saying: 'Never mind; give the bastard half an hour to get back to sleep, and then I'll have a go.' Which he did, with more success. Perhaps the man had the wit to see a pattern developing.

Doing it by the book, c. 1976 *Arnold Shaw*

Another of the intellectual giants from West Gorton Operations spent a long time explaining that Corporate Systems was short of computing capacity. His way to deal with the overload would be to send support staff down to Stevenage to use the machine there. I pointed out that we had an unofficial arrangement to use Executive machines across the yard, paid for in beer. He spoke to me as to a child, explaining the sanctity of budgets and the iniquity of using 'unofficial arrangements', and how wicked the practice was. He intended to stop it, and he did. The bit of my brain that's supposed to understand these things must be missing. Perhaps that's why I never got on.

Telling the truth, c. 1976 *Arnold Shaw*

West Gorton had its share of rough diamonds. I treasure one particular memory of one of our brethren toiling over a terminal when his hovering manager, unwisely, asked if he could help. The labourer turned on the squire in uncontrolled rage. 'You can't run a ******* MOP.' he snarled. 'You can't run a ******* job. You can't write a line of ******* code. How does a ****** like you think he can help?' The content of the abuse was, alas, perfectly accurate in every particular.

A tribute, c. 1976 *Arnold Shaw*

I once came across a copy of the code of the executive of the Ferranti Pegasus, 'Initial Orders' as it was called. It was written by a man called Felton. I studied that code for hours; I wish I still had the document. It was a piece of code of such transparent elegance that it seemed to me, as a young programmer, to rank with any piece of engineering of any time. Certainly I never forgot what the gold standard of programming was and always tried to get somewhere near it.

Not a tribute, c. 1976 *Arnold Shaw*

A few light years away, at the opposite end of that particular spectrum, among the many bosses I acquired at different times was a man from Putney whose name I have genuinely, but happily, forgotten. It might have been Harry something (at least, he kept telling me he was my boss but nobody else did, and it never occurred to me to check). He used to recite to me some rubbish called 'Toe Control', which had all the scholarship of an oriental mantra learned at the feet of the Green-Eyed Yellow Idol to the North of Kathmandu. Insofar as I could ever discover any coherence in it, the principle seemed to be that software design is merely a matter of designing the lowest level subroutines. This, according to the mantra, is sufficient; the total design emerges on its own like a jewel from a rag-bag. He used to preach at me with the light of enthusiasm in his eyes, like a missionary talking to a cannibal. What evidence he had to support his ridiculous thesis I never discovered. He quickly wrote me off as a hopeless reactionary. Perhaps he had a point.

The American era, c. 1976 *Richard Banks*

This can perhaps best be typified by the famous occasion at a meeting in the O'Heron 'War Room' in BRA01, at which a scantily clad bimbo reaching across the table popped out of her dress, to the entertainment of the assembled throng.

Going through the numbers, c. 1976 *John Deas*

On the other hand, life did have its serious side:

Geoff Cross was on a 24-hour visit to Wellington to go through the numbers. After a day of meetings he was sitting at dinner next to Dennis Hughes, chief engineer of ICL (NZ), who said something about spares margins. Geoff queried; Dennis persisted; Geoff leaped from his place saying 'Wait right there!', fetched his briefcase, and spread papers all over the table. Having confirmed that Dennis was right, he returned to his soup, saying: 'I'd never have forgiven myself if I'd looked it up on the plane tomorrow and found out you'd conned me'.

Blue borders, c. 1976 *John Deas*

A good Geoff Cross idea (management summary of the risks and rewards of a proposed sale) but it got over-bureaucratised and people learned how to conceal the problems in ever-thicker heaps of paper. I saw one (which had been approved and signed off) where buried among many pages of sizing calculations was an estimated processor utilisation of 105%, with a footnote: 'This may cause some delays'.

Terms and meanings, c. 1976 *John Deas*

I once spent an instructive afternoon watching Brian O'Heron in programme management mode, listening to a developer saying why he could not deliver in time, and patiently repeating in endless different forms of words, until the message finally got through: 'Don't *you* tell *me* it's impossible; you tell me *what it would cost*, and then *I'll* tell *you* whether it's impossible'.

The Archetypal Red Alert Telex, c. 1976   *Tom Pilkington*

Sent round by Bob McKillop, curiously on the day before he left the company, in about 1976.

MILESTONE PLAN FOR RED ALERT 999

1. PIG WILL BREATHE DUE APRIL 1

2. PIG WILL WALK DUE MAY 1

3. PIG WILL FLY DUE JUNE 1

4. PIG WILL FLY WITH ENHANCED PERFORMANCE BACKWARDS IN DIMINISHING CIRCLES UNTIL FULLY RE-ENTRANT AND EAT LESS DUE JULY 1

5. PIG WILL BECOME IMMORTAL, BREAK WORLD LONG-DISTANCE NON-STOP FLYING RECORD, FEED NOT LESS THAN FIVE THOUSAND AT A SITTING, AND NOT EAT AT ALL DUE AUGUST 1

PROGRESS REPORT

MILESTONES 1, 2 ACHIEVED. DURING HANDOVER FROM KIDSGROVE TO BRACKNELL PIG ESCAPED; NEVERTHELESS WE ARE CONFIDENT THAT IT WILL BE FLYING WHEN FOUND. ON WMG ADVICE BACKUP PIG HAS BEEN KILLED AND EATEN. TARGET DATE FOR DELIVERING SECOND PIG CONSTRAINED BY REPLACEMENT TIME – TODAY'S ESTIMATE JUNE 1 1980.

FOLLOWING ACTIONS RAISED:

CDD – REDUCE SPECIFIC GRAVITY OF PIGS

WMMG – ACCELERATE DELIVERY OF REPLACEMENT BY SHORTENING GESTATION CYCLE

WMG – FIND CUSTOMERS FOR OUR ACCUMULATED STOCK OF MILESTONES

GOD – RESURRECT OUR PIG

OPL, March 1977   *Dave McVitie*

OSROVision Productions Limited: Extracts from the programme of their Spectacular 1976 Pantomime Snow White (System Designer) and the Five Dwarves.

Introduction: OSROVISION PRODUCTIONS is a non loss-making organisation dedicated to the entertainment of release-shocked and overworked systems programmers. Although most active in the vicinity of the Red Bull (its headquarters until the end of 1975), it is an international organisation having members in many countries including Germany, Australia, New Zealand, Canada, and a branch will open soon in Luxembourg.

Stop Press: The enormous effort made by OPL to ensure customer satisfaction in this production is demonstrated by the adjustment in delivery schedule and budget, while the coherence of the product is ensured by the omission of some facilities and the inclusion of others at positively no extra cost.

Note: No part of this production implies any commitment by OPL to provide the facilities described. The policy of OPL is one of continuous development of its products which occasionally causes improvements which might appear to the customer as slippages, errors, lack of capability, or deficient documentation.

Acknowledgments: OPL extends its grateful thanks to the following, who have given help, advice, encouragement, support etc in the production of Snow White: Congleton Cricket Club (including volunteer bar staff); Marston's Brewery (for deep draughts of inspiration); The Lawton Arms and Robinson's Brewery (rehearsal facilities); and not forgetting International Computers Limited, especially 2900 SSOSS, without whom none of this would have been possible.

Jonathan Randolf-Ailing's appearance is sponsored by The Staffordshire Campaign For Injection of Life into Cheshire (under their Cultural Exchange Programme).

Do you know Frank Walker? 1977   *Chris Cheetham*

A frequent occupant of the Eight Bells in Putney was Brian Cook. When I first joined, it often happened that I was just leaving the bar when Frank Walker arrived. Brian *always* had business to discuss with Frank and, having introduced me with 'Do you know Frank Walker?', they would go on talking while I went back to work. This happened on about five occasions, during which I never actually got to talk to Frank.

Eventually Frank and I ended up one day next to each other in the queue for food at Beaumont. Each of course knew the other's name, but neither had any basis on which to start a conversation After two increasingly embarrassed minutes I was able to break the ice. 'The problem is', I said, 'That without Brian here to introduce us we can't actually talk to one another'. We became good friends and had much fun pulling Brian's leg when next we met in the Eight Bells and he again introduced us.

161

A notice and a response, 1977   *Fred Skeat*

<u>Expense Claims</u>

Due to the number of inaccurate expense claims, i.e. arithmitical errors and car mileage errors. The cashier will check all claims on presentation this may cause slight delay to staff enchasing expenses. It is the duty of the cashier to carry out this function to safeguard herself. In the event of errors being found, the employee should go back to his/her authority for amended signature, however, I am prepared to allow ~~hte~~ the cashier to amend claims which are in error of less than £1.00 beyond this errors must be counter signed by the approving authority.

<u>Expense Claims</u>

Due to the number of inaccurate sentences, i.e. speling errors and punctuation. Errors making it impossible to discern the sense all readers will ignore and cause slight delay to requests for inaction. Each reader must do this to safeguard himself. In the event of errors being found, the reader should take the letter back to his/her/its sender for amended writing and signature, however.

I am prepared to allow the reader to accept letters which are in error of less than one., or ~~beynod~~ beyond this errors must be rewrit ten by the approved signatory.

Hardly malaprop   *Tim Goldingham*

Extract from the minutes of a Bracknell Customer Service meeting:
   'The engineers are soldering on.'

OSTC/OUT/1427, 1977   *Dave McVitie*

   In the 1977 All-ICL Bullshitter of the Year Competition, this entry won the Andrews Liver Salts Prize for Sparkling Effervescence:

Document reference:	OSTC/OUT/1427
Title:	*CTM REDEFOUTITION OF IN AND OUT*
Status:	*DEFOUTITIVE*
Keywords:	*Range Definition (Range Defoutition)*

ICL: THE NINETEEN-SEVENTIES

Summary:

Out all CTM Outterfaces referoutg to the concepts BREAKOUT and BREAKIN, the terms BREAKIN and BREAKOUT (respectively) must be used out future out all cases within exception. This is an in and in ruloutg by the CTM authorities and, to avoid confusion, will not apply except out cases of names contaoutoutg BREAK. Do not, therefore, refer to Outdex Sequential Files, Outstrumentation, Logout and Login, Outtelligent Termoutals, Outterupts, Outteractive Devices, Contoutgencies, CTM Outform, Outt, etc.

We will use the syntax '-' for the old standard and '+' for the new as a hyphen out the words so that BREAK-IN is written BREAK+OUT out the new form and BREAK-OUT is written BREAK+IN out the new form. Duroutg speech, a legitimate question will be: 'Do you mean plus or moutus?' to distoutguish the termoutology out force. This syntax should be used from today until all use of origoutal termoutology has expired.

Bridge House East, c. 1977 — H.C.

In 'Doctor in the House', the pub across the road from the hospital was known as The Chapel. 'I'm sorry, you can't see Doctor Sparrow just now, he's in Chapel.' From its convenient location, and for similar reasons, the 'Eight Bells' in Fulham was often known as Bridge House East. And many ICT and ICL tales it could tell.

Immediately behind it was a small Territorial Army drill-hall, which was another of the places the BBC used from time to time for rehearsals, so that one might encounter in the Eight Bells such people as Sid James, Eric Sykes, Hattie Jacques and others.

That drill-hall was probably the target for the bomb that went off one evening in the underground car-park of Bridge House North but speculation has always suggested that the Eight Bells was involved as well. Rumour imagines that the bombers spent too long in the Eight Bells, realised that the timer was running out and they didn't have time to plant it on the TA, and so just dropped it over the railings into our car-park. Boom! No injuries but a lot of superficial damage.

But was it wise of ICL to give the re-glazing contract to an Irish company?

What goes up..., c. 1977 — John Spilsbury

In the early days of the 2900 systems there was a room at West Gorton containing a 2950 processor, some MT13 tape decks, etc., etc. The air conditioning was in the ceiling and had been known occasionally to fail. On one such occasion the 2950 had been powered off for a considerable time and covered with plastic sheeting to protect it from the water dripping from the ceiling. All was duly repaired, the plastic sheeting removed, the machine switched on again, and many users were logged in.

At this point a keen site engineer arrived with his water gauge (a U-shaped, water-filled tube for measuring the low levels of vacuum seen in the tape columns of the MT13s). Mistaking the air bearing high pressure monitor point for the low pressure vacuum monitor point he was slightly taken aback when the high pressure shot the water column vertically out of the gauge tube and up into the ceiling via the perforated roof panels. Not too worried by this (only mild expletives), he wandered off to the gents' to refill his tube.

Meanwhile along came the operator, back from some errand or other, and as he crossed a certain part of the room he was dripped on. Thinking that the air-conditioning problem had not, after all, been solved, he immediately switched off the system with the emergency stop and was three-quarters of the way towards re-covering it all with plastic sheeting when the engineer returned to the scene...

Expert opinion? c. 1977   *Gordon Scarrott*

'Why on earth should ICL have a CAFS in its product line?' said the pundit; 'IBM hasn't got one'.

The whole saga of the implementation of CAFS deserves a book of its own, and it wouldn't all be funny. H.C.

Open sesame, 1970s   *Peter Byford*

Alan R. had just taken over responsibility for the ICL computer at a very secure MoD site, so went to visit it. The two Colonels who were responsible for its security led him to the imposing security door. Each Colonel had his own key on a chain around his neck. Each bowed to the appropriate lock and opened it. The door opened and there were two ICT engineers doing some maintenance work on the machine. 'What the blazes! You're not supposed to be in here! How on earth did you get in?' 'Oh, we always have trouble with that bloody door, so we take a tile out of the false floor and crawl through underneath.'

Pride and Prejudice, 1977   *Congleton Cricket Club (via Dave McVitie)*

VME/B =   Virtuous, Munificent, Excellent and Bounteous
VME/K =   Vast, Monolithic, Expensive and Knackered

The end of the Americans, 1977   *Richard Sarson*

'When Geoff Cross leaves, the streets of Putney will run with American blood'.

Attributed to ALCH.

Information sharing, c. 1978   *Sandy Walker*

Arnold Jewitt accompanied Prince Phillip to the ICL installation at the State Statistical Office in Moscow. HRH's first question was: 'What are you doing?' There was a long and suspicious pause before the grudging answer: 'Statistics'. 'Oh, yes; what sort of statistics?' Further long pause; then: 'Population statistics'. 'Indeed! What's the trend?' Even longer pause, followed by: 'Trend is good'.

Mike makes it happen, c. 1978   *Roger Daw*

The Telephone Billing proposal was a huge one and, inevitably, the final print was delayed until just before the deadline for delivery. Which didn't matter, because Mike Forrest had given instructions that the print room was to be kept open, regardless of the hour, until the job had been done. But the print room of those days was operated, owned and guarded by a martinet who was a stickler for his own rules and, when he decreed that the working day was finished, the machines were switched off and disabled, the lights were all turned off and the odd little brick-built annexe behind LON11 which was his private empire was firmly locked.

When, therefore, we arrived in the small hours with our precious masters, there could have been frustration. But in what seemed like no time flat Mike had extracted the keys from the night security staff, opened everything up, deduced how the machines had been disabled and rectified that, and we printed at full speed till all the required copies were complete. Then everything, including the disablement, was restored in all minutiae to just how it had been, and we departed.

There were never any complaints from the martinet. Did he, we wondered, decide to lie low and let things be? Was he ever aware of the discrepancy in the machines' number-of-copies registers? Or did he really not realise what we had been and gone and done?

George Mark 7.5, 1978   *Chris Cheetham*

This little known version of George 3 was invented in the Micawber's Wine Bar in Putney by Brian Cook and me. We were just leaving the bar, having split a couple of bottles of wine between us, when the then account manager for Plessey came out from another part of the bar, also well lunched. Business need demanded that we return.

It transpired that Plessey, users of George 3, were being more than usually sceptical about the merits of VME/B. 'Ah!', said Brian, 'They need George Mark 7.5'. Now Brian was never a person to use plain English if he could find a more subtle and obscure alternative, but I was by that time pretty used to the technique and quickly understood his drift: Moving from George to 2900 should not be a big bang. By working up to it and preparing the way, it should be possible to create an environment which minimised the trauma of the eventual change. We discussed this between the three of us for some time. Protocol demanded that we split a further three bottles of wine.

By the end of lunchtime we all felt pretty happy with what we perceived as a shared idea of much merit. Brian felt pleased enough to exceed 60 mph over Putney Bridge. The account manager felt it worth contemplating a little longer in a lay-by off the A3. It was accordingly not until a few days later that I, as the HQ support manager for VME, got an irate phone call from my colleague responsible for George 3 asking what on earth Mark 7.5 was and would I provide the technical specifications to Plessey.

Bemused in a bus, c. 1978   *Margaret Whitney*

There was a party of Bulgarians in the UK for a week's visit, and the hired coach took them to a number of ICL sites, including West Gorton. Then there proved to be a vacant day in their itinerary, so the Visits Unit laid on a sightseeing tour. They were in a cheery mood, and liked what they saw of Chester. But as the coach continued into North Wales for a look at the grandeur of Snowdonia, the party fell curiously quiet. This persisted until they recrossed the Dee in the late afternoon on the way back to the hotel, when smiles broke out again. As they alighted at journey's end, the leader of the delegation asked the guide to thank the coach driver for so successfully bribing the border guards to stay out of sight, because they didn't have visas for Wales.

The English have never been very good at geography   **Tim Goldingham**

When the Cardiff district office was opened, the Bristol manager (presumably Joe Kendrick) dictated a memo to his secretary and told her to send it to 'the new South Wales district office'. Six weeks later it arrived, via Australia.

Can't you hear what I'm telling you? c. 1978   **Chris Johnson**

In the 1970s I was a support technician with IAL, which later became an STC subsidiary and subsequently part of ICL Network Services. One of my responsibilities was providing a diagnostic and repair service on our SECMAT speech-plus-data multiplexors. These devices interfaced their speech circuits to PTT switchboards.

One day I received a call from an irate customer in Ireland with a problem on his speech circuit. He described it to me, and then there was the following interchange:

Me: 'So, to summarise then: You can speak to him but he can't speak to you?'

Customer (in a very broad Irish accent and with more than a hint of sarcasm): 'No! That's not right at all! We can both speak to each other perfectly well. The problem is I can hear him.'

Stockholm ta very much, 1978   **Chris Horrobin**

The timetable for the project was very tight, because it had to tie in with a customer's building move. Unfortunately the new official software release proved to be fatally flawed. That news was immediately fed back to the co-operative development team in Dalkeith, who prepared a new development beta version.

Also unfortunately the Swedish project had ruffled the feathers of a senior ICL manager, by implying that similar ambitious projects in the UK would suffer similar disasters. So the official decree was made that Sweden would have to wait several weeks for the next official release.

The Swedish project junior was despatched to Scotland with directions on how to find the development computer room, housed a short distance away from the main building. He arrived; the airport taxi was told to wait; there was a swift transaction involving discs and bottles of whisky; and the Swedish project was a complete success, to the customer's great satisfaction.

Hook, line, and bumper, 1978   ICL News

It looked like an everyday occurrence: a bent car, anxious drivers, a policeman with a notebook, but this one was *different*.

ICL Engineer, Paul Schutte, parked his car on the bank's of Europe's busiest waterway while he went fishing. Unfortunately, the German cargo ship *Craigaboy* ran out of control and, in a last-ditch attempt to avoid ramming the bank, dropped her anchor right on top of Paul's car.

Luckily Paul and his companion got out of the way in time and nobody was hurt. In fact it was probably just a case of the two drivers exchanging names and leaving it to the insurance companies to sort out, except that Paul probably had some problems in filling out his accident report, especially drawing the little diagram showing which vehicle was on which road, who was indicating a turn in which direction, and what the condition of the road surface was at the time.

Old Essex customs   Michael Brew

While working as ICL's salesman for H.M. Customs & Excise I discovered that they had a problem with fleas in a carpet in one of their offices in Southend. The bugs were successfully eradicated from the problem floor, but it was then decided that all floors would be treated with the insecticide spray over the next weekend. As the insecticide to be used could damage some textiles, an internal memo was sent to all staff with the instruction : 'Before leaving the building on Friday afternoon, staff must remove all items of clothing.'

It was not reported whether anybody obeyed the instruction literally, but there were many who hoped that somebody might.

The all-ICL bullshitter of the year award, 1978   Dave McVitie

This was run by an entirely fictional character, Dr W. (Bill) S. Hitter, from his virtual office in KID01. The ICL internal mail unfailingly managed to deliver his mail into an appropriate in-tray (mine), despite our recurrent failure to get the good doctor into the ICL phone-book, due to Personnel's vigilance.

Every year, a panel of expert judges reviewed all the entries and published the winners in various categories in the virtual document 'OSTC/IN/1000', with an issue number of the year in question (the real OSTC/IN/1000 was supposedly 'The History of VME', but each yearly increment covered less than twelve months of history due to the problems of trying to keep up with real time. Only the front-sheet was ever issued, in fact).

News of the awards seemed to reach most parts of ICL, thus encouraging a satisfactory flow of further entries.

The popularity of the scheme may be gauged by a quote from Ed Mack: 'What *do* I have to do to get the main award instead of one of these minor prizes?'

ICL goes East , c. 1978   *Chris Cheetham*

I was fortunate enough to go with Graham Morris, Brian Lewis and four others to China, just after the end of the Cultural Revolution when normality was beginning to return. We travelled on an almost empty SwissAir 707, in which we were able to rearrange the seats so as to group the eight-person team into two bridge fours. Harry Ellis had joined the flight at Geneva, direct off a flight from Australia and the Middle East, pausing only long enough to change to his Passport *without* the Israeli stamps. Not until he arrived in Peking did he remember that all his vaccination certificates were in the passport he had dumped. He received a full load from Chinese immigration, at eight o'clock at night, after 72 hours almost continuous flying. He was past caring.

We took just about everything we might need: not just coffee and toilet paper, but overhead and 35 mm projectors. This was the right decision. I know because a desperate UNIVAC salesman asked me in a lift in the Peking Hotel where he could buy them. One up for ICL.

Although the Chinese were probably genuinely in the market for a small number of computers, they made no secret of the fact that their overall objective was to acquire technology and the skills to build it. This led to audience expectations that the visiting team could not always satisfy. A classic exchange followed the Brian Lewis presentation of 'Slave Stores on the 2900': a piece of best quality marketing bullshit that we expected any salesperson to be able to spout, and Brian had probably written it. Could he explain why the 2980 processor required so much slave store? Easy: because it was such a fast processor. Could he explain why the 2960 required little less? Ah, had to think that one out, because although it was much slower the main store was relatively even slower. In that case, why was the slave store of the 2970 not intermediate between them? Brian was at a loss. What they really wanted was not theory but hard fact, preferably with the graphs the engineers had drawn when designing the systems.

I thought I was in trouble when they refused to accept my claims that VME/B could handle any workload: Transaction Processing, Batch, Interactive, whatever. While an experienced speaker has the great advantage of knowing far more about his subject than the audience, that includes awareness of certain skeletons in the cupboard of his knowledge. Could it be? Fortunately it turned

169

out that our hosts were in possession of an ICL document dated almost ten years earlier when ICL was planning one operating system for every letter of the alphabet, one for each combination of workload.

[*Yes, one of the hazards of speaking in any of the Communist countries was that in the Ministry of Industrial Espionage they* collated *notes of every Western session attended. Thus an offhand reply in Putney could return months later to haunt you – or someone else – in Warsaw or Budapest. H.C.*]

Conversely, I thought they were deeply impressed (or at least were reduced to an impressive rate of scribbling) by my description of ICL magnetic tape systems, which I was deputed to cover, there being no room in a team of seven for a specialist. Lacking any knowledge, and on a subject somewhat deficient in the lofty conceptual advantages that were my forte, I ingested enough to become for half an hour an encyclopaedia of knowledge on magnetic tapes, NRZI and Phase Encoded, 1600, 1200 and 800 bpi. I knew start times and stopping distances, instantaneous acceleration rates and allowed error detection limits. All of this invaluable knowledge in a non-critical tehnology I imparted verbatim. They lapped it up. Today I cannot remember a single fact, but they probably have an indexed record in the archives of Shanghai University.

Harry Ellis was the best possible colleague on such a trip, himself starting dog-tired but a constant source of intended and unintended amusement. In the Peking Hotel is was he who tried to teach our (Chinese) interpreter how to use chop-sticks. When we got to Shanghai, we went out for a stupendous dinner in a magical Chinese restaurant. Until now, our hosts had chosen our meals; now we were presented with a menu in Chinese, and were more than a little lost, except Harry who was expatiating on the typography. 'Isn't that beautiful?' he was saying, just as a passing waitress took it from him and turned it the right way up. Harry seemed to have a communication problem about food throughout: on one occasion, and despite the waiter's disbelief, he insisted on Lychees and Ice Cream (sounds reasonable) and was duly delivered cheese and ice cream. Harry left China in pretty much the same condition he had arrived, ready for relaxation. This, I regret to say, he and others of us eventually took, naked at midnight, in the swimming pool of Her Britannic Majesty's High Commission in Hong Kong, on the occasion of the party to celebrate Her Majesty's Official Birthday.

Like it is, c. 1979.   *Chris Cheetham*

It is to Richard Dean that I owe the single most useful perception of my business life. 'The trouble is', he complained, after yet another bloody session with the User Group, 'They think ICL are being devious when we are merely being incompetent'.

Misfire, c. 1979   Mike Forrest

Roger Houbert instructed me, while I was in Stockholm, to fire the then Managing Director of ICL Sweden, which I would have done, except that it is illegal under Swedish law to cause stress to anyone currently under the care of a Doctor.

A plaintive complaint, 1979   The victim

Dear Sirs:

Some weeks ago the computer was delivered to our offices at ... and, as you are probably aware, we had some difficulty getting the machine into the office, and the counter had to be removed, and the swing doors, and our Mr Parkinson was kind enough to lend a bag of his own tools to enable this to be done.

When it was all over the tools had disappeared and cannot be found. Would ICL please check if they were inadvertently removed when the job was completed, and please can we have them back.

Oh dem boxes! 1979   Alan Trangmar

ODB (the Orders Data Base system) was one of the first major in-house online applications within ICL. It was developed in COBOL about 1974 using the then new Pericles framework superimposed on the rather basic Communications Driver product on 1900 Series.

In about 1979 we were called on to help with a project conceived by Bernard Bassett, namely to print the whole of ODB. I spoke to him and wrote down the details of the requirement. This was converted to a program specification and we got someone else from Stevenage (who can remain nameless) to write it. He had a bit of trouble and only got it to compile just before the weekend during which it was to be run. Bernard decided to proceed regardless. The job duly ran and, come Monday morning, there were about 20 boxes of printout in his office.

Unfortunately it took only a brief examination to establish that there was a bug in the program, as a result of which the 20 boxes were completely unintelligible and useless.

171

The program was duly corrected, conventionally tested, and re-run the following weekend. Bernard acquired another 20 boxes, but at least this time they were accurate ones.

But I never did discover what the underlying business problem was, or what happened to the 20 boxes once he had them.

Leave no spade unturned, c. 1979   Charles Bazalgette

In the late 1970s I worked for a while for a certain project manager whose single-minded approach to getting the job done was legendary. While he had many admirable qualities, he often caused some consternation by demanding that his team attend progress meetings at peculiar times and places, the most memorable being during the night at a maternity hospital while his wife was upstairs trying to give birth to their first child. His team also needed strong heads, in that we were sometimes detailed to try a get a DP manager drunk in order to learn of plans which he would not have divulged while sober. The snag with this was that if any information of significance did emerge we were too drunk ourselves to notice it or to remember it afterwards.

He was full of vogue project management phrases, such as: 'You've got to get into bed with these guys'; or: 'You've got to get their inside leg measurements'; or: 'You've got to put a peg in the ground'. At his leaving do we made sure that he received a variety of apposite gifts, including a nightcap, a tape measure, a tentpeg, and a bullet for biting.

A handbag! c. 1979   Mike Forrest

I was interviewing a guy in Marseilles and, having very early on decided that handbags were more efficient than pockets, I had my bag in its usual place on the table in front of me. The chap seemed absolutely right for the job but, throughout the interview, he gave the impression that he didn't think the job was right for him, and there were lots of strange emphases: for example, that *his wife* wouldn't like him to be working such long hours. It was only afterwards that I learned that in the south of France at that time male handbags were considered a sure sign of homosexuality.

Things that gang AWOL in the nicht, c. 1979   Chris Cheetham

It had been Ken's Majority do at Beaumont and it had gone on late into the night. At about one o'clock in the morning Ken stepped outside and, having relieved the immediate pressure, realised that it was a fine night, a fine warm night, a fine warm moonlit night, and indeed just the ideal fine warm moonlit night for a stroll in the fresh air. He was not wearing his jacket.

Indoors, other party-goers gradually became aware that the guest of the evening was no longer among them. Some while later, when he had still not reappeared, they bethought them to look for him. A search of Beaumont and its grounds yielded no trace. They became a little concerned. After all, they were still sufficiently alert to realise that Ken had not been in the best condition for going home to Uxbridge. They searched again. Still no trace. At about three o'clock John went surreptitiously to Ken's home and still found no sign of him but, in the process, couldn't help alerting Jo, Ken's wife, to the fact that Ken was missing. John returned to Beaumont. It hadn't escaped his attention that beyond the grounds at Beaumont lay the River Thames. He contacted the Police. A discreet enquiry revealed no reported incidents, but it was arranged that a boat would be sent to cruise that stretch. And so a disturbed night was had by all, searching for Ken on foot, on the roads, and in the river.

Eventually, at about 6.30 a.m., Jo was awoken by the arrival of the milk on the doorstep. But when she went down to take it in, what should she also find in the porch but Ken, deeply asleep, having walked all the way from Beaumont to Uxbridge. Of course, he'd left his key in his jacket at Beaumont. What Jo said to Ken is a private matter between the two of them.

What is beyond dispute is that Jo then rang John's wife. John, after all, had been unexpectedly and unexplainedly absent all night. It was a brief message, but perhaps less than tactful: 'Tell John not to worry. I can't explain, but everything is all right'.

Thus did both the wholly guilty Ken and the wholly innocent John have as a common agenda for their meeting the following afternoon their relationships with their respective womenfolk.

The end of rugger, c. 1979   H.C.

It must have been David Hilliard (well it would be, wouldn't it?) who suggested, at the end of a very wet evening, that the front hall of Hedsor, marble floor and all, would be the ideal place for a bit of scrum practice.

He always was a persuasive blighter and managed to round up 16 mugs, all much the worse for wear. We formed up, he put in the 'ball' (whatever it was) and told us to shove. Now the second row on the opposite side consisted of Gerry Gilbert and Chris Crawford, two massive fellows. They didn't need to push; they just leaned in our direction, we went rapidly backwards, hit the wall, collapsed and, for me, all the lights went out.

When I started to come round, I was being helped to my feet. Allen Davies on one side was saying in concerned tones: 'Stop turning blue!'. On the other

Graham Green was murmuring solicitously: 'Don't you think you're getting too old for this sort of thing?'

The cracked ribs were a nuisance for a fortnight.

Comica Telephonica, c. 1979   *David Brown*

On his appointment, the new Dataskil Managing Director demanded a private telephone line in his Reading office, bypassing the company's switchboard.

Let us ignore all the bureaucratic hurdles, obstacles and delays, on our side as on theirs, and leap forward to the day when the Post Office engineers ran special bits of cable from an external junction box to the MD's office. They made the final connections and left a shiny new instrument on his desk.

After a few moments it rang. A few minutes later it rang again. Indeed, it rang every few minutes for the rest of the morning.

Back at the exchange, someone had blundered. The supposedly private line was in fact connected to every emergency phone on the M4 motorway between Maidenhead and Swindon.

Things that go bump in the night, c. 1979   *Chris Johnson*

I was staying in a small hotel on the outskirts of Manchester, where I was installing a Data Comms system for British Aerospace, or one of its precursors. The hotel was twinned with another about a hundred yards down the road; they shared a single security man-cum-night porter.

One night my sleep was disturbed by a muffled banging and rustling which, as it fitted in with my dream, I at first ignored. But eventually I was moved to look out of the window. There were two villains with the back window out of my Cortina, busily removing all my kit. I banged on the window and shouted, at which they ran off.

Not pausing for a moment, I dashed out of the hotel in my boxer shorts into the pouring rain, raced round to the back and gave chase. After about half a mile I lost them, and in any case my bare feet were not up to it. I walked back to the hotel, feeling very angry and not a little foolish.

On arriving back at the hotel, my feelings of rage and foolishness were not abated when I realised that the door had locked behind me and I couldn't get in. There was a speaker/mike box by the door to call the porter at the nearby hotel, which I used. He said he would be along shortly.

About five minutes later I heard him coming along the road with a colleague. From some distance I could see them giving me strange looks, and overheard one say to the other: 'I saw him in the bar about 10.30 and he didn't look too bad then'.

Ever since then, when staying in Manchester I always go to bed fully clothed and with running shoes on.

A legendary visit, c. 1979   Mike Forrest

David Caminer reached ICL's Paris HQ at Puteaux rather late in the evening. They hadn't booked a hotel room for him. He had to sleep in the office. All right so far. But when the cleaning lady came in early next morning and found his unattached leg in the outer office she broke the local decibel record.

Night-shift games, 1970s   Brian Russell

Mag Tape Bowls was a bit like ten-pin bowling. For skittles we used the centres from console teleprinter rolls. The bowls were mag tapes (in their cases!). Unless a grumley was fitted, a mag tape had to be rolled in the correct direction to prevent it unwinding.

Cricket was played with a ball made from a very large number of rubber bands. The bat was some part of a lineprinter and the wickets were the same centres from console teleprinter rolls.

The game went curiously out of fashion when the ball went through a window between the R & D machine hall and the tape tunnel.

United we stand, do we? 1970s   Iain Drummond

The technical authors were unionised. Their annual pay awards were agreed and formally notified, but never appeared in pay packets because some Director higher up the tree refused for some reason to give the final authorisation. They were therefore all going to withdraw their labour. One of them turned up, with his union rep, to make a formal protest, and was (with equal formality) suspended. 'Now my rep is also going to complain', he said, 'and I'm his rep'. 'Oh no, you're not; you can't be; you're suspended', said I, making it up as I went along. Said Tom Stocks in Putney: 'That was *terrible* industrial relations!' 'Maybe so', said I 'but it was bloody effective practical management'.

Inscrutability, 1970s   H.C.

A delegation of some twenty Chinese came to the UK and visited a number of British companies, including ICL. Far from all looking alike, their faces varied enormously in character, from northern Eskimo to southern Vietnamese. But they were uniformly expressionless. Whether the interpreter was making sense of any part of the presentation one could not decipher at all. Rather unnerving.

Then at the end of their visit they gave a reception at the Chinese Embassy for representatives of all the companies they had seen. The food, including 'hundred-year-old' eggs, was wonderfully colourful but difficult to identify. The embassy staff wore charming smiles, but didn't seem to speak any English. The guests wore no name badges, so (being British) we couldn't talk to each other. The man from the Confederation of British Industry gave the most embarrassing and boring speech I've ever heard, including a monumentally unfunny reference to Mao's Little Red Book.

And then there were the toasts, in what we were told was 'wodka'. Only it wasn't, it was the rice spirit called 'mao tai' which has very little taste but an absolutely appalling smell: a gut-wrenching, stomach-curdling effluvium, like last year's sewers in a heat-wave. So picture these silent Brits, as the speeches drone on, all with their glasses held, not in the conventional crooked arm in front at waist level, but at full arm's stretch and as far behind the starboard buttock as each one could reach. Never again, Antonio.

Red alert, 1970s   *Arthur Humphreys*

A *very, very* senior Chinese politician came to Carlton Gardens for a VIP reception in the ICL suite on the seventh floor. The lift in that building was tiny, so this important guest had to be sent up unaccompanied. Somehow, he got out at the sixth floor, which was out of bounds to ICL. I now know exactly why security people talk of a 'flap' because they were all in headless chicken mode until he could be extricated.

A little more deference, please, 1970s   *Arthur Humphreys*

Thanks to Reg Watkins, I am a lifetime chief of the Irabi tribe.

How it used to be in the East: 1, 1970s   *Iain Drummond*

The menu in the CKD canteen consisted of pig's blood soup and dumplings, inedible pork and dumplings, mouldy apricots and dumplings. It was uniformly ghastly, including the dumplings.

How it used to be in the East: 2, 1970s   H.C.

The visitor from Prague to Corporate Systems in Putney had come to study how we dealt with error management. Well, strictly speaking, we didn't have any policy on error management: we just put things right as quickly as possible in the best *ad hoc* manner, like everybody else. Nevertheless, he had eight weeks, or something like that, to study our policy on error management. 'It's amazing', we eventually said, 'that you can spend so much time in formal study of such a subject'. 'Ah well, you see, as long as we are learning something in theory we are potentially benefitting ourselves. If we ever implemented anything, we would only be benefitting the Russians.'

How it used to be in the East: 3, 1970s   *Iain Drummond*

The Hungarian Government Institute asked if they could send a party to the UK for six months to study production control methodology, and I was sent out to Budapest to vet the suitability of the members of the party. I was booked into the office bedroom (to save hotel bills). This resulted in the only occasion in my career when my office mail has been delivered to me (by a very attractive maid) while I was in the bath.

At nine in the morning the briefing meeting started with apricot brandy. This was repeated at all the institutes which we visited in the morning. Lunch, as I recall, was equally wet. The afternoon meetings continued in the same vein. Dinner in Buda was, to say the least, moist. Then attendance at the engineer's leaving party was obligatory, and memorably liquid. The hotel bar was still going strong at 5.00 a.m., when my remains were taken in a bucket to the airport for the 7.00 a.m. flight to Heathrow. Another taxi took me home. I went to bed on Saturday afternoon and woke up some time on Monday.

And my report? 'Five of the proposed members of the party are OK; they have adequate English and a good understanding of the subject. Number six is useless; his English is very poor and he's a complete ignoramus.' 'Oh, but he's the one who's *got* to come; he's the Party Member'.

How it used to be in the East: 4, 1970s   *Rosie Dean*

On my first visit to Moscow I was booked into the massive Rossiya hotel. Mike Bradnick came up with me to my room to make sure that everything was OK. The television wasn't working. 'Give it a kick', he said, before we went off to a meeting. When I got back at midnight it had been repaired, proving that they had been listening.

How it used to be in the East: 5, 1970s   *Rosie Dean*

To make it more sporting for the listeners, Mike Bradnick and Tony Neville used to converse in a mixture of English, French, and Latin.

How it used to be in the East: 6   *Andrew Mason*

Soon after the Red Army 'liberated' Prague from the dastardly Dubcek regime, the Soviet Commissar was going through the list of ministerial appointments with one of Dubcek's subordinates.

'Minister of Finance'. 'Yes, comrade commissar'.
'Minister for the Interior'. 'Yes, comrade commissar'.
'Minister for the Army'. 'Yes, comrade commissar'.
'Minister for the Air Force'. 'Yes, comrade commissar'.
'Minister for the Navy'. 'Yes, comrade commissar'.
'Navy? But Czechoslovakia doesn't have a Navy. It doesn't even have a coastline! How can you have a Minister for the Navy?'

'Comrade commissar, the Soviet Union has a Ministry of Justice; Bulgaria has a Ministry of Culture...'

Ah, dear departed days!

Get it right! 1970s   *Gordon Hobbs*

Working on site at BP was a pleasure! Their catering was superb and you could have had an eight-course meal at two in the morning if you felt like it. It was at about that time one night that the chef came out from the kitchen, immaculate white tall hat and all, to ask if everything was all right. 'Hmm. Superb! But could I possibly have some more of that nice dark gravy?' 'Certainly, Sir. But may I point out that it isn't gravy; it's sauce chasseur.'

'allo 'allo 'allo, 1970s   *Gordon Hobbs*

The Shell site in St Mary Axe was also very generous in the amount of food they provided for engineers working overnight and it was the done thing for somebody to take the excess home rather than leave it to go to waste. So it was really bad luck that Ian Lang, bag of food in hand in the middle of the night, should encounter a conscientious policeman at a time when pilfering of food by hotel employees had been hitting the tabloid headlines. 'Now then. What's this? Where did you get it? ' 'I got it from the Shell computer room' ..., and the conversation continued in the police station. 'Can I phone my supervisor, please?' 'OK'. 'Frank: I've been arrested; come and get me out.' So Frank

Greenway turned up at the desk. 'Yes, I'm his supervisor, and Yes, I gave him permission to take that food away with him'. 'And what is your position within Shell, Sir?' 'Well, I don't actually work for Shell', so that made two of them under arrest. Luckily, Frank had had a premonition and had primed the night-shift operator to lie like blazes on his behalf if anything came unstuck. So when the desk sergeant rang the computer room he got a magnificently authoritative voice saying: 'Yes, this is Shell, and I formally confirm on behalf of the Shell Corporation that Mr Lang and Mr Greenway, in acting as they did in this matter of a bag of food, had our explicit corporate authority to do so.'

Anon: 1, timeless　　　　　　　　　　　　　　　　*Richard Banks et al*

He went to a meeting at West Gorton. At the end of the day he met a colleague in reception and they agreed to share a taxi back to Piccadilly Station. On the train home, he was perplexed that he couldn't find the return half of his ticket and didn't have enough money to pay the guard. He had to leave his name and address. The colleague offered him a lift home from Watford Station, which was gratefully accepted. On arrival, he invited his driver in for a sherry, telling his wife how grateful he was for the lift from the station. 'Oh, whatever's happened?', she replied. 'Where on earth is the car?' Actually it was in Manchester, because he had gone there by road.

This story had to be included because it is such a well-known classic, and submitted as such by several people. But I was sternly informed by the protagonist that, although he knows that the story is told, and concedes that it is a good one, it never actually happened, or not to him anyway. However, there are others. H.C.

Anon: 2, timeless　　　　　　　　　　　　　　　　*Richard Banks*

He had a habit of occasionally going to sleep in meetings. On one occasion, in a meeting with a customer, his sleep was prolonged and, indeed, stretched through several items on the agenda. Eventually someone asked him a question. Stunned into consciousness, he entered into a lengthy dissertation on the topic which was current when he fell asleep. It was some time before anyone could stop him.

Anon: 3, timeless　　　　　　　　　　　　　　　　*Richard Banks*

He rushed to get to a meeting by car, and the only place he could park was on a meter. During the meeting, he realised that the meter had expired, made his excuses, and left temporarily to feed it. The meeting was suspended. Time passed. More time passed. After a fairly lengthy delay, someone was sent to track him down. All attempts to find him failed. But it was an important meeting and his contribution to it was particularly important, so they persisted. Eventually someone phoned his home. 'You can't talk to him at the moment', answered his wife; 'He's in the bath'.

Anon: 4, timeless   *Another anon*

He was sent out to do the weekly shopping, with a shopping list in one hand on which the shops to be visited were listed in geographical order. With the other hand he was pushing the push-chair containing the young son. He worked methodically down the shopping list until the purchases were complete and then proudly started home. But an awful feeling of something missing came over him. After checking the purchases, he suddenly remembered young Tim. Where had he left him? He set out to revisit all the shops, methodically starting at the bottom of the list and working through it in reverse order. It was in the dry cleaners that he found him.

Exit, pursued by..., 1970s   *Russell Austin*

It was late at night, but the engineer was still working on a fault. Suddenly all the lights went out. Groping his way to the front door he found that it was locked; apart from him the building was deserted. Being a dedicated sort of chap, he went back to work and finished off his repair in the dark. Then he made a quiet departure through the emergency exit. At least, he went quietly: it was the bells and sirens behind him that made all the racket.

Strategy for the 1980s, 1979   *Chris Cheetham*

In mid-1979, ICL had two operating systems (VME/B and VME/K) fighting for funds. The then Managing Director (Chris Wilson) asked me to run a small working party to advise on strategy. Among the usual suspects included were Keith Davies, Peter Ruhemann and Geoff Squire. We very rapidly concluded that ICL would have to do without VME/K.

This clearly was not the answer wanted and, though we dutifully spent three weeks listening to everyone telling us so and assembling a case, a less radical strategy was still sought. Product Marketing had a go at formulating a strategy that began with a simple statement of functional roles: 'VME/B is for...; VME/K is for...'. Intense argument resulted. Eventually Doug Comish knocked heads together and ICL went into the 1979/80 financial year with a strategy all could agree: 'VME/B and VME/K are operating systems'.

The only effect I could see was that, having sat in the Great Western Hotel, Paddington, for four days, during which I got through nearly 300 duty-free cigarettes, I gave up smoking. Keith, however, pressed ahead with one part of our strategy, turning VME/B into a much simpler system for smaller computers, and lasted in ICL long enough to see VME/K cancelled as Robb Wilmot's first major decision on joining ICL.

AN ICL ANTHOLOGY

Nine Singer Business Machines

A brief history   *Senen Novoa*

One of the companies which made the biggest contribution to expanding the market in which ICL operated was Singer Business Machines, the multinational subsidiary of an American parent. By 1977, SBM were selling a number of products which, in technological terms, were world leaders.

For example, in retail systems the Point of Sale equipment known as the Modular Data Terminal System ('MDTS') was of a revolutionary design when launched in 1970, and the advanced form of its Arithmetic and Control Unit (which was a predecessor of mainstream microprocessors) was recognised as such in the Proceedings of the IEEE. The most important customer was Sears Roebuck of the USA, who installed 60,000 terminals world-wide. Other large users were Prenatal and La Rinascente from Italy. There were other interesting machines in the range, such as the Information Storage and Forwarding device: this had a closed loop of magnetic tape which gathered information from the POS terminals and later, when polled from the central computer, sent the information via an asynchronous communication line. A variant of the same idea was the Tape Cassette Recorder, whose cartridge could be sent by mail or courier to the central site.

System 10, the long-lived forerunner of the even more long-lived System 25, operated originally as a very efficient concentrator. It was an extremely reliable machine, which greatly impressed all its users and won great loyalty from them. In retail it was used as the concentrator for all systems having more than four POS terminals. It also served as a very powerful concentrator in all the Time and Attendance and Manufacturing Control systems installed.

The terminals for the Time and Attendance and Manufacturing Control systems were derived from the POS units. In Spain, SEAT's car factories were major users, as was ENASA, another industrial vehicles manufacturer. ITT-Standard Electrica had over 1,000 such terminals in all its factories, used both for data entry and for communication with a central mainframe.

SBM acquired the 1500 product by buying the COGAR Corporation. The main model was a very small intelligent VDU, programmable in Assembler, with two integral tape cassette recorders and the possibility of installing synchronous

183

or asynchronous communication boards. It, too, was well ahead of its time in being able to form a network of up to 64 interconnected terminals when the option of a LAN had hardly been conceived, let alone standardised or implemented.

From Friden, which operated out of Rochester, New York, and in Nijmegen, Holland, SBM had even earlier acquired a range of: billing and accounting machines, some with a delay line as a memory; electrical typewriters with integral papertape punch and reader; an excellent set of calculators with various forms of display (CRT or printer or numeric); and a comprehensive keyboard to tape product line, among whose most important users was the Spanish Ministry of Finance.

Altogether, the assimilation of SBM into ICL brought into the fold a lot of innovative and inventive genius, together with experience and a satisfied customer base in many new areas. It was a very good decision!

What happens at 4.00 in the afternoon? 1965   *Henk van der Vegt*

It must have been 1965 when Singer/Friden delivered an F6010 computer to the currency exchange office located in Amsterdam Central Station.

It was programmed by wiring a removable plugboard with about 1,500 small hubs on the left hand side for the 12 operands and space for the 20 address commands on the right. The 26 available command lines with maximum 15 and minimum 3 program steps could be selected by program codes mixed with the data to be processed in an 8-channel paper tape which came in through a reader with the phenomenal speed of 10 cps.

Wiring a program was very much like first-time knitting and, as more of the program was plugged by leapfrogging wires from hub to hub, so it got more difficult to make sure that the right wire got into the right hub. However, a doorbell mounted on a battery pack with two probes enabled the programmer to check whether the right connections had been made.

It was quite an advanced application: exchange tickets were entered on adding machines with papertape output. The papertape was read and processed by the F6010, the data from the tickets was checked and amounts in various currencies were added in counters to produce daily totals. The program worked extremely well and it was an enormous step forward for the customer, saving a lot of end-of-day balancing on the adding machines.

However, the mean time between failure was low and the engineers were always being called to the customer site to try to improve the situation. The prevailing assumption was that the system was overheating because the problems always started around four in the afternoon.

The customer was not happy and I, as manager of the programming department, was asked to look at the program itself in detail. Could the way it was set up be the reason? But nothing irregular could be found.

The computer was taken apart and rebuilt. Another system was delivered but the same faults occurred on that system. Could it be (shudder, shudder) a primary design fault? Experts from the large Singer/Friden factory at Nijmegen appeared but they too were completely baffled.

The decision was taken to return one of the two systems to the factory for an extended check under close supervision by all the technical experts. As a super F6010 programming wizard I had to accompany the computer for at least a fortnight to act as operator, which was a simple (and boring) job. To do the checking the customer supplied an input paper tape of at least 10 metres in length, with a running time of 45 minutes. To automate the process we constructed an ingenious 'advanced papertape guidance system', with loops hanging on pieces of string from the ceiling.

After initiating a run with the start button I could go out for 45 minutes. And the only thing I had to do on return was to look at the printed output. If the results were OK, I pressed the start button again for the next run.

Every morning I was collected by company car from my hotel and every evening I was taken back again.

How did the system perform? Perfectly! There were no failures or errors throughout the entire week.

After the weekend I returned for a second week's trials, to be told that I was impeding the factory's operation by taking up valuable space. And besides, moving the system to my hotel would save a lot of kilometres for the company car. So the next day the system was moved. The hotel generously offered the use of their TV room in the cellar because nobody could watch TV during the day.

After the first run I looked at the results : WRONG! Second and third runs: EQUALLY WRONG and the errors were in line with those at the customer site.

Experts hurried from the factory to the hotel and eventually one bright guy found that the electric outlet was supplying about 180 volts instead of the standard 220.

It was then that we discovered that in Amsterdam, every afternoon around four, long rush-hour trains were moved from the yard to the station platforms with a high demand for electric power affecting the entire station.

After measures had been taken to stabilise the 220 volts on the outlet the F6010 errors were gone and, from that day and for many years, the system ran to the customer's entire satisfaction.

So if ever something strange happens about four in the afternoon, watch the trains!

A Very Interested Prospect, 1970s   *Henk van der Vegt*

In the early 1970s, I was general manager of one of the regional offices of Singer Business Machines (SBM) in the Netherlands. SBM Europe was merged with ICL in 1976.

One of my salesmen, called Ton, asked me to accompany him to a well-known technical trading company in the city of Utrecht.

I had seen the name of the company on his prospect list and, at a prospect review meeting, Ton had told me that the demonstration of the 'STELLA' wholesale application on our System Ten minicomputer had been very well received. A couple of days later I had signed an official proposal to the prospect for what seemed to be a very promising project.

Now Ton asked me to join him in what we hoped would be a final meeting at the customer's office. 'They said they wanted to see me to get answers to their final questions', Ton told me, 'I think we can clinch the order'.

At the prospect's premises we were led into a conference room and a couple of minutes later we were joined by Mr X, our contact. He was carrying a well-filled binder in which I recognised a lot of papers with our company logo: brochures, letters and other documents. Mr X had studied the documentation thoroughly, and had formulated an interesting series of questions, to all of which we were able to give positive answers.

As Mr X seemed to be satisfied, I started to raise a number of questions from our side, following the rules given on a Goldman commercial course:

'Ask your prospect questions to which the answer will be "Yes", and end with a question to which a "Yes" answer will mean that you have an order.'

It went like this:

'Have we now answered all your questions, Sir?'

'Yes.'

'Are you happy about the answers we have given you?'

'Yes.'

'Don't you agree that our proposed solution will have a lot of advantages for your company?'

'Yes.'

'And that it will also save you money, Mr X?'

'Yes.'

'We've shown you that the system is easy to operate?'

'Yes.'

'Altogether all the factors are looking positive?'

'Yes.'

'Don't you agree that we should take the final step?'

SINGER BUSINESS MACHINES

I was fully expecting his final 'Yes.' Instead, Mr X said to me: 'It is a very interesting proposal and we are very impressed. We absolutely want to go ahead with it. Can you please come back next year?' Ton went pale. The only thing I could say was: 'Certainly, Sir. In the morning or the afternoon?'

The song, but not the Singer, 1977   *Phil Hopkins*

It was a cold autumn day, not long after ICL had acquired Singer Business Systems, and the Local Government unit in the South West had assembled a large number of its clients to see a demonstration of the novel (to them) Singer 1500.

This was quite a different beast to the other ICL offerings of the time, such as the 2903. For a start, it was a desktop device: OK it weighed about 50 lb. but, for its time, that made it quite small and portable. And then there were the mini-cartridge tapes which it used, slightly smaller than an audio cassette and mounted flat on top of the machine in full view. People would often be transfixed watching the little wheels spinning.

The demonstration was to show the 1500 working as a cash receipting machine for the acceptance of rents and rates payments in Local Government offices, a new application area for ICL. The demo would be given by John, an ex-Singer salesman, known as the singing Welshman: quite a vivid character; able to talk the hind legs off a donkey; not yet imbued with the ICL culture and, therefore, perhaps treated by us ICL die-hards with a touch of suspicion.

On the morning of the demonstration my boss (Mike) and I were prettifying the room where it was to take place, moving chairs, distributing brochures, etc., before the customers arrived. The demo was to be preceded by a presentation of the features and benefits of this new ICL approach, at the culmination of which the 1500 in all its glory would be unveiled.

During final preparations Mike decided that the 1500 on its table at the back of the room should be moved a few feet away from the wall. So we picked the table up, 1500 and all, and moved it. We were conscious of a little resistance and then heard a loud bang. Suddenly we realised why the table had been so close to the wall: the 1500 was plugged into a power socket at skirting board level and it only had a three-foot power lead. We had not only pulled the socket out of the wall, we had put undue tension on the 1500's power lead.

Now in most modern computers this would present no particular problem, the power lead normally fits into a standard socket. But on the 1500 it was directly soldered to the motherboard! By straining the power lead we had blown the motherboard itself. No panic (yet), there was an ex-Singer engineer at the Bristol office not a hundred yards away. We called him in; he studied the damage, ruminated, and pronounced that a new motherboard was the only

187

solution. 'OK, let's get one!' said Mike. Fifteen minutes later, after umpteen increasingly frantic phone calls, the situation became clear: there was only one spare motherboard in the UK and it was in Sheffield.

It was at this point that we noticed the queue of customers at the door. Our colleagues had been fending them off with coffee and excuses for about 20 minutes while we tried to solve the problems. John came over to assess the damage: he was the one who would have to present and 'demo' a dead machine. 'We'll have to go ahead as best we can', he said, so the punters came in and sat down. John's spiel was magnificent: how wonderful the 1500 was and how local authorities couldn't do without it. But then came the point in the script where he would normally show money being accepted and receipts being printed. 'We have a slight problem with the 1500', he admitted, 'however, we can show the tape reels working' and he proceeded to make them spin first one way and then the other. But this wasn't quite what the audience had come to see and didn't generate much enthusiasm.

Needless to say, we never sold a 1500 to any local authority in the whole of the South West of England.

Minus 10 = 2 times 25, 1970s   Roger Cunliffe

Long before all the hoo-ha about transporting live calves, there was said to be a computer in a cattle truck. Actually it was a horse-box.

The client had two auction marts, one of them 20 miles away from their main office and on the edge of the Yorkshire dales. The computer system was used to record all transactions with their customers at the weekly sheep and cattle auctions. It consisted of a System 10, and the processor and its disc drives lived in the back of the horse-box, which was driven week after week between the two sites. On arrival they would park at the side of the building and plug the cables from the computer to connect up the terminals and printers, of which there was a complete set at each site.

The end came one winter's day when, driving between sites over wild moorland, the Land Rover pulling the box hit an icy patch. The horse-box detached itself from the Landrover and rolled over and over down a slope. The contents were way beyond patching up.

So the client wisely decided to install a System 25 at each site.

The Singer, not the song, c. 1980   Keith Cooper

Our client in Bolton was putting in one of our first System 25 installations. We were eagerly waiting for it to be commissioned but apparently there were problems: the engineer installing it had spent a week trying to get it commissioned, during which time the sealed Micropolis drive had been replaced three times but it still wasn't accessible.

I visited the site with the engineer and his supervisor, and we immediately discovered the problem. Whilst installing a new drive, the engineer was having difficulty getting it seated properly, so was using a lump hammer to 'tap' it into place! This had apparently always worked with similar problems on System 10.

AN ICL ANTHOLOGY

Ten ICL: The Nineteen-Eighties

...and the cuddly toy, 1980   *David Bell*

OPCS (the Office of Population Censuses and Statistics) enhanced their system from a 1904S to a 1906S in preparation for the 1981 census, and the Assistant Registrar, George Redfern, was invited to inaugurate the new machine. He was, quite incidentally, the father of the lovely Anthea, then Bruce Forsyth's wife and assistant. As he pressed the 'button' the console teletype clattered into action. What it printed was: 'Didn't he do well?'

Well goodness gracious me, c. 1980   *Chris Cheetham*

To celebrate the grand opening of the 2900 system at the Delhi Institute of Technology the *Times of India* produced a special four-page spread. It had a prominent empty rectangular space on the principal page, in the middle of which appeared: 'This space is reserved for a special message from Mrs Indira Gandhi which has unfortunately been lost'.

One bridge too far?
One drum too many? c. 1980   *Jan Willem van der Brandhof*

The atmosphere was very tense indeed when Les Cole entered the boardroom of GAK in Amsterdam. You could see it on the faces of the GAK senior management, and you could feel the vibes.

There was a good reason for these stressed looks. GAK, a large, loyal and long time customer of ICL in the Netherlands, was the owner of one of the early 2900 VME/B systems and at the same time the proud developer of one of the first wide-area networks in Holland. All 30 GAK district offices were linked to the 2972.

However, the reliability of the Amsterdam installation in the early days was very bad, which was terrible for GAK, especially with its large number of online users. On average, the 2972 went down twice a day and the remote terminal users could not continue with their work. The ICL account team, under project manager Alan Bruce, worked night and day to improve the up-time. The drum in particular caused many intermittent faults. As the problems mounted, the senior management of GAK demanded a meeting with an ICL director of the highest level, which at that time meant Les Cole.

Les came over and, during a briefing session the evening before the meeting, all options were reviewed with Jaap Ellerbroek, Alan Bruce and myself. Les started with a suggestion to offer them an extra drum. This was rejected on the basis that it would probably cause more problems than it would solve. We also knew that GAK had made their calculations for a possible claim for compensation because they had 'leaked' the very substantial figure to us before the meeting.

'Gentlemen, please sit down', said the GAK Director, Mr Van Donken.

After we were arranged round the table, Les Cole started with the following introduction: 'Gentlemen, it is a pleasure to be here. The last time I was in Holland I came down by parachute near Arnhem in September 1944.'

The whole situation changed. The tension evaporated. The straight dark-looking faces became friendly. Some even managed a smile. We then had a very constructive meeting at which an action plan was made and no mention was made of any claims.

GAK is still a very important customer.

A taxing task for IDMSX, 1980   *Mike Kay*

One of the most demanding contracts was the Inland Revenue bid in 1980–81. This was politically very high profile, with the incoming Thatcher government determined to eliminate any suspicion of preferential purchasing in favour of British companies. IDMSX was a critical component of ICL's offer. The sizing indicated that 47 mainframes would be needed, distributed around the country, and the profitability of the bid (ICL's biggest contract ever) depended entirely on the accuracy of this estimate. Moreover, the customer demanded exacting demonstrations that the system tendered was capable of doing the job. We had a great deal of data on IDMSX path-lengths and the sizings were calculated to an accuracy of 5%. But when the first measurements were done, I received a horrified phone call saying the path-lengths were 30% greater than estimated. If true, this would either have lost us the contract or eliminated any profit from the deal. I asked a few questions about the workload and soon discovered that they had designed the database to make extensive use of variable-length records, a feature we had always regarded as rarely used and therefore not included in our measurements. I wasn't in the least surprised that the measurements were out but the problem was what to do about it? In the end, careful investigation revealed that although the records were nominally of variable length, in practice their length very rarely changed and so the overheads in IDMSX to allow records to change their length could be avoided. I wrote a 20-line patch which eliminated the 30% overhead and put us back on track to win the contract. I always reckoned that each line was worth about £10,000,000 in turnover and £1,000,000 in profit. But, of course, it was the salesman who took the commission.

There was just one further little problem: we had to run the Inland Revenue test with general release products; no special modifications were allowed. This we neatly side-stepped by putting the patches on general release.

The reliability of IDMSX   Mike Kay

For nearly 20 years now ICL has had a team making enhancements to the product to reach ever higher levels of performance, database size and availability. I once rashly coded a statistical counter in a 32-bit word, reckoning that it would only overflow if someone ran 50 transactions per second continuously for four months without a system break. At the time, these seemed wildly optimistic estimates both of throughput and of reliability. But, sure enough, within a few years the counter overflowed. These days we would think twice about holding it in 64 bits.

SIDA (Some IDMS Definition Alternatives)   Anon

A memorable tribute to a great character

The whole ball of wax	IDMS software
Play Tarzan round the arrows	Navigate the database
Follow the yellow brick road	Use the ICL Data Management Approach
A bit of a shoe-in	Schema generation from DDS is very usable
Bang	STORE a record
Whack it in	STORE another record
Bung it over there	STORE on an overflow page
Cop me a record	OBTAIN a record
Here's a string of bits – cop this lot back	CALC algorithm
Daisy chain	CALC chain
Clever-Dick serial	Location-mode DIRECT
Fishes out	Reads a page into the buffers
Lights go out	System break

193

Look at that son of a bitch	Read the quick-before-look file
Boot it off	Start a program
Punter	Customer
SSC on a bike	Product support
Sludge Army	Central Marketing
Rowing the boat	Project Management
Them geniuses at Bracknell	The development unit
Holiday camp	ICL Beaumont
Bunch of yo-yos	COBOL programmers
Clever buggers	Experienced users
User type equals wally	Inexperienced users
Sausages and forks	Entity model
Puts a curtain on it	Subschema
Boy's book of numbers	Result codes listing
Boy's book of deliberate mistakes	Known error log
Mass of hieroglyphics	Virtual machine dump
Sh*t-sifter	Alteration to CLUC protocols to trap errors
Box of light bulbs	Indicator files
Piece of string	Of unknown magnitude

Steam will never replace sail, c. 1980   *Malcolm Turner*

The progressive manager of the computer operations branch at Kidsgrove decided he would like to bring some modern technology into our Heath-Robinson world. So he duly appointed one of our more intelligent operators to try out and report on a piece of software which he had obtained.

The operator spent a couple of weeks on the project. His discontent with the subject of the trial grew steadily more virulent, until he would damn it with colourful language whenever the subject came up. Thus the report, when it was submitted, was not favourable. In a nutshell it declared that word processing was an utter waste of time: the electric typewriter was a far better bet.

Compatible is as compatible does, c. 1980   *Alan Long*

Way back, in the days when the 2903 had been around for some time and its successor, the ME29, was being developed, I was involved with developing and supporting sort programs. One of them (probably #XSMM) was being used to compare the performance of ME29 versus 2903 when it was discovered that ME29 was not actually performing correctly. On investigation I found that, in certain circumstances, a particular group of three instructions consisting of a pre-modification, a comparison and a branch, gave a different answer on ME29 compared with 2903. I reported my findings. Subsequently I heard that the problem was in the handling of a particular bit. Which bit? Not bit 0. Not even bit -1. It was bit -2. Whatever on earth is that?

Let's parler Franglais: Lesson 16, c. 1980   *Anonyme*

La Conference du Release, avec Monsieur le Chef du Projet et Monsieur du QA

M. *de QA:* Bonjour, Monsieur le Chef du Projet. Comment ça va, la VME/K?

C. *du P:* Très bien, Monsieur le Gendarme du QA. C'est le meilleur release que ever frappé le fan - pardon - le field. C'est le meilleur chose depuis que le pain à tranche.

M. *de QA:* Eh bien. Je suis très heureux. Dîtes-moi, Monsieur le Chef, c'est très reliable, cette VME/K, n'est ce pas?

C. *du P:* Mais oui, Monsieur; le break, c'est une chose très rare.

M. *de QA:* Excellent, Monsieur. Qu'est ce que c'est le MTBF?

C. *du P:* Dix, Monsieur.

M. *de QA:* Dix! C'est formidable! Dix heures entre les breaks?

C. *du P:* En actuel, c'est dix minutes.

M. *de QA:* C'est un different kettle du poisson. On ne peut pas infliger cette système sur les clients.

C. *du P:* Hold vos chevaux, Monsieur. Dix minutes entre les breaks - c'est très reliable.

M. *de QA:* Reliable! Pah! Vous parlez en votre chapeau.

C. *du P:* Mais non, flic! C'est necessaire prendre en considération sa vitesse. VME/K va comme le merde sur le shovel. Elle fait beaucoup de travail en dix minutes: plus que le VME/B et le Georges Troisième put together (je réferes a Mark sept, qu'etait un region de désastre).

M. *de QA:* Je différes. C'est une pointe noire pour vous. Puis-je considerer maintenant le question des bugs?

C. *du P:* Bugs? Quelles bugs?

M. *de QA:* Les bugs qui sont outstanding dans votre système. Il y a beaucoup?

C. *du P:* Mmmm... C'est conceivable qu'il y a un ou deux; ou peut-être trois.

M. *de QA:* Seulement trois? C'est incroyable. Vous êtes bien sûr?

C. *du P:* Est ce que j'ai dit 'trois'? Pardon - c'était une glissade de la tongue. Il faut dire six; ou, pour rester sur le sauf side, seize.

M. de QA: Seize?

C. du P: Pardon; soixante.

M. de QA: C'est presque bug-free, Monsieur. Vous l'avez fumigé?

C. du P: Aha! Un moment! Je regards le réport de mon Chef du Support. La photocopy n'est pas très bien (c'est une machine infernal d'IBM). Je pense qu'on a perdu un petit zero.

M. de QA: Six cents! 600 bugs?

C. du P: Oui; c'est bon, n'est ce pas? Peut-être on dit une mille, pour rester sur le safe side.

M. de QA: Mille bugs! C'est une catastrophe! Je crois que vous avez fait l'oreille du cochon. C'est une autre pointe noire.
Maintenant les tests-beta. Ils y ont cinquante en total, n'est ce pas? Comment ils vont?

C. du P: On a fait dix-sept.

M. de QA: Seulment dix-sept? Quand avez vous commencés les tests?

C. du P: Il y a dix-sept jours. Mais demain nous allons faire un petit spurt: nous allons faire soixante - et soixante-treize le day after. Ca sera une victoire glorieuse, n'est ce pas?

M. de QA: Non - une débacle. Vous pensez que je crois qu'un escargot va aller comme un bloody greyhound? C'est votre troisième deficiency grand. Un plus et vous êtes pour le chop.

C. du P: Petit bureaucrat! Vous connaissez rien de software! Si nous avons trouvés mille bugs, il n'y a rien remaining! Après maintenant VME/K sera très reliable. En actuel, elle court aujourd'hui pour dix heures sans break.

M. de QA: Formidable! Elle fait le travail comme un user?

C. du P: Très similar - c'est dans un petit loop pour dix heures. L'exécution des petits loops est un marketing requirement.

M. de QA: Bon. Et maintenant le documentation. Comment ça va?

C. du P: C'est un oeuvre significant de la littérature du vingtième siècle. Je lis un tasty morsel pour vous:

> *'Il y avait une jeune fille called Auty*
> *Qui un jour fait une chose un peu naughty ...*

M. de QA: Monsieur le Chef, je vous en prie!

C. du P: Pardon! J'essayes une autre quotation:

> *'Il y avait un jeune homme called Hucker...*

M. de QA: Taisez-vous, Curly! Ce documentation-là, c'est très smutty.

C. du P: Oui. C'est un autre marketing requirement. Aussi, ils y ont des avantages; on l'import de Hong Kong. C'est moins cher que Market Street.

Aussi, en Hong Kong on deals avec l'homme blanc; en Market Street ils y ont seulment les Gallois et les Irlandais.

M. de QA: Est ce que vous avez les approvés?

C. du P: Oui. Mais marketing n'est pas en accord.

M. de QA: C'est la quatrième pointe noire. Le produit est sub-standard.

C. du P: Ballons! Je vais by-pass le QAD. VME/K va aux soixante clients cette semaine. Si vous n'êtes pas en accord, tant pis. Mon ami, le docteur Wilson va parler avec votre chef et le frapper sur les kneecaps. Nous avons un idéal dans cet projet; c'est: 'Nous ne le voulons pas bon - nous le voulons Thursday'.

M. de QA: Calmez vous-même, Chef. Je suis bien sûr que je ne veux pas tangler avec Papa Doc. La qualité, c'est OK, mais quand arrive le crunch, je prefers mon skin. Maintenant dîtes-moi des activités du Centre pour Distribution du Software et de la Littérature (du Royaume Uni).

C. du P: Ils ont repliqués trente-six copies de la release tape - toutes uniques et différentes. C'est un exploit extraordinaire, n'est ce pas? Ils ont développés le plus advancé technique d'encryption du monde: ce s'appelle le ongoing random cock-up.

M. de QA: Trente-six! Toutes différentes! C'est héroique! Dîtes-moi, est que l'encryption est un marketing requirement?

C. du P: Oui - c'est un KSV16 drop-in.

M. de QA: Bon. La réplication des release tapes a achévé notre standard normale. Mais, comment vont les clients lirer les tapes?

C. du P: Ne demandez pas a moi. C'est une problème du Marketing. Au revoir, Monsieur.

M. de QA: Au revoir.

Never the twain shall meet, c. 1980   *Myra Brooks*

The visitors from Eastern Europe wanted to do some shopping in Putney High Street. I let them go on ahead so that they could have a look for what they wanted, while I tried to exchange some money for them.

When I caught them up a few minutes later there was a terrible shemozzle going on. They had found a clothes shop they liked the look of, where all the garments were very carefully wrapped and they were trying things on to see what suited them best. They couldn't understand why the sales staff were making such a fuss. The shop was Sketchley's.

The misperception of distance, c. 1980 — *Peter Woodhouse*

1. There was a desperate need for a 1904A in Adelaide to support the development of 1900 DBMS. Neil Lamming in Sydney didn't think it very funny when he received a call saying: 'It's all fixed: the 4A is now in Perth'.
2. Telex from Putney to Vancouver: 'WHILE YOU'RE IN CANADA, WHY NOT DROP IN ON... IN MONTREAL'. Reply from Vancouver: WHY DON'T YOU DROP INTO MONTREAL YOURSELF; YOU'RE CLOSER TO THEM THAN I AM'.

Vive la difference, 1981 — *H.C.*

It was quite by chance, in an interval of a SICOB Exhibition and Conference, that I met Terry Ward in the Champs Elysées. We sat down for a cup of coffee and watched the world go by. After a time, he asked ruminatively if I knew the difference between American women and French women. 'No', I truthfully replied. 'Well, look at them: American women have legs that go all the way up to their bottoms, and French women have bottoms that go all the way down to their legs.'

Software Name Clearance, 1981 — *Ron McLaren*

From: Deputy Manager, Group Patent Services
To: Manager, VME/K Support and Planning
Date: 2.7.81

In ICL News June 1981 I noticed that in an article concerning the release of the latest version of VME/K the important new features of SV18 listed include IPA, KIND and ADRAM. We have carried out clearance checks on the names IPA and ADRAM but it appears that we were not requested to clear use of the name KIND.

Accordingly I have carried out our usual searches in respect of KIND through our records and through the registers of registered trade marks, company names and business names. No doubt you will be relieved to know that these searches did not reveal anything which would prevent our use of KIND.

*

From: *Manager, Logistics, Medium and Distributed Systems Segment*
To: *Deputy Manager, Group Patent Services*
Date: *3.7.81*

Thank you for your memo of 2.7.81

I am concerned to hear that no clearance check on KIND had been requested; it seems very praiseworthy of you to have spotted this and to have performed the check on your own initiative.

Returning to VME/K, I have to tell you that the name 'K' has been in use for some time by a breakfast cereal manufacturer; as a result of this we have been forced to withdraw our product completely.

Switch selling, 1981   Paul Rappaport

Gareth did very well to get a competitive knockout by selling two 2900s with DME2 but, when he gleefully reported this, he got no end of a rocket for not selling them VME/K. That very afternoon VME/K was cancelled. Next morning he appeared in triumph before the sales manager and announced: 'I've done it!'

The all-time impossible product award, 1981   Chris Cheetham

This was won outright by the man who managed to sell a quadruple 2966 running VME/K with CAFS and DAP during that narrow window in time between VME/K being cancelled and the decision being announced.

A natural emergency, c. 1981   Russell Austin

While working on some equipment at a very major bank the engineer realised that he needed a 'comfort break'. He was told that to get out of the computer hall he should depress the red mushroom button by the door. When he got there, the red mushroom button on the floor was hidden by a box but the other red mushroom button (on the wall) was not. Feeling fairly desperate he pressed the only red button he could see. In this vast computer hall everything went very quiet for about ten seconds. Then all hell broke loose as every machine powered down.

The bare facts   Tim Goldingham

Bruce Stewart, the boss of software development, took exception to the proliferation of pictures of naked ladies printed on Bracknell's line printers and issued an edict banning them. I responded as follows:

> How sad that out inamorata
> Should now be persona non grata;
> For who but the lewd
> Could think the nude rude?
> To us she was just so much data.

On the button, 1981   H.C.

It was a forlorn hope, really, expecting that any part of British Rail would take a serious interest in CAFS 800 but at least they had been persuaded to lend us some of their data so that we could show them what CAFS could do. So a file of property rental details was obtained from the British Rail Properties Board in Nottingham, converted to 1900 format and thence into CAFS self-identifying format at Bracknell and we started testing it to see what sort of interesting questions might be possible.

'Are there any properties with annual rentals of less than £10?' seemed a pretty unlikely question but, to our surprise, it threw up two responses which were sufficiently oddball to put them into the proposed demo script. One referred to rabbit-shooting rights along a short stretch of the southern embankment of a particularly obscure branch line; the other to goat-grazing rights in similar circumstances. For each of these British Rail was receiving the princely sum of £5 per annum.

So in due course about ten people from the Properties Board came down to Putney for a demo and gathered in a conference room where there was a VDU connected to the CAFS service at Bracknell. Barrie was doing the presentation and driving the keyboard; I was a hanger-on in the background. The visitors were basically bored with the whole proceedings even before they started and slouched glumly in their chairs, plainly looking forward to the time when they could catch the train home. Nevertheless, the demo proceeded with as much light-heartedness and enthusiasm as was possible under the circumstances.

Suddenly, a nondescript little man in the second row shot upright in his seat. 'Can that thing pick out all the properties where the tenant's name is 'British Transport Hotels' or 'BTH' or BT Hotels' or that sort of thing?' 'Certainly, Sir', said Barrie and, with hardly a pause, formulated a question which exactly mirrored the little man's requirements. His fingers flickered for a moment on the keys, the search started, and almost immediately the list of hit-records began to parade down the screen.

'Ooooh!' said the chap in the audience; 'Can you let me have a list of those, please, because I've got to start charging them all a commercial rent from next Monday!' We should, of course, have made the 'Yes' conditional on their signing the order.

Ooooops! c. 1981 — Sue Woodhouse

The DRS had just been launched with tremendous flair. Massive press coverage. More advertising than ICL had ever used.
Customer: 'I'm having trouble with my DRS'.
Support Desk: 'How do you spell that, please?'

Retail butchery, c. 1981 — Chris Cheetham

I lay claim to early leadership in the game of not taking Robb completely seriously. After his first public presentation, a speaker at the same conference fell ill and I was obliged to fill in. This was an opportunity to talk about some of the things which Robb had omitted. There were the advanced workstation for three-dimensional scientific computing (PORQ), incredibly small computers (Hearing Aid Micros), CAFS deployed in betting-shops for punters to do instant 'form' searches, and new information-transport facilities called Geographically Uncommitted Networks for the Information Processing Architecture. It ended with IPA being used at GUN-point to bring the PORQ and HAM to the street-corner CAFS.

VME turns the corner, c. 1981 — Chris Cheetham

I was fortunate enough to become VME Worldwide Marketing Manager (great title, pity about the grade) just when VME was finally coming good. Although I was thrown in to sink or swim, good luck led to my being thrown in the shallow end. An ex-ICL Press Office journalist splashed a scurrilously critical article in *Computer Weekly*. This appeared on my second day, when I was due to visit Kidsgrove. On arrival there I was faced with Robb Wilmot and David Dace, saying: 'OK, Mr VME, what the hell do you propose to do about it?' I nervously called a few of my former user colleagues to ask if they would be prepared to talk to the said journalist and put him straight. I need not have bothered. Both Martyn Thomas (later founder and Chairman of Praxis) and Brian Parlett (Chairman of the 2900 User Group) were almost incandescent with rage and burning for action. All this resulted in the best VME publicity we ever had. I was able to persuade Robb to do some press briefings and, although it took years more before journalists themselves started praising VME, we never looked back.

IBM *announce the best news VME ever had, c. 1982*   Chris Cheetham

Potential customers took a long time to be convinced of the merits of VME and anyone who had the job of selling it had some prospect who, after a day or more listening to a very good story that VME was better than MVS, would turn round and say: 'Yes, but if that's so, why isn't IBM doing it?' Certainly I spent weary hours researching ways of proving our case and fending off criticisms that our software was priced too high.

Then IBM announced MVS-XA at twice the price of MVS. Suddenly we had the entire marketing power of IBM telling their customers and ours how important were all the features which they were going to put into MVS-XA (features which we already had in VME and claimed as reasons for its superiority) and why they should be happy to pay double. So we increased the price of VME, and by and large made it stick.

That damned radiation, c. 1982   Sue Woodhouse

Bracknell had acquired a Faraday cage (a room protected against the incursion or escape of electro-magnetic radiation). Barrie and Sue had acquired a very early pair of mobile phones. A very early conversation on these went like this:
Barrie: 'Where are you speaking from?'
Sue: 'Inside the Faraday cage.'
Barrie: 'Oh shit!'

Missed career opportunities, 1982   Barrie Archer and Brian Russell

There are job vacancies in an exciting and expanding area of DSDD:

CANCELLED PRODUCTS SECTOR

ICL has a large budget to spend each year on cancelled projects and it has been decided to consolidate the expertise into a single sector. All projects undertaken by the sector will be cancelled just as they are ready for release. The obvious benefits are:

Other sectors do not need to worry that their projects will be cancelled.

There is no maintenance

You don't need to worry about beta tests and QA

There is no IPC manual vetting (though a cancelled manuals team is being considered)

Projects are normally leading edge technology that would give ICL a significant market lead.

Only suPer quality implementers need apply, as a prime requirement for cancelling a project is that it should be on time and significantly better than competing products. Experience of at least two cancelled projects is an advantage.

CAFS 800: Early days, 1982   *Tony Colvile*

The General Enquiry Program (#XJCQ) was still not very reliable when the Falkland Islands were invaded in April 1982. Members of one particular user organisation were rather frustrated by the poor initial system availability: they could not access their intelligence about the Falklands. When the system's reliability was improved, however, they continued to be frustrated. This was because they were able to discover that they had almost no intelligence about the Falklands.

CAFS 800: Early days in North Yorkshire, 1982   *Tony Colvile*

His Holiness the Pope visited York on a Bank Holiday weekend in May 1982 and a huge throng came to York Racecourse to see and hear him. North Yorkshire Police were still conducting system trials on their CAFS 800 service and decided to try out a relatively simple and free-standing application to help on the great day. Its task was to record details of lost children, as reported by distraught parents, and found children, as brought to the central crèche, and to try to match them together. Before the day was over the system crashed and the data file was corrupted. I was involved in telephone support over that weekend, diagnosing problems as they arose. I managed to supply a repair for one problem but couldn't recover the corrupt file. As I recall, the telephone was ringing very frequently as Barrie Boorman, Dick Morgan and George Whitley reported one problem after another. Despite the problems and despite the fact that human nature was probably more successful at solving the problems of reuniting parents with the right children, it was possible to claim that the CAFS application had been successful, and everybody went away happy.

Wilmotiana: 1, c. 1982   Chris Cheetham

Robb was anything but pompous. You could say anything to him provided you could prove you were right. You could get away with being wrong as long as you admitted it. And you could certainly make jokes at his expense provided they were good enough. At one of Robb's parties, Andy Roberts brushed a fly off his jacket and said: 'I didn't think there *were* any flies on you, Robb'.

Wilmotiana: 2, c. 1982   Chris Cheetham

Amother fly featured briefly in one of Robb's first public appearances. After months of intense internal activity, of which the main outward sign was the disappearance of former directors, Robb addressed a major external audience for the first time at a User Group Conference. None of us knew what he was like at public speaking, let alone what he was going to say. Without either script or slides, he simply stood at an overhead projector with a blank roll of view-film and spoke (very well) and drew (less well). At one stage, to illustrate a point about local area networks, he chose to draw ICL's multi-storey Putney HQ. A small fly landed on the view-film near the top of the drawing, and Robb squashed it with his finger, in the process creating a smudged red line the height of the building. 'Whoops!', he said, 'There goes another ICL Director!'

Wilmotiana: 3, c. 1982   Chris Cheetham

On one occasion, Robb took the only vacant chair at a meeting and inadvertently sat on the microphone, thereby making a truly awesome rude noise. 'Ah!', said Noel Tomes, 'I didn't know you talked out of that end, Robb'. It says a lot for his style that not only did he collapse with laughter but so did the rest of the meeting, and moreover without feeling the need to wait for his lead.

Wilmotiana: 4, c. 1982   Chris Cheetham

His ability to understand what he was being told while simultaneously going through his in-tray was legendary. On one occasion he looked up and interrupted Warwick Morgan in full flight. 'Hang on, you are telling me *this* but ten minutes ago one of your people said something else. How do you reconcile the two?' After a very short pause Warwick admitted: 'Basically, Robb, I think it can be explained by the fact that I don't have the faintest idea what I am talking about.' He got away with it.

Insistence on a signature, c. 1982   *Peter Woodhouse*

It was the half-year, or the year-end, and it all depended on getting this vital contract signed before the books closed. Reg Selby was very explicit: if Mike Pollitt didn't get it signed he needn't show up in the office ever again. The customer wasn't at his office, he'd gone on holiday to South Wales. Mike set off in pursuit and scanned every beach, searched every hotel register and interviewed every landlady from The Gower to St David's Head. He drew a blank. In something approaching despair he rang Reg to report his lack of success. 'But I told you! It's *got* to be signed. Oh, sign the bloody thing yourself and bring it straight back here!'

Beyond Euphemism, c. 1982   *Paul Tomlinson*

An ICL engineer was called out by his boss with the unforgettable message: 'Get down to ... in Holborn right away; they're in the shit'. The expression was a little stronger than usual but he trotted off dutifully to see what he could do. It had started with the customer's caretaker who had been unable to clear a blocked toilet with the usual remedy of lots of caustic soda. Professional drain clearers were called in and cleared the blockage not by rods but by a more modern compressed air technique. Which would have been all right, except that the pressure sprung a joint in the main waste pipe, which happened to run through the false ceiling of the computer room. The engineer was greeted by a scene from a horror movie, with indescribable slime plopping and dripping from the ceiling onto the equipment below.

Falling off the end of time, 1983   *H.C.*

In 1964, at the start of the 1900 era, I wrote a set of date conversion subroutines to mediate between the public calendar and the internal 13-period calendar. Being a far-sighted chap, I gave them a 20-year driving table, one year back and 19 years forward (this happened somehow to be convenient for the fifteen bits available in each word).

In 1983, when I was long gone from internal systems, I received a very tentative phone call from someone in Letchworth. 'Please, do you know anything about the internal calendar?', the voice said, 'because this batch analysis job we run after the payroll doesn't seem to be working any more'.

'Ah, the little more and how much it is,
and the little less and what worlds away!' 1983   *Chris Cheetham*

On one occasion, an important lady arrived for a critical review at which
she was to speak to and defend the latest PDG position on CAFS. Although she
had dictated the content of the fax, it was despatched unchecked after she had
left for the meeting. What she probably *meant* to convey was that, in order to
bring the CAFS situation back to an orderly state, we were to agree 'not to
promote the *count* feature'.

Quest, 1983   *Doug Urquhart*

You are in a small log cabin in the mountains. There is a door to the north
and a trapdoor in the floor. Looking upwards into the cobwebbed gloom, you
perceive an air-conditioning duct. Hanging crookedly above the fireplace is a
picture of Whistler's mother, with the following inscription underneath: 'If
death strikes and all is lost - I shall put you straight'.

If you recognise the above, then you've come in contact with some of ICL's
other software, the games!

Inspired by *Adventure*, Keith Sheppard and I decided to produce an ICL
adventure game, not restricted to the mainframe environment and easily ported
to new environments in the future. I won't bore you with the architectural
details but it would appear we were fairly successful, since the game is still alive
and well, having survived System 10, System 25, DRS 20, CPM, DOS and now
Windows. It took shape over about three years during which we were joined
by Jerry McCarthy and finally *Quest* was released to the waiting world in 1983.

It's hard to describe the impact of the game (no graphics, no sound effects,
no windows), just textual descriptions of what was going on and a heavy
reliance on human imagination to fill in the blanks. Within a very short time it
spread throughout the world. Even now, I occasionally come across it on
customer sites in places like Tulsa or Oklahoma City.

Quest is, as they say, functionally rich. We packed over two hundred places
into our small part of Cyberspace and peopled them with dragons, elves,
insurance salesmen and some of our colleagues. One particularly hated manager
was placed, name anagrammatized to avoid legal action, in a rubber goods shop
down a sleazy alley near the railway line. He's still there, if you care to look.

As PCs became available, *Quest* moved onto them but soon found itself
surrounded by a gang of newcomers: games which exploited the graphics
facilities of the new environment and games produced by people who were
actually paid to do so! It was an unequal contest. *Quest* still lives, but in a
manner akin to those beautifully polished steam engines maintained by

preservation societies, good for a gentle run on bank holiday weekends, but not really suitable for everyday use.

No connection with any actual product launch, c. 1983   H.C.

This goes to the jaunty tune of Noël Coward's '*There are bad times just around the corner*'.

Impressive Occasion

There's a Press launch happening on Friday;
There are actions flying through the air;
And in Putney and Reading they think we may be heading
For a major catastrophe, and we don't much care.
In the Slough of despond the chaos is beyond
Belief, and everyone's wrapped in gloom;
For as the Press get their invitations day by day
We're waiting for impending doom.

There's a Press launch happening on Friday,
But the slides won't be ready till the day;
And our concentration slipped while we were typing up the script
So that's it full of regrettable things we just can't say.
No Director'll be there to chair the affair,
So Chris is taking it on instead;
But when the Press and the commentators have their say
He'll wish that he could drop down dead.

There's a Press launch happening on Friday,
But the Management Centre system's on the blink;
When we tried to connect an alternative projector
There were bangs, sparks, and flashes and a frrrightful stink.
Ian Bidgood's lot are going to have a shot
At concealing the damage behind a screen;
But when the Press and their photographers are on the spot
There's bound to be an appalling scene.

There's a Press launch happening on Friday,
But the demo has never been known to go;
And it won't be enough to rely on subterfuge and bluff
Because the bloke from Computing will be the first to know.

It'll still be a cock-up, even if we lock up
The gear and pretend that we've lost the key.
Because Robb's sure to open up the other side
And show the Press the bits they shouldn't see.

There's a Press launch happening on Friday,
And Terry's going absolutely spare;
In fact his latest impression of the prospects for the session
Was a stream of obscenities that would cloud the air.
They may just get it right, by late on Thursday night,
But up you! Jack! I'm on my way:
Because before they had a chance to say it was all my fault
Some silly ass went and signed my OTA.
I'm off to China! On a perfectly valid O T Aaaaaaaay!

ERIC, or little by little, c. 1983
Elly van der Mark

The European Retail Industry Centre, based in Amsterdam, received an invitation from a major European retail organisation (an ICL prospect) to give presentations and demonstrations to their Belgian management team. This was to take place at a hotel in Louvain-la-Neuve, a university town to the south of Brussels.

Three members of the ERIC team, Alan Bruce, Andrew Colleran and myself drove down there with a car full of equipment (don't tell the Belgian Customs!). All afternoon was spent setting up the equipment and rehearsing for the next day.

In the evening our host, the client's head of IT, invited us out to dinner. With his assistant, all five of us would fit easily into his enormous black Oldsmobile. It was quite a long journey but well worth the ride, as Mr C was a connoisseur both of good food and good wine and was taking us to the best restaurant in the area.

It was our first experience of Nouvelle Cuisine but the restaurant was excellent and the service outstanding. When the main course was served, three waiters simultaneously lifted the five dome-shaped covers off the plates. We could hardly suppress a laugh when all that was revealed was half a potato, three beans and a minute portion of meat in a strangely-coloured sauce. So we didn't eat a great deal but we certainly drank a lot of excellent wine and, about midnight, set off in very good form to go back to the hotel.

About half an hour later, in a quiet stretch of the Belgian countryside, a police car with headlights on full beam emerged without warning from the surrounding darkness, shot past us and braked savagely. Another screeched to a halt just behind us and we were forced off the road to a grinding standstill.

Why? What we had failed to realise was that, at that time, a notorious band of thieves known as 'The Nijvels Gang' had been active in the area. Their speciality was violent robbery in supermarkets and, by now, the Belgian Police were very keen to find them. Five people driving at dead of night in a large American car were obviously suspicious. We were forced out of the car and lined up at gunpoint. While they were examining our documents, Andrew noticed that one of the police cars contained a small computer and, in his typical way, started to sidle over to the car murmuring: 'Mmmmm, that's interesting! Mmmmm, let's have a look!' This made them even more nervous. All guns swivelled his way and he was forced back into line. Eventually Mr C convinced the police of our innocence, and we continued our journey.

Back at the hotel we encountered the 40 people who would form our audience in the morning. So it took several rounds in the bar to tell them the whole story and relieve our tensions. Despite the hangovers, the presentation went extremely well and the demonstrations were brilliantly successful. But it was one of those cases where decisions made in another country meant that we never did get the business.

However, it was a difficult story to forget and now, more than ten years later, we still recount our adventure to newcomers to ICL. Indeed, some would say the story gets better and better with each repetition.

Bye bye M-Drives, 1983 _Tony Colvile_

Two M-Drives were being returned to stores (these were the special EDS60 drives modified so that they could read from ten disc surfaces concurrently which allowed CAFS 800 to achieve its scanning speed of 3 Mbytes per second.)

Bracknell requested that they be sent on to BRA01 for use with the CAFS 800 system being used for software development. By phone, the stores foreman agreed that this would be done. Unfortunately, the units arrived when the foreman was at lunch, and he hadn't passed on the request that they were to be kept. Instead, the chap who handled the receipt of the hardware took one look at the Type/Bar/Serial numbers, recognised that they were incredibly old, and consigned the drives immediately to the rubbish skip. What a waste!

CAFS 800: Triumph in North Yorkshire, 1983 _Tony Colvile_

A minibus drove several of the CAFS 800 development team up to Northallerton. The afternoon was spent discussing the latest problems, but in the evening we went to a party at Police Headquarters. George Whitley had a sizeable win on the fruit machines, despite having been warned not to try them, and Dick Morgan won two prizes in the raffle. The food, (not the high spot of the evening), was pie and mushy peas. The occasion was to celebrate the success of their online police system, including twenty-four hours running without a system fail.

A master at work, 1980s   Chris Cheetham

Richard Dean's VME presentations were legendary. The standard issue presentation pack was long and thorough; Access Control rings jostled with Virtual Machines and Slave Stores; there was a wealth of technical detail, embedded in top quality marketing bullshit. Richard had more than enough technical competence to deliver it straight. His own slides, however, consisted of a Rolls Royce side by side with a Mini, an old-fashioned but adorable timber-framed house beside a smart modern building, and several oddly-shaped eggs all, except the one marked VME/B, sitting uncomfortably in their egg-cups. Quite how he transformed these into a wholly persuasive exposition of a thoroughly modern operating system I could never remember five minutes after he finished, which made every performance a new pleasure. Another good piece of advice is that people remember the person first, the slides second and the content last. People bought VME because they remembered Richard Dean and his oddly-shaped eggs.

Yet another Plessey disaster, c. 1983?   Chris Cheetham

The Operations Manager at Bracknell regarded the Plessey standby contract as a dubious asset. They were notoriously hard to please, and demanded patience, bonhomie and diplomacy to an extent which was not reflected in his job description. Everything seemed to go wrong for them, and he was perpetually being called out to fight fires not of his making. Came the day when Sales rang yet again: 'The roof's fallen in at Plessey'. 'Surprise, surprise! What is it this time?' It took several attempts before it finally dawned that for once it wasn't another complaint about the software but a real, physical building-collapse disaster and, for the first and only time, they were making a legitimate demand under the standby contract.

Take-off '83: Conference Report   *Henk van der Vegt*

This conference was held at Fort Regent, St Helier, Jersey and was attended by delegates from more than 50 countries. The event was based around announcements from Office Systems of new developments in DRS20 departmental systems together with a lot of promotion for the DRS 8800 word processor. A number of model office setups showed the advantages of the ICL solutions. The Thompson Agency explained all sorts of initiatives in external communications, based on the new logo with ICL 'coming out of the box'.

At that time Ninian Eadie was director of Product Marketing Division (PMD) at Slough; Roger Hill was managing Small Systems Marketing within PMD; Rob Kinnear was director of corporate communications. Other *dramatis personae* need no further introduction.

The starting session of the conference was done from a simulated airplane cockpit, with all presenters wearing airline shirts. At the farewell dinner there was great enthusiasm for the conference song, written by Pip Rowett, then of the East European sales unit.

Given the form of the chorus, even Sassenachs ought to be able to identify the tune.

Chorus:

It's Systems in the Offices
Products to the wall;
If you never take off on a Saturday night
You'll never take off at all.

The nine Verses were not quite as bawdy as the originals, but even more scurrilous.

The INDEPOL launch: 1, 1984   *David Bell*

The audience (consisting largely of frightfully important VIPs from the armed services) was assembled, the lights went down and the opening video (which ran for about eight minutes) started to play. I was on the podium, nervous and dry-mouthed, looking for the umpteenth time at the script which I would have to read as soon as the video finished. Then a door at the side of the hall opened a crack, there was a subliminal 'Psssst!', and I saw a sinister finger beckoning urgently. What the heck? I sidled quietly out.

'Your radio mike's not transmitting! Where've you got it?'

'Round here.'

'Inside your pants? Right, get your trousers down quick and I'll change the batteries'.

Not pausing to consider that this was in a very public corridor in the Metropole Hotel, Marylebone, I complied. He changed the batteries in a trice, told me to wait, and disappeared into the control room behind the projection screen. In a moment he was back again.

'No good; still can't hear you. Come in here... but keep absolutely quiet.'

Another set of batteries made no difference. Then (*agitato ma sotto voce*): 'Oh! *******!! I was pushing up the wrong fader!!!'

I hoisted and fastened my trousers, slipped back into the hall and resumed my place on the podium with barely (if that's the right word) a minute to spare.

As a means of maximising the flow of adrenaline I can recommend this procedure. I can't think of anything else to say in its favour.

The INDEPOL launch: 2, 1984 — *David Bell*

I was doing the presentation, in which the facilities of INDEPOL (such as they were at that time) were demonstrated in a complicated story involving a private eye, a blonde, a corpse, part of a car's numberplate and a hexagonal brass bolt. A crucial part of the plot centred on an enquiry being repeated and getting three hits on the second try as opposed to two on the first, thus proving that online updating worked. The creation of the new record was done by George, at a terminal behind the scenes but within earshot of the presenter's podium. The process was fragile and fraught, and I could follow its progress by the scarcely muffled cursing. On the first day the update was completed just in time and we followed the script to the letter. On the second day, though, George was better co-ordinated (that's a euphemism) and completed the update at record speed. Only I didn't hear him do it, and to prevent an embarrassing hiatus switched smoothly into busking mode. The autocue operator thought I'd gone bananas. She went into fast forward and then fast rewind, looking for this totally unexpected stuff. She threw up both hands in despair and then, thinking better of it, gave me two fingers. I went further and further into the realms of fantasy and it was probably while I was deducing the link between INDEPOL and the Great Exhibition of 1851 that I got the requisite signal and returned to earth. 'Don't ever do that again!' was her parting shot; 'I've never worked with anyone who got so far from the truth as you did'.

Clearly a problem, c. 1984 — *Russell Austin*

One of our engineers went to a customer's site to investigate an intermittent fault with a terminal. It was reported that the screen would regularly go blank after a full page of text had been typed but before the Enter key could be pressed. Many hours of testing failed to reproduce the fault, so the operator was asked if she could demonstrate it. She duly agreed, and typed in a full page of text (no problem so far) but, as she reached for the Enter key, her right breast nudged the Clear-Screen key and the screen went blank. 'There you are!', she said. She was informed that the fault was probably due to a 'spurious proximity effect', and asked to raise her chair a little. No recurrence was reported.

Before the cock crow thrice, c. 1984   *Chris Cheetham*

I gave a talk at the strategy conference in Arnhem and it seemed to go down pretty well with everyone except Robb Wilmot, who strode to the front. 'We are not paying enough attention', he said, 'to CAFS. I hoped we would cover it in this session. We will have an extra session on CAFS tomorrow morning. This means we will start at seven o'clock instead of eight o'clock'. Not a hint of a groan. But Mike Forrest stood up and said: 'In that case my seven o'clock meeting is brought forward to six o'clock.' It was.

An Irish story, c. 1984   *Richard de Fraine*

As Worldwide Spares Services Manager I had occasion to visit Dublin with Dick Cromwell of ICL (UK), to review, and see if we could improve, the spares service for Ireland.

While there, Dick and I were invited out to help say farewell to a storeman who was leaving the great ICL to join Digital who, at that time, were just starting to grow in Ireland. Off we went to a local beer shop and had a great time cutting the tops off Guinnesses with a knoife. The room was crowded but it was one of those steamy damp Dublin evenings when it's better to be in than out. Everyone was having a great time; the bonhomie was grand; relaxation was in full swing.

In due course the local CS manager rose and made a small speech thanking the dear departing for his contribution and wishing him well in his new position. The clapping stopped and there was a short pause as the response was about to be made. From somewhere in the middle of the crowd came a rather loud stage whisper: 'Well, his going raises the average level of intelligence in both organisations'. The room dissolved; the response was inaudible. But never mind.

The thrut will out, 1984   *Michael Bywater*

Transcribed from Punch, *11 April 1984. As part of the marketing campaign for CAFS-ISP, we published a poster showing a large conventional sewing needle, with the caption: 'We Can Even Find a Noodle In a Hatrack'. This led to the only occasion when an ICL product was 'reviewed' in* Punch. *H.C.*

When the dog barks, when the cat howls, when the eyeballs ungum and see 'We Can Even Find a Noodle In a Hatrack' gazing from the cheap matutinal newsprint, the natural assumption is that the brain has yet to surface. Wrong. What it means is that the bright sparks at ICL have come up with a means of getting the right answer out of your computer even if you ask the wrong question, spell the name backwards or turn blue and die at the keyboard. With a whirr and a bleep, primeval fears are once more unleashed.

What fears? Of men out there, writing it all down in greasy little books; men in grubby flannel trousers with binoculars pressed to their red-rimmed eyes who ring up the office from their Cortina, and say things like: 'It is Mister Fanshaw here, is that Mr Bywater, Mr M.K.H. Bywater? As you have failed to...'

How nasty. How unutterably horrid. The instinct is to bellow down the phone: 'How dare you call yourself 'Mister'? You're not entitled to that honorific. Go to hell, scumbag! And, anyway, this isn't Mr Bywater; he's *dead*, you and your sort killed him with your telephone calls and plain brown envelopes and stupid questions and lies about bills and blondes and agreements and overdrafts, he could have been one of the great ones, he could - given time - have grown a moustache and buggered off to the Gilbert Islands, but you wouldn't give him a chance ... '

... but it wouldn't do any good; it's all down in the little book, ready to be telephoned over to some pimply draggle-haired frippet called Janine or Torvill, who will type it into the machine where it stays for ever or until it is retrieved by some brooding glob of malevolence, whichever is first.

One fights back, after one's fashion.

One has certain venial little misdemeanours at one's command. Nothing so outmoded as the false beard, blue spectacles and slouch hat here; new technology demands new weapons, the Date Of Birth filled in, now American style, now European; the Previous Address If Less Than Three Years altered slightly but significantly from form to form; the postcode recalled in just the wrong order, the name spelt differently on each credit card. Thank you, Mr N.K.H. Bowater, that will do nicely.

Nothing, you understand, that wouldn't stand up in Court, my memory, Your Honour, no, I can't really understand it, I suppose the girls at Head Office must have misread my handwriting, Nichael Tywater of *Pinch* magazine, how silly, haha, all a misunderstanding of course, no deception intended, the fact that our names are on the same registration card *of course* doesn't mean that we checked in at the same time, the room numbers must be wrong, oh dear, I shall certainly sue, defiling the memory of my dead brother like that. What? I claimed he was killed at Bloemfontein? No no no no no, died of sprue while selling Bakelite butt-buffers to the Flemish infantry at Floem Beinton, good market, generous commission, opportunity to proceed up the management ladder were it not for a tragic clerical error, yes he *did* leave a lot of debts and angry husbands but nothing to do with me, understandable confusion but I don't really see what I can do.

Not any more.

Used to be a time when computers were literal, GIGO we called it, Garbage In, Garbage Out, a comforting little algorithm to murmur as one crouched, blotto, beneath window level, crawling from writ to summons past the bit where the Sherendale escritoire used to be before they took it away, did I say Sherendale, my mistake, I meant Hienz Baked Banes, it's all we eat now since the gas was cut off.

By mistake.

Because now they have Fuzzy Search, which sounds like something the Brixton Police might use and in fact is. All sounds jolly cosy (We can even find a noodle in a hatrack, ho ho, aren't we lovable rustic types, our gleaming red noses all ready to poke into other people's business *but only in fun of course*, nothing sinister here, no need to worry, just buy! buy! buy! persecute! muckrake! hound down!) but what it means in short is that, if you want to lay down a smokescreen, you're going to have to lie like mad.

Don't pretend that you haven't thought it all out while lying in the darkened drawing room with legal seals on your sleepless eyelids, ignoring the doorbell. Don't tell me that you haven't sat there, night after night, doing pathetic 'accounts' which are nothing more than a list of your ghastly liabilities put in alphabetical order and bound in a special legalistic folder which has plunged you another £5.57 further into debt. I know the interior monologue which pertains to these occasions:

...If I can fend off the Gas for six weeks then the cheque from the insurance company will arrive providing they don't notice that I've put two 'L's in Rolex which should fool the computer into not discovering that I've already claimed for it and anyway the false receipt will fool it, anyway, they always check the Postcode first, and then I can pay off the furniture people and then I can get an Access card because if I spell my name Brawn instead of Brown they won't find those outstanding judgment debts, but they're going to write to the Bank aren't they they're going to write to the bloody bloody bloody Bank, they'll say they haven't got a customer called Brawn, but then the address is nearly right, nearly...

maybe the Bank'll assume it's just a spelling error, then I can have an Access card and take out cash on tick and pay the bills and then it'll be all right because this time next year things should be OK if I can get rid of that bloody Sandra Oboe, she's costing me a fortune and I'm sure Mr Oboe's getting suspicious, I shouldn't have given my mother-in-law's address when we checked into the hotel, I'm sure that little bloke was following me, O God O God O God...

And it won't work any more, any of it, because next time you spell yourself Smoth or Jines or Frad Bleggs the computer is going to click, whirring, into CAFS (Content Addressable File Store) and come up with all the alternative people you might be or have pretended to be, and then where will you be? No way out. Only one thing for it.

(Lorches towerds bittle of Glinfeddoch and tikes hoge sweg, in vain hipe thit nabedy nutices, but it's too late. The machine has locked in. Outside in the thickening dusk men in raincoats prod their pocket computers and transmit valuable data down the RS232 ASCII TTY Modem, wasting not a second in filing that all-important information which in today's fast-paced world of sneaking, spying and skilldoggery could make all the difference between escape and detection. All innocent of the tragedy unfurling within the precincts of 27 Acacia Mansions/21 Acaica Masnions/72 Accaico Mensions, Mrs Sandra Oboe trips lightly up the path, sparing not a glance for the three men crammed into the telephone kiosk fighting to plug in their data lines. She knocks on the door of number 27/21/72. No answer. Lets herself in.

Oh horror! Depending from the ingenious antlers on the wall are (a) a Homburg; (b) an old greasy trilby, peppered with Strand cigarette burns; (c) the hopeless greying corpse of her illicit beloved. 'Oh you noodle!', she weeps fondly, 'I never thought to find you in a hatrack!' which just goes to show that computers will never beat us humans when it comes to the real thing.)

Divine assistance, c. 1984   *Nick Bretherton*

A 2900 system, of a model which did not have the greatest reputation for reliability, was sold to a customer in Nepal. On a follow-up call the salesman was surprised at the customer's delight with the good and reliable performance of the computer. The office proudly displayed photographs of the elaborate religious ceremony performed on the inauguration of the service. The salesman also noticed that the cabinet had a large dark mark on it: that was apparently where the goat had been sacrificed.

Laying down the law, c. 1984   *Malcolm Turner*

The computer operators at Kidsgrove had trades union affiliation. So when the company entered into a rationalisation programme, involving a number of redundancies, the operators decided to oppose them. I seem to remember it entailed a lot of visits to the pub and some very militant language but the outcome was inevitable. Though it didn't last all that long, the picketing was memorable, including the wag whose placard read: 'ICL Laidlow! But we Wilmot be moved!'

Le Mot Juste, c. 1984   H.C.

There was a much needed break in the Conference, which for perfectly sound business reasons was being held on the Australian shores of the Pacific, at Surfer's Paradise on Queensland's Gold Coast.

Entirely understandably, Yvette decided to take advantage of the respite and get in a bit of overdue sun bathing. Choosing a suitable site, she positioned herself comfortably face down in her bikini on the sand, and relaxed into a gentle doze.

Now marketing people, as we know, are ever on the alert for opportunities to reinforce their business messages and it was, therefore, only to be expected that advantage would be taken of the unusual appearance of this respected colleague. A photograph was obviously called for. But not just any photograph. It was probably Alan Wakefield (it would be, wouldn't it?) who purloined a label from one of the conference tables and placed it gently on her bra strap just before the shutter clicked. It was extremely topical and relevant:

It read: 'DECISION SUPPORT'

The heart of the matter, 1984   H.C.

It must have been at about the same time that an internal conference was held at Brighton or Eastbourne, and Decision Support was the crucial buzzword of the day. Richard Stilgoe had been engaged to provide entertainment during the evening and he arrived early enough to do some preliminary investigation. The high point of his performance, therefore, was the brand new song describing ICL marketing people in conference, each with a glass in one hand and the other elbow resting on the Decision Support.

Keeping a copy of the software, c. 1984   *Henk van der Vegt*

When 5$^1/_4$ inch floppies were in common use, an ICL customer was handed such a floppy as a software backup with instructions that it be kept in a safe place for use in any emergency.

At an unhappy moment the system went down and an ICL engineer was called to restore it. To do this he needed the backup floppy and so asked the customer for it.

The customer was happy to show that he had followed the directions to keep it in a safe place. As he took a binder out of a fireproof drawer, he opened it and handed the floppy to the engineer.

The only problem was that the secretary had punched two holes in it in order to keep it securely in the binder.

Sending a copy of the software, c. 1984   *Henk van der Vegt*

A customer suspected that his software wasn't working properly, so phoned an ICL software support engineer.

The engineer asked the customer to send him a copy of the floppy containing the suspect software. A couple of minutes later a fax arrived with what proved to be a photocopy of the floppy taken out of its cover.

Oh, how sweet! c. 1985   *Paul Gath*

When the DRS300 was launched, hexagon shapes featured very prominently in the literature. The theme was taken further in very large models, complete with model bees inhabiting the honeycombs made by the hexagons, for use at launch ceremonies. There were also matching models of flowers. Generally the launch presentation went down very well with the invited audiences. But in Portugal it was received with inexplicable hilarity. Later it transpired that 'Flowers and Bees' was the name of a very famous Lisbon condom manufacturer.

At the Barbican, 1985   *H.C.*

In May 1985, a Management Information Meeting (or 'MIM') was held at the Barbican, with the intention of impressing the ICL attendees with the grandeur of the STC environment which they had now joined. It didn't turn out like that. Almost without exception the STC Directors on parade came across, putting it kindly, as ignorant and elderly incompetents. When the incisive, well-illustrated and well-argued ICL strategic presentation was made the contrast could not have been more vivid. All round the hall one could hear STC chins dropping onto STC chests. One might say that the ICL takeover of STC began from that moment. And when the question session started, among the staid Directorial sub-fusc there was one brilliant flash of colour...

The following comment goes to the perky little tune of 'Popular Song' from Walton's 'Facade':

Mim-sy Whimsy

Sitting together so sedately
   Saturday morning, only lately,
      Hearing the lovely news of S T C;

Terrible shocks!
   Jack-in-the-box!!
      Up in the morning without any warning
         Pop Wilmot's red socks!!!

Telecommunications theory   .
   Certainly sounds extremely dreary
      Told by a man of nearly ninety-three,

God, what a bore!
   Was that a snore?
      Feelings are sinking, we're all of us thinking
         What are we here for?

etc.

Dealing with a Robbogram, c. 1985   ***Peter Woodhouse***

'UK Division is to present its five-year marketing strategy at (specified date, time, and place). Take 3 hours. Attendees RW, Bonfield, Biggam, Watson, Eadie.'

Alan Roussel said to me: 'Please create this presentation. I don't care what we say so long as it's excellent.' So out of our discussions two main themes emerged: we should shift from a geographical organisation into industry-focussed selling; and we should delay the 3900 for 12 months. The presentation was put together and rehearsed and rehearsed and rehearsed.

On the day, Alan introduced it and then said: 'I'll hand over to Peter, because it's his show. And I'll sit at the back, because it'll be news to me too'.

That accidental business, 1986 David Bell

The State Insurance Agency in Victoria was concerned at the mounting claims for injury compensation. We said INDEPOL could probably help and they provided a tape of claims records for us to use in a demonstration to them. When they started making enquiries, it quickly became apparent that fraud was being perpetrated on a massive scale. Whiplash injuries to the neck following a car accident were a particularly favoured cause for claim, since a doctor can neither prove nor disprove the asserted pain. It soon became clear that certain doctors and solicitors were manufacturing large numbers of claims, presumably for a percentage fee. There was one short street in the suburbs of Melbourne (was it Ramsay Street?) where every house on each side had submitted a claim over the preceding three years. During follow-up investigations they found that some of the road 'accidents' were totally fictitious. Others had been staged using old second-hand Holdens (notorious for their strength and solidity); strike two of them together and they make a splendid clang but nothing gets actually broken. And, with real Aussie flair, some of these 'accidents' had been staged at intersections where a policeman was on point duty; after all, what better corroboration could you get?

And did we manage to sell INDEPOL to them? 'Oh no! The cases you've found so far will keep our investigation and prosecution department busy for at least two years. We couldn't possibly cope with any more'.

The paint and the polish, 1986 H.C.

CAFS-ISP had won the Queen's Award for Technological Innovation and in due course a Royal Visit to West Gorton was arranged, so that the actual trophy could be presented with the proper pomp and circumstance. Accordingly the ground floor of MAN05 was cleaned as never before and the whole of the route that the VIP party would follow was painted (I sometimes think that Her Majesty must be under the impression that her subjects live constantly with the smell of new paint.) The gents' loo outside the conference rooms was cleaned and burnished within an inch of its life and then locked so that no mere mortal might sully its magnificence.

On the day there arrived in splendour the Deputy Lord Lieutenant of Greater Manchester with his grand entourage, the Lord Mayor of the city with a second magnificent entourage, and then Prince Michael of Kent with a modest staff officer.

David Dace led them on the pre-planned tour of the painted areas. When they returned to the foyer outside the conference room he asked the visitor, in the prescribed form, whether he would care to retire for a moment. The answer boiled down to 'Yes'.

And then nobody could find the key, and HRH was locked *out*. So that eventually there was an entirely unscheduled trip in the lift to another un-polished loo on the second floor.

At closing time, at the end of an engineers' reunion lunch in a pub in Abingdon, I found myself telling this story in the gents'. When we all emerged the staff had all gone shopping and we were locked in. H.C.

The best-laid plans, 1986   H.C.

GRiD REFERENCES

On the sunny side of Reigate there's a company called GRiD
Whose well-disciplined employees always do as they are bid;
Except on the occasion when their moral standards slid,
And they lent us a complete machine - the silly fools! - they did!

The scene shifts to Illustrious, in sunny southern seas,
And some barmy goings-on beneath the balmy Arab breeze.
With Cliff and Martin Whosit rather over-keen to please
When the Admiral exclaimed: 'I rather fancy one of these!'

When the exercise was over and they all had gone ashore
For the analysts to work out who had won, and with what score,
The GRiD stayed in the kitbag of Lieutenant Philip Shaw,
And it soon appeared unlikely that we'd see it any more.

There then began a period of misery and tears -
It looked as though retrieving the machine would take us years -
And the fact that it was AWOL reduced some of us to fears
That the loss of the machine might mean the loss of our careers.

By telex - and by telephone - in person - on her knees
Sue issued a succession of emotion-laden pleas;
And her passionate entreaties, by extremely slow degrees
Caused the Navy's icy tentacles to partially unfreeze

But to show what complications an unfriendly fate can weave -
(The next chapter of the tale would make a marble statue grieve) -

We thought we'd nearly got it, but were told - would you believe! -
That the gentleman concerned had nicked it when he went on leave.

He played with it at Christmas in some Cantabrigian fen,
(In the intervals of chatting up a rather dishy Wren),
But his sense of duty reappeared in January; then
He brought the Odyssean unit back to Devonport again.

Up to now our repossession had been nothing but a flop,
And their ever-changing arguments had kept us on the hop;
But there now emerged a way whereby the silliness might stop:
We couldn't just retrieve it, but they would allow a swap.

Like lightning one of ours went winging westward, but in vain.
The Navy's mighty intellect was wracked with might and main.
It would have been too easy to return the thing by train,
So they chose a mix of motorbike, and courier, and plane.

Enter the British climate, unexpected, unannounced,
The worst storm of the winter chose its moment and then pounced.
Incoming flights were classified 'diverted', 'crashed', or 'bounced'
So the plane returned to Plymouth - not just beaten - more like trounced!

Meanwhile the men from GRiD were most persistent on the phone:
Their questions by degrees assumed a more aggressive tone:
'Was Sue just playing games with them?', and: 'Was she really prone
To treat other people's property as though it was her own?'

So she thought a diplomatic disappearance might be due,
And instructed us to answer: 'No, we think she's got the flu',
Or 'Her car has had an accident in Hampton Court or Kew',
Or 'She's visiting a customer in darkest Timbuctoo'.

Then the unit did arrive, and she was on it like a flash,
And drove it round to Reigate in a supersonic dash;
But her smile of satisfaction was proved premature and rash:
For, when opened, all the glass fell out - Whoosh, tinkle, tinkle, crash!

Which shows how reputations for robustness must be won:
It's easy to survive a simple thing like being run
Over by a mighty Chieftain; but you've only just begun
Till you beat the baggage-handling gang at Heathrow Number One.

But at least the man from GRiD was so polite as to confess
That the reason for the aggro and the urgency and stress
Was that the thing did not belong to them! They'd borrowed it, no less,
From a customer, and that was what had started all the mess!

So now here comes the moral - a good one, though hardly new:
Take a tip from old Polonius, who knew a thing or two;
Don't lend, and never borrow; they're both foolish things to do;
And **don't** *go causing bother and embarrassment to Sue.*

Rotating knives in glass doorways, 1986   *Bernard Cosgrove*

A procedure circulated in West Gorton following the installation of security turnstiles at the entrance to the design offices.

It has come to the attention of the Administration Management that, due to an oversight on Administration's part, no procedure has been compiled to explain the method of ingress or egress to the New Building via the rotating knives (codename: TURNSTILE).

Below is a draft usage procedure which should be adopted:

1. Stand at the entrance to the knives with both feet together. At no time allow the 'inter-foot gap' to become greater than 1 inch. Failure to comply with this rule will result in the knife system removing a substantial area of flesh from the trailing ankle.

2. Place both arms tightly against the sides of the body with the hands pointing downwards. Failure to comply will result in either:
(a) the leading arm will be ingested by the cleverly-designed mechanism, or:
(b) if the leading limb is extended vertically to prevent ingestion, the following quadrant of the knife system will give the participant a sizeable poke in the right ear.

The latter case also usually results in the upper left cranium area receiving a hefty blow on the outer surface (according to the law of equal and opposite reactions).

3. Throw any briefcases or packages through the bars, ensuring that they clear the revolving area. (This may take some practice.) Failure to comply may result in the aforementioned packages becoming uncomfortably intimate during your passage.

4. Now shuffle towards the mechanism. If you are unfortunate enough to attempt use when electrically activated, your first shuffle will result in an abrupt stop against the solid bars. In this case, if attempting ingress, shuffle backwards, fumble for your card, insert it into the slot, and re-assume the position. Quickly.

If attempting egress, you may have to poke the 'press' button. This has been installed merely to make ingress and egress equally difficult; it serves no useful purpose as the knives are on a ratchet anyway.

5. Users may be interested to know that the pressbutton and card system is soon to be replaced by an audio system which will activate the rotor when it detects the phrase: CHOP-CHOP-BUSY-BUSY-WORK-WORK-BANG-BANG.

Note: In case of fire, ensure you are first to the turnstile. If this is not possible, burn quietly.

The Software Levy Funny, c. 1986   Iain Drummond

Martyn Jordan was giving the statutory six-monthly presentation in the boardroom on the accounts and proceedings of the Software Levy Fund. His first slide was a lot less than clear and various directors expressed difficulty at reading it. 'Oh, sorry!', he said; 'I keep forgetting how old you chaps are.'

Pass, friend, and all's well, c. 1986   Malcolm Turner

I always tried to carry out my duties to the letter. When the dictate came down from on high that anyone who entered the computer room must be wearing a security pass, that was good enough for me.

One day an old colleague was showing a new face around the machine room. I spied my chance. Marching forward, unabashed, and with the security of my mandate to give me courage, I asked the interloper to leave, administering a moderately sustained ticking-off which culminated with the admonition that he was 'not to return unless he had a security pass'. But, alas! My misplaced confidence soon drained away. He gave me a forceful dressing down and sent me packing, red-faced. He was our new manager.

Fallout in Fulham, 1986   Myra Brooks

The Poles were a great deal closer to Chernobyl than we were, and naturally much more worried about its impact on their lives. So a visit to ICL's HQ in Putney was a chance to fit in some *very* important shopping.

On the day they called in at an Army Surplus store before coming on to the Visitor Centre in Bridge House South. [*It was a long running internal joke that this was at the north end of Putney Bridge. H.C.*] There was a busy morning programme of presentations and demos of some of the latest technology.

For lunch, since it was a VIP party, we elected to take them to the Hurlingham Club. While we were there I was called to the phone: 'Had any of the guests left a parcel at the Visitor Centre?' Enquiries were made; one guest said that he had indeed left a package behind; I relayed this information and we relaxed over coffee and brandy. During the conversation, the visitor explained that he had bought a Geiger counter, which he intended to use when he got home for testing for contamination in the family's meat and vegetables. No further thought was given to the subject.

It was a short distance from the club to the ICL buildings and it was a nice afternoon, so we decided to take a leisurely stroll and told the driver to meet us later on. As we reached Putney Bridge Tube Station there were the first signs of an alarm: it seemed that the station was closed; there was yellow 'Keep Out' tape linking the lamp-posts; further on there was a group of military personnel. This must be serious! They were standing over a shoebox-sized package covered in green material and clearly planning the best method for blowing it up. The thought suddenly struck... it must be the Geiger counter! Looking sinister with wires leading from it, and with some sort of gauge or counter, it had obviously been taken for an IRA bomb.

'I must have it back!', hissed the Polish customer; 'What is being done to it?' His voice showed signs of fear, would he be arrested? There was no time to be lost. I ducked under the tape, rushed forward calling out : 'It is ours!' and under the nose of the amazed army captain snatched up the object and thrust it into the hands of the Polish visitor.

It took some time for the car to arrive, since the whole of Putney Bridge had also been sealed off to pedestrians and traffic. But in due course it did appear, the Polish guests were politely despatched and disappeared into the distance. An international incident was avoided. It then took a lot more time to make an adequate apology to the army officer in charge but eventually the incident closed with amusement all round.

But who was it who told *Computer Weekly* about it? Was it Doug Lindsay? Was it Owen McKenzie? And was it a deliberate bit of informing, or just another typical *Eight Bells* indiscretion?

The Balkan question, c. 1986   *S.J. Kellett*

Whatever happened to the consignment of busts of Tito that figured in an ME29 deal with Yugoslavia in the mid-80s?

Driving Force, c. 1986   *Andrina Mockeridge*

The place was Brighton; the occasion was the annual conference of the Conservative Party; and ICL was there with a number of relevant demos. The screens on which these were running were suitably disposed inside the building. The servers were in a specially adapted coach parked outside, with cables running across the pavement and through the windows into the interior.

It was really very good of Mrs Thatcher to agree to be photographed in support of ICL's efforts on behalf of her party. And it seemed to the photographer that it would offer rather a good metaphor if she was photographed in the driver's seat of the ICL coach. It was entirely the lady's own idea to put the thing into gear and drive it twenty feet along the road, breaking the cable connections of every single demo. When does conservative become destructive?

Un avis rouge, par telex, 1987   *Mike Coon*

Why a *lingua franca* is not une lingue française:

DUE TO LARGE RAIN SINCE TWO WEEKS THE TOWN OF SAINTES IS INUNDATED. CRCA SAINTES BUILDING HAS WATER UNTIL 1ST FLOOR. THE 2972s AND 2966s HAVE BEEN DECONNECTED AND HOUSED TODAY UNDER PLASTIC WITH VACUUM CLEANING. NOW THE WATER MAKES FLUSH WITH THE FALSE FLOOR OF COMPUTER ROOM. THE CUSTOMER CAN'T STOP HIS WORK ON COMPUTER AND WILL GO WORK ON CRCA AVIGNON MACHINE SATURDAY 25TH AND SUNDAY 26TH DECEMBER.

ONCE THE WATER LEAVES WE WILL HAVE TO DRY COMPUTER ROOM AND TO COMMISSION AGAIN THE SYSTEMS. IT IS LIKELY WE COMMISSION ONLY THE 2966s (IN THIS CASE SEE AVP RED ALERT) BUT THE COMMISSIONING RISK TO BE LONG TIME AS THE SYSTEMS HAVE PERHAPS ENDURE HUMIDITY.

...nor any drop to drink, c. 1987   *Iain Drummond*

The customer requested by phone a copy of the Fluid Distribution software package. It was sent at once, by post. It arrived soaking wet. The customer complained. The customer was the Kent Water Board.

Fruit Machine? 1987   *John Burleigh*

A series of telexes to and from the BRA04 Help Desk. Names and source address suppressed.

RE OPD

ME AM TRYIN TO CONNECT A ONE POR DES TO A REPUBLIC COMPUTA MANUFACTURED BY DE BANANA CORP. DIS PROBLEM HIM A COME WHEN WE DO A GRAFIC OUTPUT. AM A YELLOW CHALK ON DE YELLOW BLACKBOARD. DE SOFTWARE WE IS USING AM 'MANGO' - MANAGEMENT ACCOUNTIN NETWORKED GRAFICAL OUTPUT. ADVISE DAM QUICKLY AS CUSTOMER HIM GO UP A BLOOODY TREE BOUT DIS.

RGDS

Reply to: Fruit machine?

RE OPD

YOU FOOLMAN WORK FOR BANANA REPUBLIC. DON U KNOW ASK VOODOO MAN KILL HEN CHICKEN UNDER WOOMWOOM TREE WHEN MOON SHINE BRIGHT. DIS GIVE U ANSER PLENTY QUIK AND NO USE MUCH DOLLAR TELEX SPARKY. GO DO NOW. GREETINGS TO HUNNY BUNNY.

RGDS

MALCOLM X

Fruit machine squashed

RE THE OLD MANGO AND YELLOW CHALK PROBLEM CHICKEN SACRIFICE GRATEFULLY ACCEPTED. ORACLE SAY YELLOW NOT SUPPORTED ON OPD. WHEN CHICKEN'S NECK RUNG CHICKEN TURN RED IN FACE. THIS SAY USE RED CHALK ON RED BLACKBOARD AND PROBLEM GO AWAY WITH EVERYTHING ELSE. ALSO MANGO NOT SUPPORTED ALONG WITH EVERYTHING ELSE. BUT BERMUDA TRIANGLE ENTERPRISES HAVE ANNOUNCED A NEW PRODUCT - CHINESE HIEROGRAPHIC UNIFIED TEXT NUMERATOR ENHANCED YATTERPAK - WHICH DOES THE SAME JOB. END USER PRICE IS 10 CHICKENS FOR SINGLE NODE VERSION, ONE COW FOR SITE LICENCE, UNLIMITED COPIES; 120 VOLTS ONLY.

Out of the frying-pan, c. 1988   H.C.

There was briefly at Winnersh a manager called Bacon, and he *was* short-tempered, and he *did* take exception to the woman security guard/receptionist/telephonist (who at the time had nothing else to do) reading a novel below the counter, and he *did* get her sacked on the spot, and he *did* ring in from his car the following morning to get his secretary to put on the coffee, and he *was* livid that no-one answered his call, until his chauffeur pointed out that he *had* sacked the telephonist the previous day.

Ringing home the bacon

Ho! Ho! Ho!
The biter bit!
One can't help
But laugh at it!

Excess women?
Instant sacking:
Kick them out
And send them packing.

Ring, ring, ring,
But no reply.
Ring, ring, ring
I wonder why?

Angry voice -
There's no denying:
Sounds a bit
Like bacon frying.

Fingers burned -
Well, fancy that!
Must have been
Hot bacon fat!

Rash decision,
Rasher deed:
Service gone
In hour of need.

Ancient Greeks
Had word for this:
Poetic justice:
'NEMESIS'.

How Lewis Carroll got there first, c. 1988   H.C.

Marketing's *nine*-level segmentation is elegantly and completely pre-figured in '*The Hunting of the Snark*', an Agony in *Eight* Fits.

1. STRATEGIC STATEMENT
'He had brought them the best -
A perfect and absolute blank!'

2. EXECUTIVE SUMMARY
'What I tell you three times is true.'

3. PRODUCT OVERVIEW
'Distinguishing those which have feathers and bite
From those which have whiskers and scratch.'

4. THE OVERALL MARKETING PLAN
'He had brought a large map representing the sea,
Without ever a vestige of land.'

5. SPECIFIC TARGET MARKETS FOR THE VENTURE
'Just the place for a Snark!'

6. BENEFITS RELEVANT TO TARGET MARKETS
'Bring it home by all means, you may serve it with greens,
And it's handy for striking a light.'

7. FINANCIAL PLAN
'He offered large discount; he offered a cheque
Drawn 'To Bearer' for seven pounds ten.'

8. COMPETITIVE POSITIONING
'You'd best be preparing the things you will need
To rig yourselves out for the fight.'

9. ADDITIONAL OPPORTUNITIES
'You may threaten its life with a railway share,
You may charm it with smiles and soap.'

10. BENCHMARKS
'Taking 3 as the number to reason about -
A convenient number to state.'

11. HARDWARE CONSIDERATIONS
'He had forty-two boxes, all carefully packed,
With his name painted clearly on each.'

12. SOFTWARE CONSIDERATIONS
'He had seven coats on when he came,
With four pairs of boots."

13. ORGANISATION
'The crew was complete.'

14. LOCATION
'...pleased with the view
Which consisted of chasms and crags.'

15. STANDARDS
'That's exactly the method I've always been told
That the capture of Snarks should be tried.'

16. TRADEMARKS
'The five unmistakeable marks,
By which you may know, wheresoever you go,
The warranted, genuine Snarks.'

17. RISK ANALYSIS
'But Oh!, beamish nephew, beware of the day
If your Snark be a boojum!'

You flathead! c. 1988   *Russell Austin*

An engineer finished his daily round of calls and returned to the office. There he was confronted by his irate boss, bellowing: 'Why didn't you answer your pager? I've got a disaster I needed you to go to!' 'Sorry', said the engineer, 'but my pager was flat'. This raised the boss's temperature even further: 'How many times have I told you always to carry spare batteries?', he roared. At which the engineer pulled a mess out of his pocket and replied: 'No; I dropped it and a lorry ran over it'.

Deduction, c. 1988 — Mike Burke

The engineer was called out to a computer fault in an African country. On arrival it seemed a reasonable diagnosis that the computer's inoperability might have had something to do with the bullet hole through the cabinet.

Gasping, c. 1988 — H.C.

The new discs, of which so much had been promised, arrived at the important site in Johannesburg and proceeded to suffer numerous head crashes, which was traced to the aerodynamic design by which the heads 'fly' over the recording surface. At 6,000 feet they were well above their operational ceiling, the air was far too thin.

Barter me a Barmecide, c. 1988 — Bob Peel

There used to be a series of 'breakfast meetings', prior to each half year end, to review the supply and allocation of mainframes. Unfortunately, there was never any breakfast.

At one of these which dragged on longer than usual (and that was a long time normally), a member of International Trade who had not been warned about the absence of breakfast suddenly remembered that a barter deal had recently been done for a S39 into Yugoslavia. Part of the deal had been a container-load of Yugoslavian sausage, allegedly the best-selling Yugoslav sausage in New York.

He remembered that a few samples had been delivered to LON11 and slipped away to acquire some. His reappearance some minutes later, suitably loaded with sausage and paper plates, was greeted with cries of 'Hero!' and 'Quality Award!'. As breaking chunks off didn't seem to work, some time was spent searching for a knife. That having been found, the company fell to on the samples. But they uttered the opposite of 'Hero' as soon as the nature of the sausage was discovered.

It can only be assumed that the reason this was the best-selling Yugoslav sausage in New York was because it was the *only* one.

And we never heard how the container was disposed of. Does it still lie, gently steaming, in some forgotten corner of some great container port?

But not on the M25, c. 1989 — Tim Hargest

I used to run the information system used in the regular company-wide supply/demand balancing forum, the 'System Review'. In the late 1980s the results of the System Review were adjusted or approved by a 'Directors' Review'. On one such occasion I was called from KID01 to LON13 to attend the Directors' Review, after which a buffet lunch was served. I was very much the most junior person present and, therefore, kept myself to myself over lunch. Suddenly, though, my neighbour turned to me and said explosively: 'Nearly missed the plane this morning. Bloody taxi driver missed the Charles de Gaulle exit on the Péripherique. It was OK, though, I made him reverse for six miles up the hard shoulder!'

It ought to know what I mean, 1989   *Tony Colvile*

I was hastily summoned on site to help with a performance problem. A tedious eight hours of weekend work had been expended in what looked like fairly straightforward enquiries concerning some aspects of the Gulf War. Every enquiry was taking eight minutes, which was the time required to scan the whole file from end to end; yet from the look of the enquiries, each of them should have taken no more than ten seconds. Each of them was looking for certain records within a specified date range. 'GREATER THAN OR EQUAL TO date1 AND LESS THAN date2' ought to focus the CAFS searching onto a single small section of the file.

Why didn't it? Well, the old magnifying glass soon found out that, deep in the bowels of the Query Interpreter, the logic was being expressed as 'NOT LESS THAN date1 AND NOT GREATER THAN OR EQUAL TO date2', and those little 'NOTs' had the effect of inhibiting the use of indexes, hence a full file scan for every enquiry.

A circumvention was quickly devised and a cure took only a little longer. But why hadn't the point been discovered during system testing? Because, children, the test files were all so small that the difference in timing hadn't been apparent.

A letter from Zanietta, 1989   *Phil Watson*

Dear Mr Watson

I am sad to inform you that, I hurt my feet by the hot water when I was boiling water. In order to my feet had got any big blisters, which enable me to walk inconvenience, I could not come there in 15th and 16th August 1989.

Sorry for my sudden leave, most wish I should not give you any matters.

Nyet = Not Yet, c. 1989   *John Lawe*

An ICL engineer was called out from the UK to an urgent computer fault in Russia. He arrived at the turbine works in Leningrad only to be told: 'You can't come in; we haven't had permission from Moscow.' He spent two days in his hotel and in leisurely sightseeing until the permission was granted. Of course the system remained down all that time.

Services Information Sheet
Series 133, Number 69, August 1989   *ICL New Zealand Ltd*

Series Title: PC TERMINAL

Subject: MOUSE BALLS NOW AVAILABLE AS FRU (Field Replaceable Unit)

Mouse balls are now available as an FRU. If a mouse fails to operate, or should perform erratically, it may be in need of ball replacement. Because of the delicate nature of this procedure replacement of mouse balls should only be attempted by trained personnel.

Before ordering, determine the type of mouse balls required by examining the underside of the mouse.

Southern Hemisphere balls are larger and harder than Northern Hemisphere balls. Ball removal procedures differ depending on the type of mouse. Northern Hemisphere balls are removed by the pop-off method whilst Southern Hemisphere balls are screw-fitting.

Mouse balls are not usually sensitive to static; however excessive handling can lead to a sudden discharge. After fitting new balls the mouse can be used immediately.

It is recommended that field staff have a pair of balls to maintain optimum customer satisfaction. Product Identities and Part Numbers are as follows:

17604/004 BALL, PCT MOUSE, N.HEM Part No. 80098096

17604/005 BALL, PCT MOUSE, S.HEM Part No. 80098069

Note: Some mice have no balls. These are generally recognisable by the presence, in the place where balls are usually found, of a gap from which a red glow emanates when the mouse is switched on. Please note that all ICL-supplied mice for PWS and PCT have balls.

AN ICL ANTHOLOGY

Eleven Personalities

There are some memorable people about whom numerous stories are told or who, by strength of character, attract stories to them, or who by a gift for a turn of phrase pass into the common memory. This little section is a tribute to some of them. H.C.

Arthur Humphreys

On listening to a Divisional Director declaring that some ICL disaster might easily have been foreseen:

'What we obviously need to run this business properly is better hindsight, *sooner!*'

*

On hearing that a set of figures that had been used as a basis for an important decision were, in fact, quite erroneous:

'It ain't what you don't know that causes the trouble; it's what you know that ain't so.' (a quotation from Josh Billings).

*

'No job should be so small that the chap in charge can't make a cock of it.'

*

'Salesmen's desks are normally managed on the deep litter principle.'

*

A tribute from Geoff Cross:

'I've learned two significant things from you· the importance of cash flow, and liar dice.'

Mike Forrest

I wrote to Mike saying that there were numerous stories, that I didn't wish to offend him, and would he comment on some of these. His splendid reply said that he didn't really mind what was said about him (true or untrue), although a juicy libel case might be more entertaining than the National Lottery. The first one came from three separate informants.

He was a great trouble-shooter but had the reputation of being a bit of a tyrant and a mention of his name normally instilled fear in the listener.

Very late one evening a phone was ringing insistently somewhere in the BRA01 Machine Hall and it was a long time before an operator answered it. The gist of the problem was that a certain online system wasn't online when it theoretically should have been. The operator seemed to think this was no big deal and, anyway, what sensible person would want to use it at such a time, so was a lot less than helpful.

'Do you know who I am?' came a bellow down the line.

'No', responded the operator, 'Do you know who *I* am?'

'No'.

'Well, f*** off then', said the operator as he hung up.

But then an almost identical story is told of Robb Wilmot ringing up the Cardiff office during Friday lunch-time, so maybe this is a generic story that attaches itself to one strong person after another. H.C.

*

It is said that Mike was being introduced as a speaker at an evening occasion and the host led up to it as follows:

'Mike had to go for his annual medical with the company doctor. At the end of the examination the doctor looked at him gravely and said: "Well, Mike, you're not exactly *suffering* from stress. But I'm bound to tell you that you are a *carrier*." '

To which Mike is said to have riposted that as soon as he joined the company he saw that company people were divided into those who *had* ulcers and those who *caused* them, and he at once decided which group he wanted to belong to.

*

It was said of Mike that he had to go into hospital for a major operation. [*he denies this; he's never had surgery in his life. H.C.*] Anyway, people wondered (as they do) what was involved. All honour to him, he is credited with having invented the explanation that it was for a 'Charisma Bypass'.

*

A summer visitor to the house in Sonning gushed about how *lovely* it must be to be able to sit out in this *lovely* garden, with this *lovely* view, and all these *lovely* flowers...

'Yes', he said, 'but the wind does blow one's papers about so.'

*

Three from long ago   Ben Gunn

It was Mike's first day working at Stevenage. He went to the stores to get a soldering iron or some such thing but was kept waiting by the storeman who was holding a casual conversation with some other person. After a couple of minutes Mike banged the counter and said he had not come here to stand waiting about doing nothing. He got the service he wanted and never ever waited longer than necessary for anything. To work for Mike was a tremendous experience but not for too long or you would be dead.

*

Mike was the most dedicated person I ever met when it came to working hours and technical know-how on every subject. I was working on a printer at night in Stevenage No 5 Factory when he came in at about 2 a.m. 'What's wrong?' he asked and so I explained the problem. That was fatal. By 5 a.m. the machine was in pieces all over the floor and Mike said 'Carry on' and left me to re-assemble the whole thing with the problem unsolved.

*

On another occasion at Stevenage, in the middle of the night, we checked to see who was still logged on to the computer system we were using in Bracknell. Mike Forrest was apparently still working (or, just possibly, had forgotten to log off). At 5 a.m. we noted he logged off and, an hour later, he was logged back on again having only been home for breakfast. Obviously he didn't know the word for sleep.

*

Finally, an authorised and true one

When he was retiring, his secretary, Jane, sent an e-mail round to managers in several countries telling them of the date, time and place of the leaving party. Back from a secretary in Finland came the reply: 'We are surprised to hear that your boss is retiring as he looked quite healthy when he was here last week'.

Peter Simpson

He is not, I'm afraid, adequately represented in this collection. There ought to be much more, going back to the great days of the Hollerith Players. Even this gem may be a chestnut, but it was from Peter that I first heard it, so he gets the credit:

The three most unbelievable sentences in the language are: 'The cheque's in the post'; 'Of course I'll still love you in the morning'; 'I'm from Head Office, and I'm here to help you'.

Nowadays, we'd probably add: 'Your fax wasn't working.'

Gordon Scarrott: A few gems, from a man gifted at producing them.

'Our plans are rarely successful. We do have successes, but they are rarely the ones we planned.'

*

'Practical engineering can produce worthwhile and useful results long before the relevant science has been formulated. Look, for example, at the steam engine and its highly successful antedating of the laws of thermodynamics. Computing is still at the engineering stage. We don't have *any* recognised science of information. Therefore all talk of 'computer science' is complete and utter rubbish.'

That was said, with characteristic glee, at a meeting in the Department of Computer Science at Birkbeck College.

*

'People are naturally disordered. CAFS is a way of respecting natural disorder that can't be wished away.'

But contrast that with:

'Man is a specialist in organisation, but is certainly not very wise. As a species we ought to be called *simia ordinans* rather than *homo sapiens*.'

*

'Politicians confuse things by using 'Science and Technology' as one word. Accountants confuse things by using 'Research and Development' as one word.'

238

Roger Houbert

What fun to hear a Frenchman speaking fluent English in a Manchester accent. Let him have a néologisme as the last word.

'I won't quabble with you.'

Twelve ICL: The Nineteen-Nineties

Misdirection, c. 1990   *Andrina Mockeridge*

All was proceeding normally in the Demo Room at Bridge House South in Putney when one of the members of a visiting Middle Eastern party murmured a question to the accompanying representative of the Visits Unit. Neither his diction nor his meaning were entirely clear but, making an intelligent guess, she flung out her arm, full length, in the direction of the Gents. It was in that direction, therefore, that he shortly afterwards made his midday prayers.

The commissioner's elephants, 1990   H.C.

We took the Commissioner of the Botswana Police on a visit to the North Yorkshire Police, where he was cordially greeted by the Chief Constable, and the two senior officers sat down for a chat about common problems of policing.

'We rely heavily on microwave communications in our Force area', said the Chief Constable. 'But because the terrain is very varied, with the flat Plain of York to the east and the high hills and deep valleys of the Dales to the west, we need to site our transmitters on hill-tops in order to get the necessary line of sight communications. That means that one of our biggest practical problems is the utilities, the Gas, Water, and Electricity people, who will keep coming along with their pneumatic drills and cutting holes in our land-lines.'

'Oh yes', said the Commissioner. 'We also use a lot of microwave in my country, because of the long distances involved. One of our biggest practical problems is elephants. If an elephant takes a dislike to one of our transmitters out in the bush there's not much we can do about it.'

'I can see that', said the Chief Constable. 'We don't seem to get many elephants in North Yorkshire.'

Yorkshire tact, 1990   H.C.

On the same visit, the Commissioner and his party were to be given a demo of the North Yorkshire INDEPOL Incident-Logging System. Superintendent Gerry 'Pepperspray' Allen always thought that a demo was most effective if the visitor actually drove the system, keying in the appropriate commands as dictated.

On this occasion, therefore, in accord with this habit, he sat the Commissioner at the keyboard and started off on the usual script. It didn't take any time at all to realise that the Commissioner had never touched a keyboard in his life, wasn't going to be able to find the keys, and probably thought the whole process was beneath his dignity.

As the Commissioner changed places with someone more suitable, 'Oh', said Gerry loud and clear: 'I knew there'd be one nigger in the woodpile!'

Another view of quality, c. 1990   *Anon*

        A celebration on Zero Defects Day

        Come laugh and sing and dance with glee,
        And celebrate with QIT;
        We're shining pure and error-free
        On Zero Defects Day.

        A great new age has just begun,
        An age of freedom, sport and fun;
        (You can't through to HIT01
        On Zero Defects Day).

        One little thing - the LAN is down
        And both ITs are out of town;
        But cast aside that worried frown -
        It's Zero Defects Day!

        There's something wrong with ITD,
        And nothing right with C03,
        X25? - You're kidding me!
        It's Zero Defects Day!

        The net result's no comms at all,
        The whole bang shoot is up the wall,
        So fill your glass and have a ball
        On Zero Defects Day.

        Just cos there's nothing getting through,
        That's no excuse for feeling blue;

It means we've got no work to do
On Zero Defects Day.

Nowt done at all means nowt done wrong!
That's 'Zero Defects' all day long!
So just relax and sing this song
On Zero Defects Day.

Compute the figures how you will,
Our Price of Non-Conformance bill
Adds up to absolutely nil
On Zero Defects Day.

So shout and sing and dance with glee,
And celebrate with QIT;
We're shining pure and error-free
On Zero Defects Day

Another view of NYP, 1991   H.C.

The Brigadier of Police was from Namibia and we took him to Newby Wiske to show him the North Yorkshire Police's Incident-Logging System. With admirable candour he explained to us, during the preliminaries, that his Force consisted of '25% policemen and 75% reformed terrorists'. At the end of the demonstration his verdict was: 'That is an excellent system. We will be ready for a system like that in my country in about seventy-five years.' End of immediate sales campaign.

CAFS 800: The end (only not quite), c. 1991   *Tony Colvile*

There was to be a grand switch off ceremony for the last and largest CAFS 800 installation, which had given loyal service for the best part of ten years. I happened to be working on site when the ceremony became due and was invited to join the ICL engineers Brian Ward and Mike Tuffnall for the occasion. A Very Senior Officer was shown into the computer room which contained the single DME mainframe, the three CAFS 800 controllers, and the 42 operational EDS 60 disc drives, plus some spares, in long serried ranks. The VSO spoke to the three of us and to the operators, said a few words about the demise of the system, and then pressed a big red button. This wasn't actually connected to anything, but by other means all the lights were made to go out and there came the sound of the air conditioning running down. With the aid of several torches we made our way out of the room and went off to have lunch, which was followed by a demo of the INDEPOL replacement system.

Half an hour later, when the VSO had left, the CAFS 800 system was powered up again, because they hadn't finished extracting data from it for conversion to the new system.

A *cautionary tale, 1991*   H.C.

It was another visit-to-Lancashire day, and I was piloting the visitors' cars to Police Headquarters. We stopped at traffic lights south of Preston, with the Slovak car and the Czech car in column behind me. In the inside lane was an inoffensive yellow Metro.

The lights turned green, we moved off, and as the road narrowed the Metro tucked in behind me. Over the humped-backed railway bridge there was a straight for a quarter of a mile, and the Slovak car overtook the Metro in order not to get too far detached from the pilot.

At the next roundabout I checked in my mirror to see that the visitors were still following me and Lo! the Metro had overtaken the Slovak car again, forced it to stop at the side of the road, and a very angry policeman had got out. He stormed over to what he thought was the driver's side, only it wasn't, which made him even more angry. He then raged round to the other side of the car and began a ferocious harangue about dangerous overtaking which was completely unintelligible to the Slovak driver who just smiled sweetly.

I ran back, and began apologising to the officer: it was all my fault; I'd got too far ahead of the foreign policemen whom I was piloting to a meeting at Police Headquarters at Hutton; the Slovak car had only been trying to catch up for fear of getting lost.

'Oh! 'oo are you going to see at 'utton?'

'Chief Superintendent Donnelly.'

'Never 'eard of 'im!'

'Well, he runs the Communications Centre; he's in charge of the Control Room and all the Computers and the Telecommunications.'

'Oh! And 'oo's this, then?'

'He's the Deputy Chief Constable of the Police Force of Slovakia' (and the driver produced a card which confirmed this fact.)

'Well, that's as may be, but you tell him from me (*ff*) THAT HE'S A PLONKER!!'

The visit went fine and I ended up with a delightful flower vase in Slovak native pottery for 'saving the Deputy Minister from the dangerous British Police'.

'I'll be five years late; they haven't built the road yet',1992   *Phil Watson*

I was looking for staff for our airline computer project and arranged over the phone to interview a young French lady recently arrived in Hong Kong. She was to come the following day to the ICL office in Kwo Tai Dai Ha, which I told her was the building next to the airport in Concorde Road.

The next morning Françoise phoned and said she would be a bit late for the interview. I said I would wait.

An hour later, she called again and apologised for a further delay, saying the journey was taking longer than she expected. 'That's OK', I replied, 'I know what Hong Kong traffic's like'.

Another hour passed. Then another call came: 'I'm at the airport now, but I can't find the building'. She explained that neither she nor the taxi driver could find *any* building, or *any* road, or in fact *any* sign of civilisation.

Had they driven off into another dimension? No. Françoise had gone to the wrong airport. She had gone to that desolate patch of half-reclaimed landfill in a remote and inaccessible part of Lantau Island, which is all that exists of Chep Lap Kok airport. Another interview was arranged, and she got the job.

And my reason for taking her on? 'I've been here years, and I have no idea how to get to Chep Lap Kok. She's only been here two months and she got there in less than half a day and on her own. If that's not efficiency and intelligence, I don't know what is.'

CS ANNOUNCEMENTS   *Anon*

CS Announces New Organisation

Headed up by ReceptICL, the ICL CS Holding Company, the new organisation consists of five arms:

ServICL	Professional and Software Services
BuysICL/HeretICL	Sales and Marketing
TentICL	The eight Systems Engineering regions
TricICL	Third Party services
BisICL	Business Information systems

CS Announces new Schedules

To reflect new working practices, the following schedules for service delivery have been identified:

SabatICL	only available at weekends
MonICL	only available on Mondays
TrICL	delivered a bit at a time

RhythmICL	*only available three days a month*
QueuetICL	*awaiting delivery*
MonastICL	*no services provided at any time*

CS Announces New Services

To emphasise our corporate image, the following services have been renamed:

ArtICL	*Design services*
ArtifartICL	*Marketing's interpretation of design services*
BiblICL	*God only knows!*
BicICL	*Jointly delivered services*
ClerICL	*Services delivered to your church*
ComICL	*East European services*
ClinICL	*Health check services*
DiabolICL	*CS standard services*
DramatICL	*Performance services delivered on different platforms*
EcclesiastICL	*Religious services*
EgotistICL	*Senior management services*
ElectrICL	*Environmental services*
EthICL	*Services sold by CS rather than Sales*
FanatICL	*User Group presentation services*
FarsICL	*Remote diagnostic services*
FollICL	*Hair management services*
FollICL	*Services for no reason whatsoever*
GenetICL	*Life Cycle services*
HysterICL	*Technology services*
HistorICL	*DRS300 services*
PterodactICL	*George III services*
HypothetICL	*TeamOffice implementation services*
ManICL	*Services that tie your customer in*
MedICL	*Beach holiday services*
MirICL	*Right first time, on time, every time services*
MistICL	*Weather forecasting services*
MotorbicICL	*Pizza delivery services*
MusICL	*System tuning services*
MuseICL	*We're still thinking about this one*
MystICL	*The wand waving services*
MythICL	*The standard service that covers every customer requirement*
NaughtICL	*Personal services*
ObstICL	*Services carried out in crowded machine rooms*

PeriodICL	Report production or documentation services
PoetICL	Proposal production services
PolitICL	Bureau services
PractICL	DIY services
QuizzICL	Investigation services
PartICL	Shoddy services
RhetorICL	Consultancy services
SeptICL	Squeaky clean services
SinICL	Very personal services
TactICL	Strategic planning services
TestICL	System validation services
TheoretICL	OEM network design and integration services
TICL	Conformance testing services
TipICL	Waste disposal services
TopICL	The very latest services
TropICL	Services for that warm feeling
TyrannICL	Project management services
UmbilICL	Early-life care services
VehICL	Equipment transport services

Putting the customer's foot in it, 1992   *Alan Bruce*

ICL Nederland was trying hard to sell ICL POS and UNIX equipment to HEMA, against stiff competition from NCR. A reference visit was therefore arranged to Fort Worth, for two HEMA directors, including the Chairman, Bas Vos. On the first evening in Texas, Mr Vos happened to tread on a cast iron manhole cover, which unexpectedly tipped up and tripped him, leaving him with one leg dangling into nothingness and otherwise shaken. During the subsequent presentations and discussions he lost no opportunity of reminding ICL of how badly they had treated him, together with general remarks on the dangerous nature of manhole covers.

Some weeks later, when the negotiations had been successfully completed, Ian McKinley decided that it was our turn to remind HEMA of the incident, which he did by presenting to Mr Vos a full size cast aluminium replica of the offending manhole cover, together with an official certificate and key, confirming Mr Vos in his new status as an honorary citizen of Fort Worth.

Saved by the Belle, c. 1992   H.C.

We have entertained a lot of Egyptian Generals at Winnersh over the years, but this group was especially important. Three very senior gentlemen were gracing us with their presence for the day, with a full entourage of ADCs, Staff Officers, Bag-Carriers, and Bodyguards. Everything had to be just tickety-boo throughout and so Sutcliffes, the caterers, had been primed to do their very best. We specified a Muslim menu (no ham, no pork) and agreed with the chef that roast chicken would be very acceptable. The starters were excellent and much enjoyed by all. After that, Pet wheeled in the hot trolley and prepared to serve the main course. Being well drilled in etiquette, she knew that the first dish should be placed before the most senior guest. So a plate bearing a most succulent half chicken was already in her hand, and well on its way to the table, when I noticed that across the top of the breast, as garnish, was elegantly draped a rasher of forbidden bacon. Fortunately she was quick to catch my look of alarm and suppressed gesture of panic. A rapid word of *sotto voce* explanation, and the hot trolley disappeared. Twenty minutes later we had steak.

Secure Terminals, 1992   H.C.

An African Government was eager to install a small network of word processing terminals in the Office of the President, but was very concerned that they should be absolutely secure: there must be not the slightest risk of the information they contained getting to anybody outside.

So they specified radiation suppression, they specified that the terminals should be fastened down to the desks and they specified that the desks should be fastened down to the floor.

These requirements we passed on to the supplier in Australia who did radiation suppression for us. 'No problem', was his reply, 'but I can make them even more secure than that. How about if I fit a tilt-switch and half a kilo of Semtex in the base of each one?'

Football: 1, c. 1992   Dave Fallon

For the past six years I have managed and played in an ICL football team originally made up of people from Elstree. In our first season together we played a home match against Sainsbury's Head Office from Blackfriars at ICL's Whitethorn Lane sports ground. It was a draw.

The return match was at Crystal Palace's Selhurst Park, no less. It was cruising into the later stages of the second half and another stalemate seemed likely. As player/manager I made a substitution; off went a tired-looking I.T.;

on came an ICL Retail engineer. From the time he reached the pitch to the time he made his first tackle (for which he was subsequently booked) could not have been more than five seconds and he left a Sainsbury's desk clerk writhing in agony on the ground. I turned apologetically to their centre half who was marking me, and who just happened to be a shift manager at one of their larger stores. Before I could say anything he remarked casually: 'Late as usual; must be a bloody ICL engineer!'

Football: 2, c. 1992   *Dave Fallon*

Again in our first season together we played a team from Iceland Frozen Foods, and during the game were awarded two penalties, the second when one of our players was brought down. Before we could take the kick, one of the opposition players, who was manager of their Walthamstow branch, quipped: 'Your computers are always going down, too.'

PSD 666, 14 September 1992   *E. van Helsing*

This magnificent document, all 44 pages of it, is the formal Product Specification of the ESP 200 Interface Outline Design. Have you already spotted the reference to *Revelation*? The following extracts cannot do more than give hints of the flavour of this masterwork:

The Technical Authority, based at Location HEL01, is the Manager, ESP Peripherals, B.L. Zeebub.

The Document Cross References include:

[1] DRE 16.162 The VAMPIRE strikes back

[2] DRE 16.163 PHANTOM of the operator

[3] CP/IN/666 Invasion of the VISA-snatchers

[4] CP/IN/667 I was a pre-release VAMPIRE

[5] PSD1222 ESP Interface - what's at stake?

[6] OSTC/666 ESP 50 Outline Design Specification

[7] CP/IN/999 Plasma Driven Device Control Language (Type AB negative)

[8] CP/IN/998 Foolsrush (in where wise men fear to tread) Specification

Introduction:

The ESP package consists of a set of interfaces: software, hardware, and Ectoware, which allow the system manager to communicate directly with the mainframe module. The system manager is able to exorcise greater control over his machine. Faults and their resolution are communicated to ICL via a telepathic link.

It is only suitable for SX systems and their successors. As it is an intelligent interface it cannot be adapted or modified to run on UNIX processors.

System Management:

Day to day allocation of resources is covered under system operating; however, the system manager is expected to control the general performance and running of the machine. In order to implement this requirement, a new subsystem (INSPECTRE) monitors the performance of the machine at intervals of 10 minutes, 30 minutes, 1 hour, 6 hours, 12 hours, 24 hours, 1 week, 1 month, 6 months and 1 year in advance of the current date. These values may be tailored up to 7 years ahead so that the system manager can predict the outcome of any recommendations he is asked to make to his manager at IT review meetings and thereby avoid being suspended on full pay whilst the accountants are investigating tendering abnormalities several years later.

User Control:

The system manager now has complete control over his user population. Users logged in via an ETHERealNET connection can have the results they expected output from the computer rather than the garbage the program would have produced. Troublesome users can be controlled by assigning a familiar to watch over them. The familiar may be escalated up to the level of demon if they continue to cause trouble. The system manager can also use the option to monitor all the user complaints he will receive when the system he is currently designing goes live. This will allow him to correct the design faults before coding begins. The user will also notice fewer typing errors due to the implementation of before looks in the slow device RAM.

Diagnostic facilities:

The ESP unit itself can be dumped by calling the sacrifice interfaces or by hitting it hard with a crucifix.

And so on, and so on.

Perhaps the highest points of all are the specifications of those two vital new SCL commands:

INFORM_OPERATOR_BEFORE_CRASH

RECOVER_UNARCHIVED_CATEGORY

How have we ever survived without them?

There is also a scurrilous rumour that a certain organisation in Basingstoke volunteered to act as a beta test site for this software, but that couldn't possibly be right, could it?

Secure Systems International's annual travel awards, 1993   H.C.

Worst airline

After a well-deserved week's holiday in Northern Cyprus as neighbours of Asil Nadir, Iain and his wife reached the airport in good time, in the middle of Sunday afternoon, for their return flight. From the terminal building they had a perfect view as the Turkish Airlines incoming plane made a feather-light touchdown, braked smoothly before the turn-off, taxied elegantly across the apron, and drove... straight into a truck. Six hours later, after any chance of a connecting flight had long since evaporated, and when even the chance of a bed for the night had sunk without trace, they reached the:

Worst airport

Little did they know, as they watched the few Turkish staff still awake languidly gesticulating, that further drama had been unfolding beneath their feet. Vic and Neil successfully passed through Istanbul airport that very afternoon, on their way to a Middle Eastern destination... but their luggage didn't.

Subsequent surreal telexes averred that the missing cases were simultaneously:

a) in Terminal 4 at Heathrow;

b) still at Istanbul;

c) being at that very moment delivered, by way of Rome, by Alitalia, that well-known acronym for 'Always Late In Take-off, Always Late In Arrival' or 'Aircraft Landed In Tokyo, All Luggage In Alicante'.

The cases eventually caught up with the travellers, though without one of Vic's more lurid suits, just before they started their return journey. Thankful to be on their way home, they successfully passed through Istanbul airport... but their luggage didn't.

There had to be some mention of OfficePower, 1993   H.C.

Finger trouble

If every time we hit the flipping key
It did what we intended, we would find
It rather disconcerting, it would be
As though the damned machine could read our mind -
A spooky thought. I'm sure you would agree
It would not please us to be so confined.
Farewell, of course, to serendipity,
If every action was so pre-defined.
But one things really bugs me: When I know
Just what I want to do, and with great care
Depress the well-known key to find: Oh No!
That blasted function's shifted **over there**
With this release of software; I shall go
And tear out what remains of my poor hair.

Culture shock, c. 1993   *Rita Walton*

I worked in the Fujitsu office at West Gorton for approximately six years. It was interesting and amusing work, but complicated by difficulties in describing things to my Japanese colleagues. For example, one of them came into the office on a Monday morning just before Christmas and said: 'Lita-san, I have bought a Chlistmas Tlee.' 'Oh good!', I said; 'Did you buy any baubles?' Japanese colleague frowned and said: 'What are baubles?' We sorted that out. Then we had a similar sequence of question, frown, counter-question, and explanation over tinsel. Then I made a dreadful mistake and asked: 'Have you got a fairy for the top of the tree?' Explanations didn't work, so he got out his English/Japanese dictionary, scanned it, and looked dreadfully shocked when he found the first meaning was 'homosexual'. How do you explain, in deeply embarrassed sign language, that that isn't what we put on the top of a Christmas tree?

Clarity, schmarity, c. 1993   *Dave Sanderson*

A work instruction for the delivery test of a type of VDU reads, in part, as follows (though, as it has been translated from Swedish into English, it may have lost something in translation):

'... Check that the test pattern, centre and dimensionally, is within a frame specification where the outer limit of tolerance is represented by the "outer scribed line" of the picture position layout and the inner limit of tolerance is within 5mm of the inside of all sides of the "outer scribed line" of the picture position layout.'

Facilis est descensus Averni, 1993   *Peter Vassallo*

Not strictly an ICL anecdote, but supplied by a mate who's ex-Fujitsu/ICL Australia, and altogether too good to leave out. H.C.

A computer salesman died and, in accordance with the standard procedure in these matters, duly appeared outside the Pearly Gates. There was St Peter, on duty as always, and the conversation went something like this:

'Hello', said St Peter. 'What can I do for you?'

'Well, first of all, I'd like some information about the range of services you can supply.'

'OK, basically there are two. On this site we can offer Heaven. And elsewhere our associates provide Hell.'

'What can you tell me, please, about the various options and end user facilities?'

'Well, you can see Heaven for yourself', said St Peter and he opened the Pearly Gates a crack, enough for the salesman to be able to see inside and look round. Sure enough, there were lots of people in white robes, sitting around on clouds, some of them with harps, looking blissful.

'Very nice', said the salesman. 'For comparison, what's Hell like?'

'Well, I can't show you that directly', said St Peter, 'But you might care to take a look at this video.' And, so saying, he slipped the cassette into the player and turned it on.

Up on the screen came a scene of a party in progress on a broad beach, barrels of beer, beautiful birds with bounteous boobs in briefest bikinis, bottles of booze, and a bonzer barbie burning in the background – the lot!

'It's certainly a difficult decision', said the salesman, 'but after carefully matching the facilities with my schedule of requirements I think I'll take Hell, please.'

'Right ho', said St Peter and pulled the lever. The trapdoor opened, the salesman fell onto the chute and down he went, round and round, down and down, until he arrived with a thump at the bottom.

When he landed he found there were flames up to chest height; fireballs whizzing about burnt off his hair in one flash and his eyebrows in the next; there were devils in the regulation scarlet, with horns and forked tails and all, jabbing painful tridents into his kidneys and driving agonising nails through his feet. He didn't reckon much to it at all.

Just then the Devil in person strolled past in the heat of the evening, surveying his domain with satisfaction.

'Hey you!', shouted the salesman. 'Where's the beach, with the birds, and the booze, and the barbie?'

'Ah!', said Lucifer reflectively. 'I believe you must have been watching one of our demo tapes'.

Football: 3, c. 1994 — Dave Fallon

In our third year we were promoted to the third division of the Stevenage and District SFL. The Secretary of the league worked for Stevenage Borough Council who are, naturally, ICL users. In his speech he included the line: 'Congratulations to ICL United on promotion to division three, and let's hope they stay up longer than their computers do'.

Letts do it, c. 1994 — Paul Honor

ICL is part of a big European Union effort to help the Baltic states make the leap from 1950s technology direct to the 1990s. In this context we had shipped one of our biggest and most advanced servers, very new and needing to be set up with some care to make it work reliably. It was to replace an old eastern box based on DEC PDP 1970s technology. But it failed after one week and we got a support call.

When we arrived we found this half-million dollar machine in a dirty room with broken windows, plugged into an unearthed 13-amp supply that oscillated randomly between 215 and 245 volts. The building had bare wooden floors and, because the previous occupants had to be persuaded to leave with Kalashnikovs, there were bullet holes all across the front wall.

We took the covers off and found the inside of the machine covered in oily black dust: not just a little bit, it was positively thick with it. We had to use a vacuum cleaner and hand brushes, and it took ages to clean. It was so unlike anything we're used to that it took quite a long time to identify coal-dust and soot: and just outside the window was a chimney.

We were able to convince the local ICL people and the European Union representatives that a bit of extra spending on a clean room and a voltage stabiliser would be a good start. Top that off with some in-depth training and we might get the project off the ground properly.

'Nature is not infallible,
but she always abides by her mistakes' Saki, 1994   *Alan Trangmar et al*

Long, long ago, the Orders Data Base was designed to handle orders with a number of items between six and eight. These parameters were derived from study of orders for typical 1900 Series systems, which were current during the design stage in the early 1970s. The design was discussed with all the authorities in planning, commercial, administrative and accounting departments, and given their communal OK.

No sooner had the system been implemented than along came the 2903, where the average number of items per order jumped to about 30. This vitiated many of the technical decisions about file structure, indexing strategy, etc., built into the ODB system, which from that moment on ran well below its designed performance. The decision to go much more modular had been well known to all the planning and commercial people, but none of them had thought what effect it might have on internal IT systems.

Then there came the splendid 2900 Series, and it wasn't long before a 2980 order arrived with more than 1,000 items on it. But the item number field only held three digits and even that had been considered a bit far-fetched. No-one could justify re-writing the system, so such orders had to be arbitrarily split.

ODB was eventually ported from DME to VME in the late 1980s and finally closed down in 1993. But the decision to close it down didn't take account of all the ramifications, and a year later people were still sending enquiries about missing interfaces. *Ave atque vale!*

All out and all over, 1994   *Donald Scott*

The ICIM Delhi Sales office is on an upper floor of a shared building. As I mounted past the first landing there were some 30 Indians sitting cross-legged on carpets. They were on strike because they hadn't been paid for three months. At the next landing I noticed what looked like a bundle of rags piled in a corner. My colleague explained that it was a man who had died from the cold (it was winter in Delhi) and they expected the body to be collected in a couple of days.

Sales Managers are so helpful, 1994   *Donald Scott*

The occasion was a presentation and demonstration of a SUN software package to all the senior Brigadiers and Generals of the Indian Army Ordnance Corps at Army Headquarters in Delhi. When we arrived the equipment was already set set up, connected to the mains, but also to a UPS powered by a car battery brought in for the purpose: a useful precaution, as power fluctuations are quite frequent in Delhi (ask anyone who's been stuck in a hotel lift). The kit hummed quietly to itself throughout the presentation.

There was a short break before the demo, during which I noticed a horrible acidic smell. Looking round for the cause I spotted one of the men who had been humping the equipment. His trousers were covered in a large dark stain, completely covering his thighs and extending down his lower legs. He smiled as I asked what had happened. He had spilled a lot of acid over his trousers as he carried the battery up from the ground floor, but it was all right as he had another pair of trousers at home!

Forty minutes later the primary demo was completed; all well so far. Some junior staff had requested to see further detail, so there was a break while we said goodbye to the senior officers. Out of the corner of my eye I saw ICIM's northern area Sales Manager walk to the Sun and calmly switch it off. Anyone who has worked with UNIX systems will know the inevitable panic when the system loses power while an application is still running. As the other staff watched in open-mouthed horror I walked over to the machine and asked innocently if it had problems. The Sales Manager, deeply embarrassed, confessed that he had switched the machine off, he didn't know why.

All the ICIM staff had by this time gathered round (this happens frequently in India because everyone feels he needs to know what is going on, but no-one actually contributes to solving the problem) and were watching my face intently. Paying equally close attention were all the Indian Army officers still present. I realised that they were wondering what I was going to say to a senior manager who had been so stupid, and also what had happened to this wonderful software whose virtues I had been extolling for the last couple of hours. Pausing for a moment (purely for dramatic effect) I took a deep breath and said: 'No problem, lads, just power the system up again and it'll be fine'. This display of confidence, not to say bravado, did the trick. The switch was pressed, and the system came up to the login prompt. I logged in and opened the application without any problems. Great big smiles all round and no loss of face for the Sales Manager. Discussing it later in the day with a colleague, he said: 'That's fine, but weren't you worried at all?' I replied: 'I wasn't worried about my application but I was praying they hadn't screwed up UNIX'.

A back passage to India, 1994   *Donald Scott*

You perhaps need to know that, for Donald, food is important. H.C.

I had to do a series of demonstrations to the Indian Armed Forces in Delhi. The technical preparations were straightforward. The medical ones were more extensive. I had all the necessary jabs administered (of course this won't hurt at all!) by the Occupational Health Nurse at BRA01, a small lady with a muscular forearm. I was given an ICL Travel Pack, a very useful collection of medicaments for minor emergencies. And I was given The Warnings:

Don't drink the water unless it's bottled, and check the seal is intact before opening;

Don't open your mouth in the shower;

Don't take ice in your drinks;

Don't eat salads, because you don't know whether they've been washed in mineral water (unlikely because of the expense) or tap water (more likely because of the expense);

Don't eat any fruit that you can't peel the skin off; and remember even peeling doesn't work with mangoes;

Anything cooked and hot is normally OK;

Otherwise be wary.

After an uneventful flight to Delhi I unpacked at the Holiday Inn Hotel and was then whisked off to the ICIM guest-house where the demonstrations were to take place. This was a two-storey building with its own garden and half a dozen guest rooms, set deep in the suburbs of Delhi where all the new housing estates are called (shades of Kipling) cantonments. The company maintains these all over India, and uses them to avoid costly hotel bills.

The equipment was set up successfully and thoroughly tested; all went well. I was asked if I would like a meal, informed that the guest-house cook was the son of a highly trained army cook and assured that he could provide the best. Indeed, the curry was superb, fearsomely hot, and was washed down with copious bottled mineral water.

Thirty-six hours later I woke at 5.30 a.m., drenched in sweat, shivering like a jelly and with that pre-volcano feeling in the stomach. The moment of truth came. Let us draw a decent veil over the next two days.

As is always inevitable in India, it was the 'can do' and 'economy' attitude that had prevailed on my visit to the guest-house. The housekeeper was given an allowance at the beginning of the month to purchase all necessary provisions, including bottled water. As the money runs out at the end of the month the bottled water is topped up with tap water. Just my luck, I had arrived on the 27th.

A December story, 1994   *John Maguire, via Henk van der Vegt*

The telephone rings:
'Good afternoon. John Maguire. Can I help you?'
'You the 'elp line?'
'Yes, I am. How can I help you?'
'I got this computer'
'Yes'
'It's bust, innit?'
'What's actually wrong with it?'
'Fink it's the cable'
'Could you tell me which cable you think may be faulty?'
'The black one!'
It seemed time to bat this one away. But to whom?
'Are you a retailer, Sir?'
'Yea, sort of'
'Could you give me your business address?'
'Wot's that got to do wivvit? Can't yer send someone rahnd?'
'You see, Sir, if you are not one of our retailers I shall have to pass you on to another Division.'
'I got a stall, enn I? Bit of buyin' an' sellin'. Know wot I mean?'
'Where did you buy your computer, Sir?'
'Got it off a bloke in Croydon, dinn I?'
Who on earth could I pass this Herbert to and still retain a measure of credibility? I couldn't possible inflict him on the lovely Cilla on Openline. Perhaps inspiration would yet come.
'I'm going to have to transfer you to one of my colleagues.'
'Oh no, you bloody ain't! I been all rahnd the 'ouses already as it is. Get someone rahnd 'ere quick!'
Got it! Wakefield is the place! The Call Reception Centre! The lads up there will know what to do. Should have thought of that earlier.
'I'm just going to give you the correct number to ring.'
'Look, you're giving me the right 'ump!'
'I'm sorry, I can't help you from this office. If you could just take down this number...'
'Don't give me no more 'assle. I'll get that Sugar onto you. 'e'll sort you out like 'e done that Venables.'
'Is there a manufacturer's logo on your computer?'

258

'*Yer wot?*'
'Does it say who made it?'
'*It's got "Amstrad" on that big box thing.*'
I extended the compliments of the season to the gentleman, and replaced the receiver.

AN ICL ANTHOLOGY